MW00564884

בראשית | GENESIS

A PARSHA COMPANION

בראשית | GENESIS

A PARSHA COMPANION

Rabbi David Fohrman

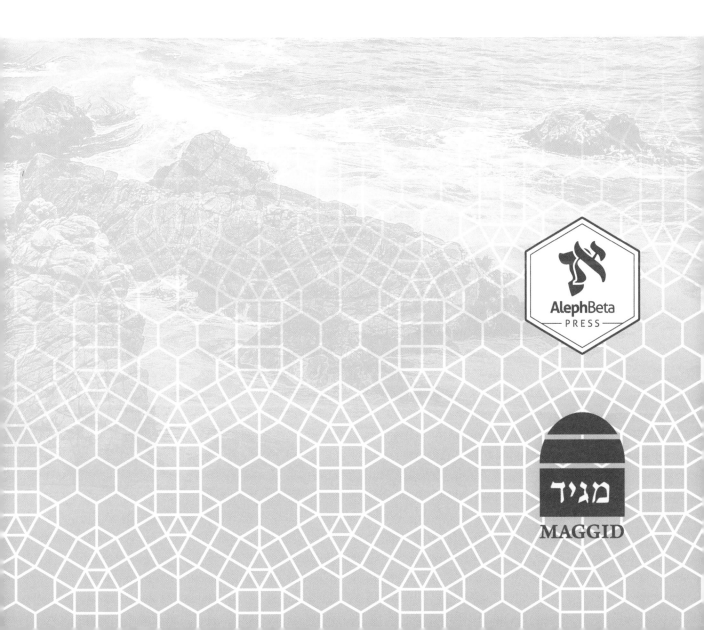

AlephBeta
PRESS

מגיד
MAGGID

Genesis: A Parsha Companion
First edition, 2019

Aleph Beta Press
EMAIL info@alephbeta.org
WEBSITE www.alephbeta.org

Maggid Books
An imprint of Koren Publishers Jerusalem Ltd.

PO Box 8531, New Milford, CT 06776-8531, USA
& PO Box 4044, Jerusalem 9104001, Israel
www.maggidbooks.com

© 2019 by The Hoffberger Institute for Text Study, Inc.

Book design by Cory Rockliff

All rights reserved. No part of this publication may be reproduced,
stored in a retrieval system or transmitted in any form or by
any means, electronic, mechanical, photocopying, or otherwise,
without the prior permission of the publisher, except in the case
of brief quotations embedded in critical articles or reviews.

ISBN 978-1-59264-544-2 (hardcover)

A CIP catalog record for this title is
available from the British Library

Printed and bound in the United States

The *Parsha Companion* series
is reverently dedicated by

Ronny & Toby Hersh

in memory of their parents

אברהם בן אהרן הלוי ז״ל
אסתר בת אברהם יהושע ז״ל

Abraham & Esther Hersh *z"l*

שמואל משה בן פסח יוסף ז״ל
חיה רבקה בת צירל ז״ל

Moshe & Rivka Zytelny *z"l*

and the many among their family
who perished in the Shoah

About Our Parents

Our parents surmounted great tragedy and hardship to live exemplary lives. They loved us, nourished us, and sacrificed much to help us flourish and become committed Jews. In their example, we saw sacred values of the Torah brought to life. We live in the shadow of their deeds.

ABRAHAM AND ESTHER HERSH hailed originally from the Carpathian mountains. They were both survivors of Auschwitz, and they met after the war in a displaced persons camp in Germany. Shortly thereafter, they made their way from the ashes of Europe to the Land of Israel, where Abraham fought in Israel's War of Independence. He was a fierce lover of both the land and the Torah of Israel. Together, Abraham and Esther lived difficult lives but, through it all, somehow always maintained a deep faith in Hashem. Their strong values — commitment to family and to Judaism, and an abiding love of the State of Israel and the Jewish people — made powerful impressions upon their children.

RABBI MOSHE AND RIVKA ZYTELNY made their way from Europe to America. Toby's father was, in his younger years, a yeshiva bachur in Kletzk. Before Lakewood was a gleam in the eye of history, he became a close student of Rabbi Aharon Kotler, and a *chevrusa* of his son, Rabbi Shneur. He escaped the ravages of war by heading, with his yeshiva, first to Siberia and then to Kazakhstan, where he met his wife, Rivka. The couple moved from Kazakhstan to France — and all this time, despite war and constant upheaval, Rabbi Aharon remained like a father to him. To this day, Ronny and Toby cherish letters in their possession that Rabbi Aharon sent to Rabbi Moshe in France, advising him on major life decisions. Eventually, Rabbi Moshe and Rivka came to America, where he rejoined his rebbe and yeshiva in Lakewood. There, he became part of an unlikely success story, as he helped reestablish a vibrant center of Torah on new and distant shores. All in all, Moshe was the only one in his entire immediate family to survive the war. Together, he and Rivka raised seven children.

Our parents lived through harrowing times and emerged with a steely, strengthened faith; they sacrificed much to pass on their vibrant heritage. We remember them with love, and are honored to carry their legacy forward.

Ronny & Toby Hersh

The Bereishit volume of the *Parsha Companion* is lovingly dedicated by

Barbara & Tuvia Levkovich

Zahava & Alan Goldschmidt, Gabrielle and Ava

Arel Levkovich

Talia & Akiva Fried, Lielle and Adina

IN MEMORY OF

גדליה בן ישעיה אבא וממציא ז״ל

Jerry Pinsky

יבדלחח״א

IN HONOR OF

יוסף בן שמחה ושייבדל נ״י

José Levkovich

About Our Fathers

OUR FATHERS, GRANDFATHERS & GREAT-GRANDFATHERS raised us to cherish Torah, to live by its mitzvot and by its ideals, and to understand that Torah is not just to be learned, but loved—and passed on. With admiration and profound gratitude, we lovingly dedicate this volume to them.

JERRY PINSKY, *zichrono livracha*, Barbara's father, was a stalwart of the Jewish community for many years. He was among the initial group of people who helped get the Young Israel of Woodmere off the ground, serving on its board and helping wherever necessary. Over the years, he and Barbara's mother, Sandy, *aleiha hashalom*, became diligent advocates for inclusivity in Jewish education and were founders of P'tach. Over the course of his life, he loved and lost, burying Sandy and two beloved children, Linda and Morris — but he somehow bore those tragic losses with a quiet grace and dignity.

Jerry served his community institutions humbly and without fanfare, and he brought wisdom and impeccable honesty to that service. He was *kove'a itim* to Torah, practiced *chesed*, and demonstrated integrity in all his actions. His commitment to the *klal*, and the devotion and dedication he brought to that work, will always serve as a powerful example to his children, and to his family as a whole. He married again, and spent the last twenty years of his life with Jinny, dividing their time between Woodmere and Jerusalem over the last few years, underscoring their love of Eretz Yisrael. Jerry will be missed sorely by his family for his gentle disposition, his humor, and his great big heart.

JOSÉ LEVKOVICH, Tuvia's father, spent much of World War II quarrying stone in Mauthausen, an Austrian slave-labor and concentration camp. In the camp, he briefly became a part-time servant of a German officer, allowing him to steal some food and other essentials to bring back to his grateful, starving compatriots. One of the SS officers he suffered under during those years was Amon Goeth, the sadistic SS commandant of the Płaszów concentration camp, whose monstrous persona became well known through Steven Spielberg's film *Schindler's List*. After the war, when Goeth had been captured, he was pretending to be a Wehrmacht soldier to conceal his true role in the Holocaust. José identified Goeth for who he really was and testified at the tribunal that convicted him. Goeth was subsequently hanged for his crimes.

But it wasn't just SS officers José helped identify. After the war, José went back to Europe, bearing with him lists of lost children from local Jewish committees. Some of these children were scattered in the countryside, living with gentiles who took them in, and José sought to find them and reunite them with family members. In some cases, families would not easily give up the children, leading to sometimes dangerous battles. After raising his own family in Bogotá, Columbia, and then Montreal, Canada, and the passing of his dear wife, Perla, *z"l*, José made *aliyah* on his eighty-eighth birthday. José's strength and resolve in the service of noble causes continue to be an inspiration to his children and grandchildren.

Barbara & Tuvia Levkovich

Zahava & Alan Goldschmidt,
Gabrielle and Ava

Arel Levkovich

Talia & Akiva Fried,
Lielle and Adina

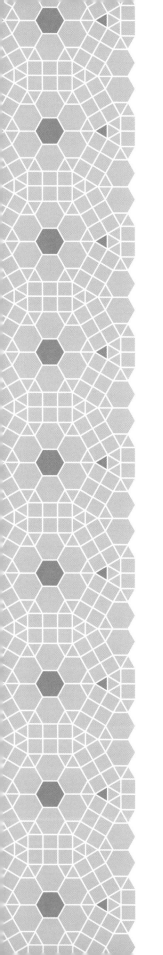

We gratefully acknowledge the following patrons who, with generosity and vision, have dedicated individual volumes of this *Parsha Companion* series:

BEREISHIT

Tuvia & Barbara Levkovich

SHMOT

Daniel & Jamie Schwartz

VAYIKRA

Mark & Erica Gerson

Chaim & Livia Jacobs

Yaron & Lisa Reich

Alan & Fran Broder

Yanky & Aliza Safier

Dr. Hillel & Chayi Cohen

Avram M. Cooperman MD & family

BAMIDBAR

Dr. Bruce Wayne Greenstein
& Ms. Monica Patricia Martinez

DEVARIM

Andrew & Terri Herenstein

We also wish to acknowledge the

Legacy Heritage Fund

which provided a generous grant to help
make this series of books possible.

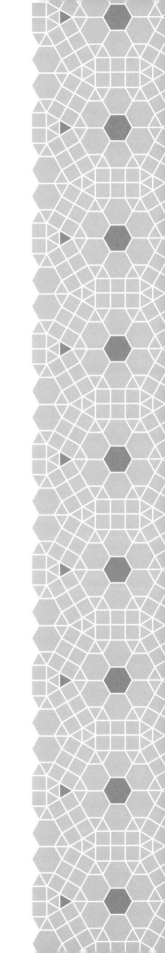

Contents

Some Words of Appreciation

CREATING THIS BOOK has been quite a journey for me. But that journey has not been a solitary endeavor, by any stretch of the imagination. I am in debt to a wonderful motley crew of partners, whose care, attention, generosity, and wisdom helped transform mere ruminations into the volume you hold in your hands.

Chief among those partners are Ronny and Toby Hersh, the "anchor patrons" of this five-volume series of books. I originally met Ronny and Toby when they joined the Woodmere community a couple of years ago. Since then, Ronny and I have enjoyed delving into the weekly parsha on Shabbat afternoons. Ronny's enthusiasm and joy in connecting deeply with the text is palpable, and we savored the delight of discovering new vistas in Torah together. In dedicating these volumes, Ronny and Toby are, in a way, opening up those study sessions to a much wider audience. If, reading these books, you too experience some of that thrill and joy in learning Torah, Ronny, Toby, and I will consider ourselves very richly rewarded.

Ronny and Toby have dedicated this series to the memory of their parents, Abraham and Esther Hersh, *z"l*, and Moshe and Rivka Zytelny, *z"l*, whose own personal stories were great journeys in their own right. I am deeply honored that this series of volumes bears their name. I hope it will prove a worthy continuation of their legacy.

This particular volume of the series (essays on Bereishit) has been generously sponsored by Barbara and Tuvia Levkovich and their children. One of the things that stands out about Barbara and Tuvia is their palpable belief that what really lends surpassing meaning to their lives, above and beyond their own personal or professional accomplishments, is the sense that they've become an effective bridge between generations. They've distilled values, beliefs, and ways of living that they saw in their parents, and passed them on to their children — and now, grandchildren.

In an expression of that belief, the Levkovich family has dedicated this volume in honor of Tuvia and Barbara's respective fathers. Tuvia's father, José, is still living; Barbara's father, Jerry, *z"l*, has recently passed away. Each has inspired successive generations of their descendants in profound ways. An appreciation of each appears a couple pages earlier in this volume. Take some time to read them; you'll be fascinated, and maybe even touched too.

I'd also like to express my profound appreciation to the Legacy Heritage Fund, which provided a generous grant that made this series of books possible. The foundation focuses much of its effort on supporting Jewish day schools in innovative and trend-setting ways. I am honored that the Legacy Heritage Fund has chosen to include this series of books among the many worthy projects they've chosen to support.

An author writes, but writing alone does not magically produce a book. Many others have helped take mere words and craft out of those words the book that you hold in your hands. I am greatly indebted to these good folks, so let me introduce you to them:

Shoshana Brody edited, proofread, and managed the production of this volume. She spent many painstaking hours working assiduously on each essay, refining ideas, challenging assumptions, and eliminating any trace of fluff or redundancy she could find in the writing. Each essay in this collection is manifestly better for her involvement. In addition to her editing and proofreading contributions, Shoshana also capably managed the dizzying administrative workflow associated with the book's production.

Shoshana was assisted in her efforts by Beth Lesch and Raquel Alfandari. Beth went through the entire manuscript, giving it another round of editing and proofreading, and also helped Shoshana coordinate administrative support. Her clear thinking and attention to detail helped enrich the essays and make them stronger. Raquel assisted in administration, and also read sections of the manuscript, contributing valuable comments and perspective.

Beyond Shoshana, Beth, and Raquel, other editors for this volume were Immanuel Shalev, Daniel Loewenstein, and Rivky Stern. Immanuel helped provide an important "50,000-foot view" of each essay, and lavished important attention on overall flow, style, introductions, and conclusions. His talent for finding potential weak links in arguments is a wonder to behold, and was an invaluable asset to me. Daniel's easy way with words helped enrich a number of pieces, including what I think of as one of the real gems of this volume: a rather complex piece on **Parshat Vayeishev** that helps elucidate Rashbam's view of the sale of Joseph. Rivky reviewed just about the entire manuscript, and her sharp eye for detail and nuance improved it throughout.

Rabbis Eli Raful and Elinatan Kupferberg contributed valuable research to this volume, combining near-encyclopedic knowledge of classic biblical exegesis with keen and seasoned judgment. Their work helped provide context for many of the essays, allowing more advanced readers to see how a given idea I propose "fits," interacting with or playing off of various writings of classical biblical commentators.

I am grateful to all those outside the orbit of the Aleph Beta office who also gave of their time to read through essays and provide important feedback. These include Zach Beer, Marc Bodner, Etta Brandman, Alan Broder, Avram Cooperman, David Curwin, Ethan Davidson, Jeremy England, Mark Gerson, Micah Gimpel, Bruce Greenstein, David Hamburger, Terri Herenstein, Sima Hertzberg, Steve Kowarsky, Carrie Lenga, Eli Mayerfeld, Robbie Rothenberg, Glenn Schoenfeld, Dani Schreiber, Daniel Schwartz, my son-in-law Yosef Segal, Esther Sutofsky, Phillip Ullman, Barry Waldman, and Esther Wein. Thanks to all of you for giving of your time, and providing to me your many prescient comments and insights.

The beautiful cover design, illustrations, and layout were created by Cory Rockliff, who typeset the volume and crafted all things related to its aesthetic presentation. Cory is the rare typesetter who also proofreads and edits; in my case, I was fortunate to have him serve as the last line of defense against errors, awkward wording, and all sorts of other sundry mishaps.

I also want to acknowledge those who stood behind this volume in other ways. LeRoy Hoffberger, *z"l*, was an incredibly important figure in my life. He was an early "student" of mine in a course I gave at Johns Hopkins University, and from then on, he never left my side. He founded the Hoffberger Institute for Text Study, which has supported my research, teaching, and writing for years now. Beyond that, he was also a great friend and *chevrusa* for me. Although I met him when he was already in his later years, he still had a kind of boyish delight in the beauty and intricacies of Torah thought. He left this world several years ago; I miss him terribly, but I continue to feel his presence in my work.

My *rosh yeshiva* at the Ner Israel yeshiva, Rabbi Yaakov Weinberg, *z"l*, introduced me to the joy and depth to be found in the deceptive simplicity of *pshat*, and Rabbis Tzvi Berkowitz and Ezra Neuberger, also of Ner Israel, reinforced that invaluable perspective. I also want to thank Rabbi Moshe Shapiro, *z"l*, for the time he spent with me reviewing and analyzing ideas in Genesis, and for his encouragement to teach the material I'd developed (and the methodological approach that underlies it) as far and as widely as possible.

Many of the ideas in this book on Genesis had their *own* genesis, as it were, in parsha videos I created with the help and support of the amazing team at Aleph Beta (you can find those videos at **www.alephbeta.org**). I want to take this opportunity to acknowledge, with gratitude, the folks behind the scene who make Aleph Beta's success a reality: its founders, board of directors, and officers. They are Kuty Shalev, Robbie Rothenberg, Steve Wagner, Etta Brandman, Daniel Schwartz, Donny Rosenberg, Alan Broder, David Pollack, and David Hamburger, along with Jeff Haskell and Josh Malin.

Finally, I want to acknowledge my family. My wife, Reena, is a wonderful, faithful partner in the greatest journey of all. As part of that journey together, we've raised seven wonderful children. How do you ever adequately say thanks for all that? She and my kids — Moshe, Shalva, Avigail, Shana, Yael, Ariella, and Avichai — have participated in shaping this book more than they might imagine, for they are *my* "parsha companions." Many of the ideas contained in these pages were born, shaped, or refined in animated discussions with them around the Shabbos table. For me, there's nothing like the thrill of pulling out our *chumashim* between the main course and dessert on Shabbos afternoon and starting a journey of discovery together. Continuing to learn Torah with my family is a constant opportunity to talk about things that matter deeply with the people I care about the most — and what could be better than that?

Rabbi David Fohrman

Inwood, NY
September 2019

Introduction

THE BOOK YOU HAVE in your hands is entitled *A Parsha Companion*. It will, I hope, be what its name implies: a faithful and engaging companion to you as you encounter the weekly parsha. That's *what* I hope this book will be, but it's not the most important thing I have to say in introducing this volume to you. There's also a how. And more importantly, there's a why.

The Power of Why

"What?" "How?" "Why?"— I once came across a short talk by Simon Sinek that meditated upon the relationship between these three simple words. He made the argument that whenever a person or a company does something, you can imagine three concentric circles:

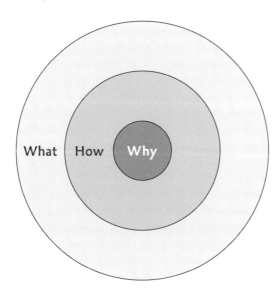

Every company, Sinek argues, knows *what* it is that they do: if I'm Apple, I know I make computers. Some companies also know *how* they do what they do: they can articulate, clearly and cogently, the process by which they go about things. But only a very few companies, he argues, know *why* they do what they do. What vision, exactly, compels them? What dream do they have that they are trying to achieve?

The most compelling thing a company or a person can do, Sinek argues, is to try and articulate that "why" and communicate it to others. Apple makes computers, yes, but their logo — the apple with a bite taken out of it — contains something of the subversive "why" Steve Jobs sought to cultivate: a commitment to rebel, just a bit, against conventional wisdom, with faint memories of the Tree of Knowledge; to "think different," in the words of their advertising slogan, and to express that way of thinking in the products the company makes. Martin Luther King Jr.'s most captivating speech wasn't his "I Have a Plan" speech; it was his "I Have a Dream" speech. In it, he shared his deepest-held beliefs, all the "whys," the hopes and dreams that animated all the "whats" he did, that gave reason and meaning to all the "hows" by which he did it. Without the "why," nothing else really matters.

Recently, I started thinking about Sinek's point in relation to my own work. For years now, I've been studying and teaching Torah. That's *what* I've been doing. There's a particular methodology I've been using — that's the "how." But what about the "why"? Why have I been doing this for all these years? What do I hope people will get from these efforts?

The answer, I think, has to do with what I *myself* have gotten from these efforts. It's something precious, and it's something I want to share. It can be summarized in a single, hard-to-pin-down word: *love*.

The Trees and the Forest

Love was pretty far from my mind back in grade school, when I was first exposed to Torah study. The way I was taught back then went kind of like this: you start, say, with a verse. God tells Abraham to go and leave his birthplace for a land that God will show him. It's a very nice verse. It seems intuitively understandable. But then you learn that it's not so simple. Rashi has one view of the verse, Sforno has a different view, and Ramban sees the whole thing in an entirely different way. Moreover, Rashi's view of the verse isn't really so clear: Mizrachi thinks Rashi means one thing; *Siftei Chachamim* thinks Rashi means something else. And did we forget about Hirsch? Rabbi Samson Raphael Hirsch has his own, unique way of interpreting all these words. OK, got all that? Great. Let's go on to the next verse, and we'll do it all again. At the end of the week, we'll have a quiz, and at the end of the month, a test.

It felt like you had to be really smart, really good at remembering lots of details, just to keep pace. Now, don't get me wrong: learning the Rishonim is important; these sainted commentators were brilliant interpreters of the text, and they are a crucial part of our tradition. But somehow, I was getting lost on the simplest of questions, like "What does the story, as a whole, *mean*?" I'm reading the story of Yehudah and Tamar in Genesis 38, and I can tell you why there might be three extra words in the third verse according to *Ohr HaChaim*, but somehow I'm hard-pressed to tell you anything about what the story is trying to *teach* me, what the story is doing there, interrupting the Joseph saga so blatantly. I was seeing a lot of trees, but somehow, the forest was passing me by.

Eventually, in an effort to regain my footing, I tried a bit of an experiment: I tried getting back to basics, as it were. These commentators of generations past — Rashi, Ramban, Sforno, Malbim, Hirsch, and others — all had the same starting point, it seemed to me: they read the text of the Torah carefully and made their best attempt to understand what was going on. Whatever else these greats were doing, they certainly *started* with that first, basic step. Nowadays, we call this basic reading comprehension. Moreover, not only did they do that themselves, they must have expected their readers to do that too. You wouldn't read a commentary on a text before reading the text itself, would you? So if that's the case, I found myself thinking, maybe I should just start there: let me clear my mind of everything else I thought I knew, go back to the basic text of the Torah, take a deep breath, and try to read it carefully.

In practice — wouldn't you know it? — I found that this wasn't so easy. Having read the stories of the Torah over and over again, it's not the simplest thing in the world to clear your mind, forget everything you know about them, and read them afresh, paying close attention to the words without leaping to conclusions. But gradually, I got better at it. I found that there was a deceptively simple set of tools — little games, almost — that were helpful in the process. You could look at a set of laws and play "Which of these things is not like the other?" You could read a story and stop halfway through, trying to guess the ending, playing "What happens next?"— and then go back and notice how very different the actual ending is from the ending you would have predicted. You could take a biblical story, pay close attention to the words, and play "Where have we heard these words before?," identifying in this story an uncanny echo of an earlier one, or a foreshadowing of a later one. All of these "games" are things little kids learn to do on *Sesame Street*. I began to find that everything you needed to know to start learning Torah, you learned in kindergarten.

Over time, I began to discover something that caught me by surprise: this "basic reading comprehension" was yielding results that weren't so "basic." It was helping to open up the deeper meaning of stories for me in entirely unexpected ways. It was as if, just under the surface of the Torah's most familiar stories, lay whole other layers of meaning, just waiting to be discovered — and these basic reading techniques were the spades, chisels, and brushes that helped me carefully lay bare some of these layers. And as I began to poke around still further, I began to realize that I wasn't the first to see any of this! The ancient rabbis of the Midrash, in their own inimitable way, had pointed to many of these deeper themes thousands of years ago. It was as if, concentrating on these kindergarten basics, I was rediscovering elements of an ancient but powerful methodology for approaching our most sacred texts.

Eventually, I began to notice something else: all this was changing me. It wasn't just that I was starting to *understand* the text better, or even learn its lessons better. It was something beyond that. I found myself kindling a romance with the Torah's text. I found myself falling in love with this book.

Who Falls in Love with a Book?

It's a strange sensation, to fall in love with a book, but that's what was happening. There was something . . . special about this text. Of course, on some level it sounds silly to say that — as an observant Jew, I always held the Torah to be sacred, to be a divine work. But it's one thing to *believe* that a sacred text is unique and special, and another to *see* that with your own eyes. I found that I didn't need be preached at to believe there was something deeply sacred in this work. If I just sat down and *read* it, the text would invariably leave me with something unexpectedly profound, and along the way, with a wink and a nod, it would find a way to remind me that this was no ordinary book. Its layers of meaning would dazzle me.

I had an interesting experience along these lines a number of years ago, back when I was teaching a non-credit class on the book of Genesis at Johns Hopkins University. I had been modeling the basic technique I described above: clear your mind, start fresh, ask the basic questions, sift the text for clues, observe the language carefully — and let the larger picture the text is painting slowly reveal itself. As I was about to begin the sixteenth and last class, someone in the back of the room — Jerry, a professor at the Johns Hopkins School of Medicine — raised his hand and asked, "Could you say a few words about the authorship of the Bible?"

Truth be told, the question of authorship was something I had been assiduously avoiding in that class. It just didn't seem appropriate to bring it up. Here I was, an observant Jew, teaching under the aegis of Johns Hopkins, a secular university. While I had my own religious convictions about the Bible being a divine work, this wasn't something I was keen to share with students there. They weren't coming to be preached to; they were coming to learn. So my approach was to take the question of authorship pretty much off the table. One way or the other, I had told them, the Bible is the greatest bestseller in the history of the world. There's got to be a reason for that. Let's study the text and see what we make of it.

But now Jerry was threatening to blow my cover. I hesitated a bit in answering him. To buy a little time, I asked him to clarify. He responded, "Well, I had always learned that the Bible was put together by a scattershot collection of authors. There was an E author and a J author, Isaiah found Deuteronomy, there was maybe a priestly author, too, and then all this was kind of pieced together by some redactors," he said. "But I'm having a hard time seeing how that could possibly be so. I mean, it's all so *interconnected*. The word patterns and structural features of Genesis are woven into those in the book of Numbers, which are woven into those in Exodus. It all seems so amazingly … unified. I don't see how more than one author could have possibly written this!"

I turned around and joked to the class that I didn't even pay Jerry to say that, and we all moved on. But Jerry's comment taught me something: it wasn't just *me* who noticed what was special about this book. The people in that classroom — my fellow explorers in this journey through the biblical text — saw it too. Despite my best attempt to remain mute about what I saw as the sacred quality of the Bible, what was special and uncanny about this book was shining through. There, in a nondescript room in Shaffer Hall, the text had begun to work its magic on a disparate group of students from backgrounds as diverse as you could possibly imagine. They were beginning to fall in love with this book too.

That sense of romance is what I want to try and share with you here in this book. More than anything else you get out of reading this *Parsha Companion*, above and beyond any particular insight you may perceive, or any methodological tool you might glean, I hope you get this: a sense of wonder and adoration for this shared treasure we have in our possession, the Torah.

The thing with adoration, though, is that it's ephemeral — and it's something not easily communicated directly. After all, how interested are you in listening to someone swooning over the wonderful qualities of their beloved girlfriend or boyfriend, wife or husband? A person in love *can't stop talking* about their beloved. They'll happily chew your ear off for what seems like hours. But most listeners . . . well, after a while, they'll just roll their eyes. Give them any chance to change the topic, and they'll take it.

I don't want to make that mistake with you. I don't want to preach to you, lecturing you on how special the Bible is. I just want to . . . learn with you. I want to embark on a shared adventure with you.

Come with me. Let's give it a whirl.

The Limits of Objectivity

The essays you'll find in this book are written a little differently from many expository treatments of Torah. Usually, an essay is written to make a point. Objectivity is prized; cogent, ruthless thinking is paramount. And to some extent, that remains true in this book: I *do* want to make a point and argue a case. But I'm also trying to do something else: I'm trying to share with you what some of these narratives mean to *me*, and why. My tone — often conversational, sometimes personal — will reflect that, or is meant to. I'm not so much making an argument here as inviting you to think along with me, to discover along with me. I'll end each essay with something of a meditation on what this all means to me. Perhaps it will resonate with you, or perhaps you'll find that to *you*, it means something altogether different. The Torah has a way of allowing for multiple perspectives, each worthy of contemplation. So if you travel along with me, rest assured that if you find yourself at odds with my conclusions, I'll be just as thrilled as if you find yourself nodding in agreement with my every word.

Does Man "Acquire" Woman?

זֹאת הַפַּעַם עֶצֶם מֵעֲצָמַי
וּבָשָׂר מִבְּשָׂרִי לְזֹאת
יִקָּרֵא אִשָּׁה כִּי מֵאִישׁ
לֻקֳחָה־זֹּאת:

This time, it is bone of my bones and flesh of my flesh. This one shall be called *ishah* [woman] because this one was taken from *ish* [man].

GENESIS 2:23

Does Man "Acquire" Woman?

I WANT TO GRAPPLE with something that is perhaps just a tad controversial, what would seem to be a decidedly un-egalitarian aspect of traditional Jewish marriage. The issue stands out pretty clearly in the opening words of the first mishnah of tractate Kiddushin:

הָאִשָּׁה נִקְנֵית בְּשָׁלֹשׁ דְּרָכִים A woman is acquired in three ways	Mishnah Kiddushin 1:1

The mishnaic text here is characterizing marriage (or to be more precise, *kiddushin*, or betrothal — the first stage of marriage) as an act of *acquisition* of a woman undertaken by a man.[1] Now, doesn't that make you cringe a little? It almost sounds as if a woman is being treated as mere chattel, like she's some kind of object that can be *bought*. Is that what we think is happening under the chuppah? That romantic moment when the bride circles the groom seven times, when her eyes meet his over a gleaming goblet of wine, when the crowd hushes as he gingerly slips a ring over her finger . . . What is he doing right then? Is he really "acquiring" her? A man buys himself a carton of milk, a pair of shoes . . . but a *wife*? Is that *really* the Torah's understanding of marriage?

An answer to this vexing conundrum can, I believe, be found in **Parshat Bereishit**, where the Torah describes what is arguably the first marriage in the history of the world, that between Adam and Eve. Let's take a look at that text together.

---

1   The mishnah is based on Deuteronomy 24:1, which also describes marriage using the language of "acquisition": כִּי־יִקַּח אִישׁ אִשָּׁה וּבְעָלָהּ, "When a man *takes* a wife and marries her . . ."

9

The Dating Game

What is the story of Adam and Eve's courtship? It's unconventional, to say the least. After bringing Adam into the world, God assesses His new creation and concludes:

Genesis 2:18

לֹא־טוֹב הֱיוֹת הָאָדָם לְבַדּוֹ
אֶעֱשֶׂה־לּוֹ עֵזֶר כְּנֶגְדּוֹ:

It is not good that the man should be alone; I will make him a helpmate for him.

Now, imagine that you're God. You've just created man, and you've decided that he shouldn't be alone. He needs some kind of companion. What would you do next? *This would be a good time to create Eve, wouldn't it?* But that's not what God does. Instead, the world's first romance takes a decidedly unromantic turn. God decides to create some animals:

Genesis 2:19

וַיִּצֶר יְקוָה אֱלֹקִים מִן־הָאֲדָמָה
כָּל־חַיַּת הַשָּׂדֶה וְאֵת כָּל־עוֹף
הַשָּׁמַיִם וַיָּבֵא אֶל־הָאָדָם
לִרְאוֹת מַה־יִּקְרָא־לוֹ וְכֹל
אֲשֶׁר יִקְרָא־לוֹ הָאָדָם נֶפֶשׁ
חַיָּה הוּא שְׁמוֹ:

And out of the ground the Lord God formed every beast of the field, and every fowl of the air; and brought them to the man to see what he would call them; and whatever the man would call every living creature, that was to be its name.

The Almighty takes this opportunity to create a whole menagerie, every beast of the field and every fowl of the air. The Lord then parades each animal before Adam to see whether it might be Adam's mate. One can imagine the scene: first comes the hippopotamus, then the flamingo, and then the giraffe. One by one, Adam names the animals — and finds himself disappointed in them. It sounds like some sort of bizarre dating game.[2]

Genesis 2:21–22

Alas, there's no companion for Adam to be found among the animals. So what does God do? He puts Adam to sleep,° removes one of his ribs, and makes it into a woman. He presents the woman to Adam, just as He has presented all the animals. And how does Adam react?

---

2   For more on this, see my earlier work *The Beast That Crouches at the Door*, pt. 1, ch. 5.

וַיֹּאמֶר הָאָדָם זֹאת הַפַּעַם
עֶצֶם מֵעֲצָמַי וּבָשָׂר מִבְּשָׂרִי
לְזֹאת יִקָּרֵא אִשָּׁה כִּי מֵאִישׁ
לֻקֳחָה־זֹּאת:

And man said, "This time, it is bone of my bones and flesh of my flesh. This one shall be called *ishah* [woman] because this one was taken from *ish* [man]."

Genesis 2:23

A very beautiful, romantic declaration, no doubt. But it's followed immediately in the text by something decidedly puzzling:

עַל־כֵּן יַעֲזָב־אִישׁ אֶת־אָבִיו
וְאֶת־אִמּוֹ וְדָבַק בְּאִשְׁתּוֹ
וְהָיוּ לְבָשָׂר אֶחָד:

This is why a man leaves behind his father and his mother and clings to his wife, and they become one flesh.

Genesis 2:24

What, exactly, is happening here? Up to this point, the Torah has been telling us a story — but all of a sudden, the narrator, as it were, steps out and "breaks the fourth wall," speaking directly to the reader. *By the way, folks, here's something you should know, a great timeless lesson for you: this is why a man leaves his parents behind. This is why a man gets married.*

Evidently, the Torah considers this message to be so compelling that it doesn't simply leave it to the astute reader to infer, but instead drills the point home overtly and explicitly: *This is why people get married; get it?* It's as if the Torah itself is telling us why this story is so important — it's not just filling in some idle historical details about the love story of the first man and woman; it's telling us about all our love stories, for all time. It's telling us something about why man seeks to marry, something we need to know right here, right now, and in every generation.

But for all the urgency the Torah attaches to this lesson, the question persists: What, exactly, *is* the lesson? The Torah's intent seems a bit obscure. It says עַל־כֵּן (*al kein*), "*this* is why," a man leaves behind his father and mother and chooses to get married. But what exactly is "this"? Because of *what* does man leave behind mother and father? Seemingly, it's because of the last thing the Torah said — or to be precise, the last thing Adam said: "This time, it is bone of my bones and flesh of my flesh. This one shall be called *ishah* [woman] because this one was taken from *ish* [man]." The

Torah is telling us that there is something in those words, in the declaration Adam made, that explains why it is that men desire to get married. Were it not for that mysterious "something," we are asked to believe, a man would never get married. He'd never want to leave behind his mother and father; he'd just grow old in his childhood home.

So what is this mysterious something?

The Drive for Marriage

What *did* Adam find so attractive about Eve? How did he know that she was Mrs. Right? The Torah doesn't leave us to speculate about this; it tells us. When Adam first sees Eve, he recognizes, with a sense of immediate understanding mixed with astonishment, that she is different, she is special…Why? Because, Adam says, she *came from him*.

And, of course, she did. Adam and Eve were once a single, unified being. God put man to sleep and took his rib from him. In doing so, one might say, God took the feminine part of man from him and made it into a separate being. Adam sensed the loss of his feminine side and desired to recapture it in marriage.[3]

Think back to those animals that God paraded before Adam. Why didn't they seem like suitable mates to him? The answer now seems clear: because they were fundamentally foreign to Adam.

Not so with Eve. When Adam sets eyes on her for the very first time, he feels an immediate kinship with her. He senses that she is a lost part of himself, and so he yearns to reunite with her. Therein lies his drive to marry her.

To Leave Mother and Father

Now let's come back to that narrative aside, the moment the Torah "breaks

---

3   The midrash in Bereishit Rabbah 8:1 and Vayikra Rabbah 14:1 goes even further, stating that Adam was initially created as a dual being, both male and female. The midrash seems to be grounded in an intriguing ambiguity in the biblical text:

וַיִּבְרָא אֱלֹקִים אֶת־הָאָדָם בְּצַלְמוֹ בְּצֶלֶם אֱלֹקִים בָּרָא אֹתוֹ זָכָר וּנְקֵבָה בָּרָא אֹתָם:

"And God created man in His own image, in the image of God He created *him*; male and female He created *them*" (Genesis 1:27). The use of a singular pronoun followed by a plural one suggests that man really was once a singular being, but a being that was also a plurality: he was indeed "one" with his feminine side. Hence, in the creation of Eve, he experiences a genuine sense of loss, which he feels bound to recoup.

the fourth wall" and addresses the reader: "This is why a man leaves behind his father and his mother …"° We wondered before: What is it about
Adam's declaration upon seeing Eve that explains, of all things, why a man
would "leave behind his father and his mother"?

But now, it's not so strange anymore: there really *is* a fundamental
commonality between man's relationship with his wife and his relationship with his mother and father. What is that commonality?

What is the common denominator between man's relationship with
his wife and his relationship with his mother and his father?

Move over, Freud; the Torah was here first. The answer is that he was
once *one* with them. He comes biologically from mother and father; before
birth, he truly *was* of one flesh with them.

That unity is very compelling. There is, indeed, a part of man that never
really wants to leave home. It is that childlike part of him that wants to stay
unified with his source, his parents, where he comes from. But the truth is
that he can't really recapture that unity. So what's going to get man off his
parents' couch? There is only one thing that can convince him to move
forward in life and establish a home of his own — and that is the chance
to really, truly, attain an alternative unity, the unity that a man can experience with his wife. In recapturing the union of masculine and feminine,
man truly attains oneness in this world, the unity of his original being, the
oneness that he enjoyed before Eve was ever taken from him.[4]

So the Bible portrays marriage as man reuniting with his lost self.
Seems kind of romantic, doesn't it? But — to come back to the question
we started with — when you open up tractate Kiddushin, the Mishnah's
portrayal of marriage seems anything but romantic. Why use a word like
"acquisition" to describe marriage, this most romantic of acts? It sounds
so harsh, so transactional.

So I want to suggest a theory here. It's a bit of a radical theory, but
bear with me.

Revising Our Understanding

We misunderstand the concept of acquisition. We think acquisition is
about owning things, about controlling them — and to some extent, when

---

4   Cf. Ibn Ezra and Radak to Genesis 2:24. Both make the point that when the
    Torah states that man and woman will "therefore … become one flesh," this idea
    is grounded in the prior verse, where Adam describes Eve as "flesh of my flesh."

acquisition is about *things*, maybe it is. When I buy a lawnmower, I control it. But there are other kinds of acquisition that have very little to do with "control." Take, for example, man's relationship with the Torah itself. Consider this statement from Pirkei Avot (Ethics of the Fathers):

Pirkei Avot 6:6	הַתּוֹרָה נִקְנֵית בְּאַרְבָּעִים וּשְׁמֹנָה דְבָרִים	The Torah is acquired with forty-eight qualities

There's that word: נִקְנֵית, "acquired"— the same word that describes a man's "acquisition" of a woman in marriage. The Torah, according to this mishnah, is *itself* something to be acquired. But how would you translate "acquired" in this context? Do I, the one who learns Torah, *control* it? If anything, *it* controls *me*! The Torah demands a certain lifestyle of me — and yet I "acquire" it!

This kind of acquisition has very little to do with *control*. It seems, instead, to be about *responsibility*. I don't "control" Torah — that would be an act of defilement. The Torah that I learn is mine, perhaps, in the sense that it "completes" me, and my responsibility is to treasure it, to appreciate it for what it is, and to keep it safe.

To Have and to Hold

Perhaps something similar is going on with "acquisition" in the context of marriage. Yes, a man "acquires" a woman — but what does that mean? Are his rights to her paramount, or his obligations to her? She *completes* him, and because of that, he is to treasure her immensely and keep her safe.

Completion. Indeed, at its deepest level, maybe that's the great hope that lies at the root of all "acquisition." *Whenever* we seek to acquire something or someone — the Torah, a wife, or a Lamborghini — what, really, is our motivation? Beyond financial gain, beyond economic security, we seem to be responding to a deeper need. We are trying to feel *complete*. But we are apt to delude ourselves in that quest, and that delusion can have sad consequences. Ironically, it can rob us of the happiness we seek: the person who has fifty million dollars and, in his waning years, works like mad to make fifty-*one* million, sacrificing time he could spend playing ball with his grandchildren to do it — what delusion is he suffering from? We humans can often feel that we are *missing* something, that there is a void within us, and if we can only acquire a certain thing (and then the next thing, and then the thing after that) we will somehow feel whole. But it never really works.

It doesn't work because *things*, for the most part, don't complete us. They are foreign to us, like the animals were to Adam. Animals were always external to Adam, so they could not possibly make him whole. Only one acquisition really completes us, and this is *the* acquisition par excellence: man's "taking" of woman. Marriage.

In marriage, masculine and feminine come together as one. In the end, marriage is the one moment in our lives when the great hope of acquisition can truly be realized. It is the moment we become whole.

Apocalypse Plow
Noah & the End of the World

זֶה יְנַחֲמֵנוּ מִמַּעֲשֵׂנוּ
וּמֵעִצְּבוֹן יָדֵינוּ
מִן־הָאֲדָמָה אֲשֶׁר
אֵרְרָהּ יְקֹוָה:

This one will comfort us from our work and from the sadness of our hands, which comes from the ground which the Lord has cursed.

GENESIS 5:29

Apocalypse Plow

Noah & the End of the World

THE TORAH talks to us about Noah's name and tells us how, exactly, he got it. It turns out that Noah's father, a man named Lemech, made a declaration upon Noah's birth — and in concert with that declaration, he named his child. But there's something puzzling about that declaration, and I want to discuss it with you.

Here's what the Torah has to say about Lemech and the naming of Noah:

וַיִּקְרָא אֶת־שְׁמוֹ נֹחַ	And he called his name Noah, saying,	Genesis 5:29
לֵאמֹר זֶה יְנַחֲמֵנוּ	"This one will comfort us from our work	
מִמַּעֲשֵׂנוּ וּמֵעִצְּבוֹן	and from the sadness of our hands,	
יָדֵינוּ מִן־הָאֲדָמָה	which comes from the ground which	
אֲשֶׁר אֵרְרָהּ יְקֹוָה:	the Lord has cursed."	

The connection to "comfort" comes from the *nun* (נ) and *chet* (ח) of Noah's name, which, according to the text, borrows from the Hebrew root for "comfort," *nun-chet-mem* (נ-ח-מ). Somehow, Lemech senses that this child is going to bring comfort, and he names Noah for this idea. But this comfort will not just be for Lemech; it will play out on a grand scale. Noah will comfort all mankind for "the ground which the Lord has cursed."

What *is* the curse of the ground that Lemech references? It seems pretty clear that Lemech has in mind the curses we hear about in the earliest stories of the Torah: the episodes of the Tree of Knowledge of Good and Evil, and of Cain and Abel. In each of these stories, sin — eating from the tree, killing Abel — gives rise to two main consequences. One is alienation from God: immediately after eating the forbidden fruit, Adam and Eve hide from God among the trees of the garden,° and are banished from God's garden soon after. Likewise, Cain, in the aftermath of his own sin, senses that he will spend his entire life continually hiding from God.°

Genesis 3:8

Genesis 4:14

But another consequence of these sins is alienation from the land, from the earth itself. Adam is told that the land will no longer simply provide, almost effortlessly, for Adam and Eve. No, they will have to *work* it now:

Genesis 3:17

בְּעִצָּבוֹן תֹּאכְלֶנָּה
כֹּל יְמֵי חַיֶּיךָ

In sadness will you eat of it
all the days of your life.

And that curse seems to intensify in the age of Cain. Even if he works the land, Cain is told,

Genesis 4:12

לֹא־תֹסֵף תֵּת־
כֹּחָהּ לָךְ

[the land] will not continue to
yield to you her strength

But now, generations later, Lemech senses that things could be different, that somehow, we as humans could — and would — overcome this curse:

Genesis 5:29

זֶה יְנַחֲמֵנוּ מִמַּעֲשֵׂנוּ
וּמֵעִצְּבוֹן יָדֵינוּ מִן־הָאֲדָמָה
אֲשֶׁר אֵרְרָהּ יְקוָה:

This one will comfort us from our work and
from the sadness of our hands, which comes
from the ground which the Lord has cursed.

So it all sounds very nice and very hopeful. But here's the chilling part: if you start from the naming of Noah and fast-forward six verses ahead in the Torah, you get to a much darker passage, describing God's decision to destroy the world by flood. And if you take a good look at that divine choice to destroy everything, you'll notice something remarkable: God's decision to destroy the world *echoes Lemech's decision to name his child Noah.*

Hearing the Echo

To see how the echo works, let's start with that idea of "comfort" that Lemech talks about: the word he uses is *yenachamenu* (יְנַחֲמֵנוּ). It turns out that precisely this Hebrew word for "comfort" makes an appearance when God chooses to destroy the world:

וַיִּנָּחֶם יְקוָה כִּי־עָשָׂה אֶת־הָאָדָם בָּאָרֶץ וַיִּתְעַצֵּב אֶל־לִבּוֹ: וַיֹּאמֶר יְקוָה אֶמְחֶה אֶת־הָאָדָם אֲשֶׁר־בָּרָאתִי מֵעַל פְּנֵי הָאֲדָמָה	And the Lord **regretted** that He had made man on the earth, and He was saddened to His heart. And the Lord said, "I will wipe out man, whom I have created, from the face of the earth"

Genesis 6:6–7

The Almighty "regrets" having created man. And — wouldn't you know it? — in Hebrew, God's "regret" is expressed by the same word as Lemech's "comfort": *vayinachem* (וַיִּנָּחֶם), from the root *nun-chet-mem* (נ-ח-מ).

Well, that's all well and good, you might say — an interesting coincidence, but nothing more than that. Except that … it's very hard to chalk this up to coincidence, for this correspondence is, in fact, one of many: it's not just the *nun-chet-mem* (נ-ח-מ) in God's declaration that echoes Lemech; other parts of the Almighty's declaration do too.

Let me try and lay out the correspondences for you more broadly. Lemech had said about Noah, "This one will comfort us from our work and from the sadness of our hands, which comes from the ground which the Lord has cursed" (זֶה יְנַחֲמֵנוּ מִמַּעֲשֵׂנוּ וּמֵעִצְּבוֹן יָדֵינוּ מִן־הָאֲדָמָה אֲשֶׁר אֵרְרָהּ יְקוָה). Now, those four words of Lemech — יְנַחֲמֵנוּ, מִמַּעֲשֵׂנוּ, וּמֵעִצְּבוֹן and הָאֲדָמָה — you'll find *all* of them repeated in God's decision to destroy the world. And not only are they repeated; they're repeated in the exact same *order* in which Lemech used them. Let's read God's declaration again, and you'll see what I mean:

וַיִּנָּחֶם יְקוָה כִּי־עָשָׂה אֶת־הָאָדָם בָּאָרֶץ וַיִּתְעַצֵּב אֶל־לִבּוֹ: וַיֹּאמֶר יְקוָה אֶמְחֶה אֶת־הָאָדָם אֲשֶׁר־בָּרָאתִי מֵעַל פְּנֵי הָאֲדָמָה	And the Lord **regretted** that He had **made** man on the earth, and He was saddened to His heart. And the Lord said, "I will wipe out man, whom I have created, from the face of the earth"

Genesis 6:6–7

וַיִּנָּחֶם יְקֹוָה   "And the Lord **regretted**" (but remember, this is the same as the word for Lemech's "comfort")

כִּי־עָשָׂה   "that He had **made** man"

וַיִּתְעַצֵּב אֶל־לִבּוֹ   "and He was **saddened**" (there's *itzavon*, "sadness," as in Lemech's statement)

מֵעַל פְּנֵי הָאֲדָמָה   Finally, as if on cue, God declares, "I will wipe out man מֵעַל פְּנֵי הָאֲדָמָה"—"from the face of the **earth** [*adamah*]." That word *adamah* is also borrowed from Lemech.

Lemech's Declaration

Genesis 5:29   זֶה יְנַחֲמֵנוּ מִמַּעֲשֵׂנוּ וּמֵעִצְּבוֹן יָדֵינוּ מִן־הָאֲדָמָה אֲשֶׁר אֵרְרָהּ יְקֹוָה: This one will **comfort** us from our **work** and from the sadness of our hands, which comes from the ground which the Lord has cursed.

God's Declaration

Genesis 6:6–7   וַיִּנָּחֶם יְקֹוָה כִּי־עָשָׂה אֶת־הָאָדָם בָּאָרֶץ וַיִּתְעַצֵּב אֶל־לִבּוֹ: וַיֹּאמֶר יְקֹוָה אֶמְחֶה אֶת־הָאָדָם אֲשֶׁר־בָּרָאתִי מֵעַל פְּנֵי הָאֲדָמָה   And the Lord **regretted** that He had **made** man on the earth, and He was **saddened** to His heart. And the Lord said, "I will wipe out man, whom I have created, from the face of the **earth**"

What's Going On?

It's impossible to resist the conclusion that, for some strange reason, God's declaration of His intention to destroy the world has as its prototype Lemech's naming of Noah. It's almost as if God is mimicking Lemech in some way when He decides to destroy the world. But why would that be? Why would God build the decision to destroy His creation out of Lemech's innocent hopes for his newborn child?

I'd like to propose a theory to you. The theory grows out of a comment made by Rashi — seemingly a very innocent little comment — concerning Lemech's declaration that Noah will bring "comfort." How, Rashi seems to wonder, will Noah bring that comfort?

Rashi, quoting the sages of the Midrash, explains the "comfort" this way:

עַד שֶׁלֹּא בָא נֹחַ לֹא
הָיָה לָהֶם כְּלִי מַחֲרֵשָׁה
וְהוּא הֵכִין לָהֶם.

Before Noah, men did not have plowshares. Noah prepared [such tools] for them.

[Midrash Tanchuma, Genesis 11]

Rashi to Genesis 5:29

Lemech saw prophetically, the Sages say, that Noah would be the creator of the plow, and the plow would be a form of comfort for humans; it would be a salve for the curse of the land. The curse of the land meant that it wouldn't be easy, going forward, to grow crops. Thorns and thistles would mix with the earth's bounty. The invention of the plow, though, would help solve that problem. It would ease mankind's cultivation of the soil. Living in a post-plow world, humans would no longer feel as much of the sting from that curse of the land, and in that, they would find comfort.

It seems like a harmless hope that Lemech expresses. I want to argue, though, that Lemech's hope somehow becomes an inflection point — the straw that broke the camel's back. It was a hope that somehow triggered God's decision to give up on the world as it was, and to start anew.

Why? Because there was something insidious about this hope. *A plow will provide the comfort we are looking for.* Lemech, apparently speaking on behalf of a frustrated humanity, sought to find comfort where none could really be found. If a plow could comfort them, somehow, for the curse of the land, then there was no hope left for humanity.

Why?

What Does Comfort Really Mean?

Let's examine, for a moment, the notion of "comfort." What is comfort, anyway? Why do we want it, and how do we go about achieving it?

Comfort is the antidote for loss — or if not the antidote, it is the balm we humans use for loss, allowing us to bind our wounds and move on. Getting over a terrible loss isn't easy. A colleague of mine once memorably said that a mourner asks an impossible question: *Why? How could this possibly have happened?* And really, there's no answer to such a question. So, in the absence of an answer, the only thing the mourner can do is somehow reconcile themselves to the simple fact that, inexplicably, it *has* happened. That, indeed, might be why the mourner, in Hebrew, is known as an *avel*. The word אָבֵל (*avel*) is spelled *aleph-bet-lamed*, which also spells אֲבָל (*aval*), "but" or "nevertheless." Being an *avel*, a mourner, means embracing nevertheless-ness: *Why? How could it happen? I don't know. Nevertheless, it happened.*

Comfort, then, involves a change in perspective. I stop trying to change an uncomfortable fact, and instead accommodate myself to it. But if this is the nature of comfort, then we must also recognize that comfort is not the answer to all types of pain. Not all uncomfortable facts *should* be accommodated. Some kinds of hardship are meant to challenge us; some kinds of pain have root causes we are meant to seek out and solve. And that was the kind of hardship, I want to argue, that was expressed by the curse of the land.

Sadness and Toil

Ask yourself: Was the curse of the land just a blind fact, or was there some sort of . . . overarching purpose for it?

There's a clue in the language God uses in imposing the curse. The Almighty suggests that in the wake of the first humans' sin, they would experience something called עִצָּבוֹן (*itzavon*) in working the land. Translations conventionally render that word as "toil," but literally, it means "sadness":

Genesis 3:17   בְּעִצָּבוֹן תֹּאכֲלֶנָּה   In **sadness** will you eat of it
כֹּל יְמֵי חַיֶּיךָ   all the days of your life

So let's consider that: What is so *sad* about working the land? It might be *difficult* to work incessantly, but why is it *sad*?

When work is just work, then no, it's not sad; but when work is *toil* — when work *could* have been easier, but is instead a hardship — well, *then* there's something sad about that work. There's a kind of futility involved in it. And our sadness, our disappointment, is a recognition of that futility, a recognition that things could have, *should have*, been different.

The curses in the wake of the episode of the Tree of Knowledge and Cain's murder of Abel imposed a kind of distance between humans and two important "other beings": God and the land. Hiding from God is one way we felt that distance. Another way we felt it was in the "sadness" that would prevail when we worked the land. We would not be as close to the land as we might like to be; our interaction with the land would be more difficult, more fraught, than we would like it to be.

The land and God were man's twin creators: God bestowed a soul on man by blowing into his nostrils the breath of life — but the Almighty formed man's body from the dust of the *earth*.[1] There is an inherent closeness between a creature and its creator, a natural warmth and intimacy. In the wake of our early sins, though, some of that intimacy would be lost. A kind of distance would creep into the relationship between man and his creators. And *that* was the curse.

The Purpose of the Curses

So let's ponder something: Why would the Almighty do this? What is the logic in reacting to man's sins this way? Why put in place curses that *alienate* humanity from its creators? God doesn't want us to be alienated, does He?

Perhaps this feeling of alienation is a kind of homing beacon. It is

---

1 Ramban illuminates this idea with a fascinating comment. When God made man, He famously declared: נַעֲשֶׂה אָדָם בְּצַלְמֵנוּ כִּדְמוּתֵנוּ—"let *us* make man in *our* image, after *our* likeness" (Genesis 1:26). The classical commentators all struggle with the plural there: Who, exactly, is God talking to when He says "our"? If God is one, who is His partner in the creation of man? Ramban's answer is that His partner was the land. God, Ramban argues, was speaking to the land, proposing to the earth, as it were: *You contribute the body and I shall contribute the soul. Together, we shall create him.*

emotionally, spiritually *sad* to be alienated from one's Creator. We were once one with our Creator, and there is a part of us that craves a return to that oneness, that closeness, always. We always want to come back, to come home. And so, the more one becomes alienated from one's Creator, from one's source, the stronger the homing beacon becomes, the more one wants to return.

And *that*, perhaps, is the point of the curses. They bid us to understand how alienated we have become — and by extension, they imbue us with a longing to return. But in order to feel that longing, we need to experience the futility of toil. We need to feel that sadness.

The Breaking Point

So let's recount the history of that "sadness." In the wake of Adam and Eve's sin in Eden, God imposed curses on the land, curses that brought a measure of sadness and toil into our relationship with God's earth, and by extension, into our relationship with our twin creators, God and earth. As we've said, the sadness was meant to be a homing beacon; it was meant to help bring humanity home. But the next generation didn't heed the beacon. Instead, one brother killed another, watering God's earth with his blood — and when that happened, the curse of the earth intensified: Cain would experience even more difficulty farming, and would spend his days hiding from God perpetually.° The sadness was increasing. But still, mankind paid no heed ... until eventually, generations later, people found a solution: the plow.

Genesis 4:11–14

Unfortunately, the plow was man's answer to the increasing sadness — a technological solution to a spiritual problem. We asked before why Lemech's "prophecy" about the plow might have been a sort of breaking point that convinced God to destroy the world and start over — and now, perhaps, we have an answer. The plow guaranteed that the sadness of the curses wouldn't be able to do its job. Man was supposed to live with the sadness day in and day out, seeking always to reconnect with his twin creators, the earth and God, and to somehow overcome the alienation he brought to those relationships. Instead, man chose to anesthetize himself against the pain. The plow was a way of taking Tylenol to avoid feeling the sadness. Once that was the case, there was no hope anymore, no hope that the gradually escalating curses would do their job. The only way out now would be to start over — which is exactly what God chooses to do.

God didn't randomly decide to give up on mankind. God gave up only when *we gave up*.[2]

At this point, God decides to bring one family into an ark and start the project of creation anew. In doing so, the Almighty uses the same language humankind did to comfort themselves; God mimics Lemech's decision to name his child "comfort"— *Noach* (נֹחַ), from *nun-chet-mem* (נ-ח-מ) —with a decision of His own to "change His mind"— *vayinachem* (וַיִּנָּחֶם), from *nun-chet-mem* (נ-ח-מ) — about humanity and its fate. With the purpose of His curses exhausted, this world would pass into the night; God and the children of men needed to start over again, in a new world.

Brave New World

The new world would not be the same as the old one. Its potential would, somehow, be more limited. A friend of mine, R. Simcha Baer, once made the argument to me that the old world was God's world, while the new world would be man's world. In the old world, man was not to be allowed to eat animals, but that would change in the new world; Noah and his children would be permitted to eat meat. Man and the animals were cotenants of God's world. In the new world, though, God would give man the keys to the property. Man was in charge. It was his world now.

The changing of the guard is evident in other ways too. When the rain arrives and the time comes to close the door of the ark, who closes that door? The verse tells us:

וַיִּסְגֹּר יְקֹוָה בַּעֲדוֹ   God shut [Noah] inside [the ark]   Genesis 7:16

But after the rain ceased and the time came to open the door, who opens it?

---

2   So, when would a benevolent God give up on humanity? Never — *as long as we are still working to restore the relationship*. As long as that's the case, we can take as much time as we need. The only time God would ever give up on the relationship ... is if we signal that *we* have given up. In essence, that's what the invention of the plow signaled: it was humanity's way of throwing up its collective hands at the curses and saying: *This sadness will never be overcome; it's just a fact of life, so let's make things easier for ourselves.*

וַיָּסַר נֹחַ אֶת־מִכְסֵה הַתֵּבָה   And Noah opened the covering of the ark

With sadness, God mournfully closed the door on His world, saying good-bye to it; Noah opened the door on a new world, his own world. God pulled the curtain on His world because man's evil had corrupted it. But God promises that He, the Almighty, will never again destroy the world. Why? Is it because man would never again become terribly evil — evil enough to justify destruction? If it happened once, couldn't it happen twice?

God's assurance that He would never again destroy the world seems to be based not on a change in humanity, but a change in the world. Evil had corrupted God's world, so God packed up the world and closed it down. If evil were ever to corrupt man's world... well, that would be man's problem.

This new world was more durable, perhaps, but it was less... brilliant. A kind of dazzling intimacy with the divine was possible in God's own world — in man's world, less so. The potential of the old world, God's world, could not be fathomed by inhabitants of the new world. Noah was the transition figure between the worlds, the one who saw both of them.

Genesis
9:20–21

Shortly after emerging from the ark, Noah would plant himself a vineyard and get drunk.° It seems strange that he would do so. But perhaps his loss — the loss not just of all humanity, but of the chance to live in God's own world — was too much to bear. Yes, the children of men would have more authority in this new world. But the world itself — its potential for connection with the divine — would be just a shadow of its former self.

The plow was an abomination in God's world, but not in man's world. The imperative to restore our original connection with the Almighty, the kind of connection that we needed for living in close quarters with the divine — was gone now. As a result, the need for redemption from alienation from our Creator was less pressing. And all this made the plow... more legitimate, somehow, in this new world. If man wanted to use it to till his earth, why, he could do so, if he chose.

The plow was a first step forward in a great march that man would undertake in his new world. That march, however, is one that man, over time, would have to manage carefully. Technology is wonderful. But over time, the drive to invent ever-more-powerful tools, tools that make our life on earth easier, would, of necessity, compete for man's attention with the sort of things that make life worth living in the first place — things like forging a richer relationship with other people or with our Creator. Moreover, God had promised never to destroy man's world. But man — could *he* ever destroy it? One wonders whether insurance against that possibility was included in God's promise.

As man marches forward, achieving milestone after milestone in his technological march, he must reckon seriously with the increasing power of his own inventions. God had given man a new lease on life; now it would be up to man to make the most of it. It would be up to him to forge as close a connection with his Creator as possible from the confines of his own world, and to ensure that these inventions — the great-grandchildren of the plow — do not unduly avert his focus, or bring the great experiment of man's world to an unfortunate and untimely end.

Covenant with God

זֹאת בְּרִיתִי אֲשֶׁר
תִּשְׁמְרוּ בֵּינִי וּבֵינֵיכֶם
וּבֵין זַרְעֲךָ אַחֲרֶיךָ
הִמּוֹל לָכֶם כָּל־זָכָר:

This is My covenant, which you shall keep, between Me and you and your seed after you: every male among you shall be circumcised.

GENESIS 17:10

Covenant with God

HERE'S A TRIVIA QUESTION FOR YOU: What's the earliest Torah commentator you can think of? To be sure, scores of Torah commentaries were written by venerable scholars of generations past: Rashi, Ibn Ezra, Ramban, Sforno... Hundreds of years before that, there was Saadiah Gaon, and before that, the sages of the ancient Midrash. But what's the *earliest* commentary on the Torah that we know of?

What if I told you it's the Torah itself?

It sounds faintly ridiculous. How could a work comment on *itself*? But remarkably, evidence suggests that this is exactly what the Torah does. The Torah, I want to argue, embeds commentary in its own text — and in so doing, weaves a kind of meta-story into its story. And this commentary is accessible to us, if we can only figure out how to access it.[1]

I'd like to discuss with you a particular device the Torah seems to employ to create such commentary: using the parlance of the Rabbis, we might call it an *atbash* pattern[2] — or, to use modern language, a "chiasm."

---

1   Chazal, the ancient Sages, were keenly aware of both the need for, and the capacity of, one verse or passage in the Torah to act as a commentary on another. The Beraita of the Thirty-Two Middot of R. Eliezer b. R. Yosei HaGelili, for example, is an extensive listing of the various modes of exegesis in the Talmud and Midrash, and many of the tools described there are, in essence, examples of some kind of interplay between biblical passages. While the Sages were more overt about their methodology for legal exegesis, they seem to have had a parallel methodology for their non-halachic *drash* (see Sifrei to Deuteronomy 16:5–8). It is left to the readers of today to try to glimpse elements of that methodology as best we can.

2   The *atbash* approach to reading a text refers to a quasi-mystical system for relating to the Hebrew alphabet. In this system, the first letter of the alphabet, *aleph*, is seen as related to, or reflective of, the last letter of the alphabet, *tav*. Same for the second and second-to-last, *bet* and *shin*, respectively. The pattern of parallel pairs continues through the alphabet until it reaches a center point. The name *atbash* (אתב"ש) derives from these pairings:

אבגדהוזחטיכלמנסעפצקרשת

See e.g. Shabbat 104a, where *atbash* is used to structure a homiletic poem.

In an *atbash* pattern or chiasm, the first element of a text is a kind of mirror of its last element; the second element of the text mirrors the second-to-last element, the third mirrors the third-to-last, and so forth. If you wanted to represent a chiasm visually, you might diagram it like this:

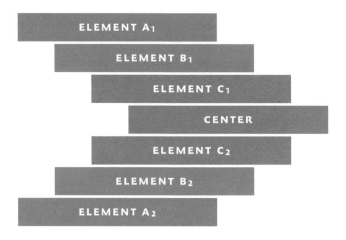

The pattern builds, and all the parallels converge toward some central element that lies, somehow, at the "core" of the text.

As you look through the Torah, you'll find that chiasms abound, and they come in all shapes and sizes. Sometimes they comprise just a few verses, or even a single verse;[3] other times, they spread out over multiple chapters. Sometimes the element pairs are linked by similar language; other times, by similar ideas or themes. Sometimes a pair within a chiasm contains two elements that echo each other; sometimes, elements are the inverse of each other. One way or the other, in a chiasm, the various pairs are somehow in conversation with one another. But here's the bottom line: if you ever read a passage in the Torah and think that elements within it seem repetitious, it's quite possible that you've stumbled upon a chiasm.

Centers of Gravity

That's all very well, I hear you saying, but *why* does the Torah encode such complex structures within its text? Other than looking elegant or symmetrical, what use does a chiasm serve?

---

3   For example, here's a single-verse chiasm from **Parshat Noach** (Genesis 9:6):

שֹׁפֵךְ דַּם הָאָדָם בָּאָדָם דָּמוֹ יִשָּׁפֵךְ

One who sheds the blood of man, through man his blood shall be shed

COVENANT WITH GOD   35

The Torah doesn't overtly tell us why it makes use of *atbash* structures, but I'd like to suggest that the Torah often uses the chiasm as an *interpretive* device, as a way of helping the reader discern layers of meaning in its text. Why go through the trouble? Well, the Torah is what we might call a minimalist text: it tries to deliver its message in as concise a way as possible, without a lot of fancy adjectives and adverbs. And yet, despite its economy with words, the Torah is rich with meaning.[4] How can you say so little, and at the same time say so much? One way to do it is through a chiasm, an incredibly efficient way of conveying a tremendous amount of information in very few words. The elements of each pair in a chiasm can shed light on each other in interesting and surprising ways; perhaps most strikingly, a chiasm can point you toward the "center" of a given text.

To see what I mean, just look back at that diagram on page 34: a chiasm is like an arrow, with different pairs converging on a central element. We might think of this middle element as a center of gravity for the text, as if the Torah is drawing a bull's-eye around a particular word, verse, or section of text, and saying, "Look here! This is really central; everything revolves around *this*."

So, What Does All This Look like in Real Life?

As it happens, one of these *atbash* structures seems to present itself right here in **Parshat Lech Lecha**, when God talks to Abraham about the circumcision covenant (*brit milah*). The relevant text is on the next two pages; if you like, take a few minutes and read through it. You'll find a lot of discussion in this passage about various things — covenants, name changes, having lots of children — and as you read through it, you might notice that it all sounds a bit repetitive. Well, that in itself is a clue that you might be looking at a chiasm.

As you read, see if you can discover some of the various element pairs. You might even break out a package of magic markers and use them to highlight the pairs you find — yellow for one pair, green for another; you know the drill. Sure, you'll be coloring in this book, and I know your parents told you never to do that, but it's a good kind of coloring; don't worry too much about it. I'll meet you in the next section (page 37) and we'll compare notes.

---

4   Our Sages recognized the Torah's parsimony, and thus attributed enormous value to every detail in the Torah, even down to the letter (see Menachot 29b, Talmud Yerushalmi Rosh Hashanah 3:5).

[א] וַיְהִי אַבְרָם בֶּן־תִּשְׁעִים
שָׁנָה וְתֵשַׁע שָׁנִים וַיֵּרָא יְקֹוָה
אֶל־אַבְרָם וַיֹּאמֶר אֵלָיו אֲנִי־
קֵל שַׁקַּי הִתְהַלֵּךְ לְפָנַי וֶהְיֵה
תָמִים: [ב] וְאֶתְּנָה בְרִיתִי
בֵּינִי וּבֵינֶךָ וְאַרְבֶּה אוֹתְךָ
בִּמְאֹד מְאֹד. [ג] וַיִּפֹּל אַבְרָם
עַל־פָּנָיו וַיְדַבֵּר אִתּוֹ אֱלֹקִים
לֵאמֹר: [ד] אֲנִי הִנֵּה בְרִיתִי
אִתָּךְ וְהָיִיתָ לְאַב הֲמוֹן גּוֹיִם:
[ה] וְלֹא־יִקָּרֵא עוֹד אֶת־שִׁמְךָ
אַבְרָם וְהָיָה שִׁמְךָ אַבְרָהָם
כִּי אַב־הֲמוֹן גּוֹיִם נְתַתִּיךָ:
[ו] וְהִפְרֵתִי אֹתְךָ בִּמְאֹד
מְאֹד וּנְתַתִּיךָ לְגוֹיִם וּמְלָכִים
מִמְּךָ יֵצֵאוּ: [ז] וַהֲקִמֹתִי
אֶת־בְּרִיתִי בֵּינִי וּבֵינֶךָ וּבֵין
זַרְעֲךָ אַחֲרֶיךָ לְדֹרֹתָם לִבְרִית
עוֹלָם לִהְיוֹת לְךָ לֵאלֹקִים
וּלְזַרְעֲךָ אַחֲרֶיךָ: [ח] וְנָתַתִּי
לְךָ וּלְזַרְעֲךָ אַחֲרֶיךָ אֵת
אֶרֶץ מְגֻרֶיךָ אֵת כָּל־אֶרֶץ
כְּנַעַן לַאֲחֻזַּת עוֹלָם וְהָיִיתִי
לָהֶם לֵאלֹקִים: [ט] וַיֹּאמֶר
אֱלֹקִים אֶל־אַבְרָהָם וְאַתָּה
אֶת־בְּרִיתִי תִשְׁמֹר אַתָּה
וְזַרְעֲךָ אַחֲרֶיךָ לְדֹרֹתָם:
[י] זֹאת בְּרִיתִי אֲשֶׁר תִּשְׁמְרוּ
בֵּינִי וּבֵינֵיכֶם וּבֵין זַרְעֲךָ
אַחֲרֶיךָ הִמּוֹל לָכֶם כָּל־זָכָר:
[יא] וּנְמַלְתֶּם אֵת בְּשַׂר
עָרְלַתְכֶם וְהָיָה לְאוֹת בְּרִית
בֵּינִי וּבֵינֵיכֶם: [יב] וּבֶן־
שְׁמֹנַת יָמִים יִמּוֹל לָכֶם
כָּל־זָכָר לְדֹרֹתֵיכֶם יְלִיד בָּיִת
וּמִקְנַת־כֶּסֶף מִכֹּל בֶּן־נֵכָר
אֲשֶׁר לֹא מִזַּרְעֲךָ הוּא:

1 And when Abram was ninety-nine years old, the Lord appeared to Abram, and said to him, "I am God Almighty; walk before Me, and be wholehearted. **2** And I will make My covenant between Me and you, and will multiply you exceedingly." **3** And Abram fell on his face; and God talked with him, saying: **4** "As for Me, behold, My covenant is with you, and you will be the father of a multitude of nations. **5** Your name will no longer be called Abram, but your name will be Abraham; for the father of a multitude of nations have I made you. **6** And I will make you exceedingly fruitful, and I will make nations of you, and kings will come out of you. **7** And I will establish My covenant between Me and you and your seed after you throughout their generations for an everlasting covenant, to be a God to you and to your seed after you. **8** And I will give to you, and to your seed after you, the land of your sojournings, all the land of Canaan, for an everlasting possession; and I will be their God." **9** And God said to Abraham, "And as for you, you shall keep My covenant, you, and your seed after you throughout their generations. **10** This is My covenant, which you shall keep, between Me and you and your seed after you: every male among you shall be circumcised. **11** And you shall be circumcised in the flesh of your foreskin; and it will be a sign of a covenant between Me and you. **12** And he that is eight days old shall be circumcised among you, every male throughout your generations, he that is born in the house, or bought with money of any foreigner, that is not of your seed.

[יג] הַמּוֹל יִמּוֹל יְלִיד בֵּיתְךָ
וּמִקְנַת כַּסְפֶּךָ וְהָיְתָה
בְרִיתִי בִּבְשַׂרְכֶם לִבְרִית
עוֹלָם: [יד] וְעָרֵל זָכָר אֲשֶׁר
לֹא־יִמּוֹל אֶת־בְּשַׂר עָרְלָתוֹ
וְנִכְרְתָה הַנֶּפֶשׁ הַהִוא
מֵעַמֶּיהָ אֶת־בְּרִיתִי הֵפַר:
[טו] וַיֹּאמֶר אֱלֹקִים אֶל־
אַבְרָהָם שָׂרַי אִשְׁתְּךָ לֹא־
תִקְרָא אֶת־שְׁמָהּ שָׂרָי כִּי
שָׂרָה שְׁמָהּ: [טז] וּבֵרַכְתִּי
אֹתָהּ וְגַם נָתַתִּי מִמֶּנָּה לְךָ
בֵּן וּבֵרַכְתִּיהָ וְהָיְתָה לְגוֹיִם
מַלְכֵי עַמִּים מִמֶּנָּה יִהְיוּ:
[יז] וַיִּפֹּל אַבְרָהָם עַל־פָּנָיו
וַיִּצְחָק וַיֹּאמֶר בְּלִבּוֹ הַלְּבֶן
מֵאָה־שָׁנָה יִוָּלֵד וְאִם־שָׂרָה
הֲבַת־תִּשְׁעִים שָׁנָה תֵּלֵד:

13 He that is born in your house, and he that is bought with your money, needs to be circumcised; and My covenant shall be in your flesh for an everlasting covenant. **14** And the uncircumcised male who is not circumcised in the flesh of his foreskin, that soul shall be cut off from his people; he has broken My covenant." **15** And God said to Abraham, "As for Sarai your wife, you shall not call her name Sarai, but Sarah will her name be. **16** And I will bless her, and moreover I will give you a son of her; and I will bless her, and she shall be a mother of nations; kings of peoples will be of her." **17** Then Abraham fell on his face, and laughed, and said in his heart, "Will a child be born to someone who is a hundred years old? And will Sarah, who is ninety years old, give birth?"

The First Pair

Okay, maybe you've taken some time to hunt for some of those pairs. Now let's take a look at the text together.

Right at the beginning of the passage, in the prologue to the circumcision covenant, the text tells us that Abram[5] is quite old; to be precise, we hear that he is ninety-nine years of age. He's granted this covenant, is told to "walk before" God, and is informed that he will yet have biological children. Now, look at the end of the passage; do you see anything that seems to correspond to any of these notions? Hint: Is there any marker, by year, of Abram's age?

We do find such a marker, as it turns out, right at the end of the passage: Abraham hears from God that Sarah is going to have a biological child with him, and he laughs, saying to himself, "Will a child be born to someone [like myself] who is *a hundred years old*?" °

Genesis 17:17

There we have it: God makes a promise ("walk before Me" and you

---

5   He will become "Abraham" soon, in the course of this very conversation with God — but for the time being, we know him as "Abram."

will have many children) to a ninety-nine-year-old Abram at the *beginning* of the passage, and at the *end* of the passage, Abraham marvels as to how this promise could come to be, in light of his being "a hundred years old." [6]

In chiasm-talk, we might say that we've now found our As, our first element pair … But maybe not. It could be that what we have found is an isolated parallel, not necessarily the beginning of a full-fledged *atbash* pattern. To see whether there's a larger pattern, we need to keep reading. Does a second pair exist?

Face-Falling

Toward the beginning of the text, right after the reference to Abraham being ninety-nine, what happens?

Genesis 17:1–3

[א] וַיְהִי אַבְרָם בֶּן־תִּשְׁעִים שָׁנָה וְתֵשַׁע שָׁנִים וַיֵּרָא יְקֹוָה אֶל־אַבְרָם וַיֹּאמֶר אֵלָיו אֲנִי־אֵל שַׁדַּי הִתְהַלֵּךְ לְפָנַי וֶהְיֵה תָמִים: [ב] וְאֶתְּנָה בְרִיתִי בֵּינִי וּבֵינֶךָ וְאַרְבֶּה אוֹתְךָ בִּמְאֹד מְאֹד: [ג] וַיִּפֹּל אַבְרָם עַל־פָּנָיו וַיְדַבֵּר אִתּוֹ אֱלֹקִים

1 And when Abram was ninety-nine years old, the Lord appeared to Abram, and said to him, "I am God Almighty; walk before Me, and be wholehearted. **2** And I will make My covenant between Me and you, and will multiply you exceedingly." **3 And Abram fell on his face**; and God talked with him…

Remarkably, toward the end of the passage, we find that this exact same thing happens again — and it happens right *before* the reference to Abraham being a hundred years old:

Genesis 17:17

וַיִּפֹּל אַבְרָהָם עַל־פָּנָיו וַיִּצְחָק וַיֹּאמֶר בְּלִבּוֹ הַלְּבֶן מֵאָה־שָׁנָה יִוָּלֵד וְאִם־שָׂרָה הֲבַת־ תִּשְׁעִים שָׁנָה תֵּלֵד:

Then Abraham fell on his face, and laughed, and said in his heart, "Will a child be born to someone who is a hundred years old? And will Sarah, who is ninety years old, give birth?"

---

6   At the end, a more rounded number than at the beginning. First, the text tells us that Abram is 99 years old; at the end, he describes himself as (virtually) 100.

So it looks like we've found a second pair, right "inside" the first one:

[א] וַיְהִי אַבְרָם בֶּן־תִּשְׁעִים שָׁנָה וְתֵשַׁע שָׁנִים וַיֵּרָא יְקוָה אֶל־אַבְרָם וַיֹּאמֶר אֵלָיו אֲנִי־ קֵל שַׁקַּי הִתְהַלֵּךְ לְפָנַי וֶהְיֵה תָמִים: [ב] וְאֶתְּנָה בְרִיתִי בֵּינִי וּבֵינֶךָ וְאַרְבֶּה אוֹתְךָ בִּמְאֹד מְאֹד: [ג] וַיִּפֹּל אַבְרָם עַל־פָּנָיו וַיְדַבֵּר אִתּוֹ אֱלֹקִים	1 And when Abram was ninety-nine years old, the Lord appeared to Abram, and said to him, "I am God Almighty; walk before Me, and be wholehearted. 2 And I will make My covenant between Me and you, and will multiply you exceedingly." 3 And Abram fell on his face; and God talked with him…	Genesis 17:1–3
וַיִּפֹּל אַבְרָהָם עַל־פָּנָיו וַיִּצְחָק וַיֹּאמֶר בְּלִבּוֹ הֲלְבֶן מֵאָה־שָׁנָה יִוָּלֵד וְאִם־שָׂרָה הֲבַת־ תִּשְׁעִים שָׁנָה תֵּלֵד:	Then Abraham fell on his face, and laughed, and said in his heart, "Will a child be born to someone who is a hundred years old? And will Sarah, who is ninety years old, give birth?"	Genesis 17:17

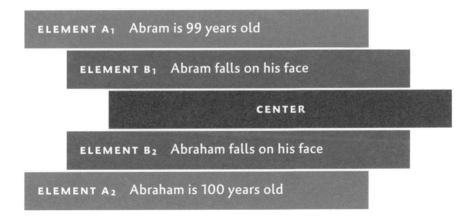

Let's continue, and see if we find any other pairs.

Behind Every Great Man…

To find a third pair, we look "inside" the space delineated by the pairs we've already found. In other words, on the "top" side of the chiasm, we look for what comes after elements A_1 and B_1, and on the "bottom" side of the chiasm, we look for what comes right before elements B_2 and A_2. If there's another pair, that's where we should find it.

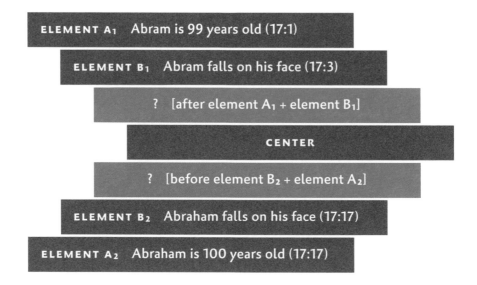

Let's start at the "top." Right after elements A₁ and B₁, we have this:

Genesis 17:4

אֲנִי הִנֵּה בְרִיתִי אִתָּךְ
וְהָיִיתָ לְאַב הֲמוֹן גּוֹיִם:

As for Me, behold, My covenant is with you, and you will be the father of a multitude of nations.

God promises Abram that he will be a father of many nations. Now, stop and ponder this a moment: Where else do we encounter a similar idea? Is there anyone else in the Torah who is called a parent of many nations?

As it happens, there's someone who fits that description, and it's ... Sarah. And she's called this right where this emerging chiasm would have you expecting her to receive this designation — just before element B₂ in the chiasm's "bottom" half:

Genesis 17:16

וּבֵרַכְתִּי אֹתָהּ וְגַם נָתַתִּי
מִמֶּנָּה לְךָ בֵּן וּבֵרַכְתִּיהָ
וְהָיְתָה לְגוֹיִם מַלְכֵי
עַמִּים מִמֶּנָּה יִהְיוּ:

And I will bless her, and moreover I will give you a son of her; and I will bless her, and she shall be a mother of nations; kings of peoples will be of her.

Each of these elements, of course, is a pair: a version of each appears at the "top" and "bottom" of the chiasm.

[א] וַיְהִ֣י אַבְרָ֔ם בֶּן־תִּשְׁעִ֥ים שָׁנָ֖ה וְתֵ֣שַׁע שָׁנִ֑ים וַיֵּרָ֨א יְקֹוָ֜ה אֶל־אַבְרָם֙ וַיֹּ֣אמֶר אֵלָ֗יו אֲנִי־אֵ֣ל שַׁדַּ֔י הִתְהַלֵּ֥ךְ לְפָנַ֖י וֶהְיֵ֥ה תָמִֽים: [ב] וְאֶתְּנָ֥ה בְרִיתִ֖י בֵּינִ֣י וּבֵינֶ֑ךָ וְאַרְבֶּ֥ה אֽוֹתְךָ֖ בִּמְאֹ֥ד מְאֹֽד: [ג] וַיִּפֹּ֥ל אַבְרָ֖ם עַל־פָּנָ֑יו וַיְדַבֵּ֥ר אִתּ֛וֹ אֱלֹקִ֖ים לֵאמֹֽר: [ד] אֲנִ֕י הִנֵּ֥ה בְרִיתִ֖י אִתָּ֑ךְ וְהָיִ֕יתָ לְאַ֖ב הֲמ֥וֹן גּוֹיִֽם:

1 And when Abram was ninety-nine years old, the Lord appeared to Abram, and said to him, "I am God Almighty; walk before Me, and be wholehearted. 2 And I will make My covenant between Me and you, and will multiply you exceedingly." 3 And Abram fell on his face; and God talked with him, saying: 4 "As for Me, behold, My covenant is with you, and you will be the father of a multitude of nations.

Genesis 17:1–3

[טז] וּבֵרַכְתִּ֣י אֹתָ֔הּ וְגַ֨ם נָתַ֧תִּי מִמֶּ֛נָּה לְךָ֖ בֵּ֑ן וּבֵֽרַכְתִּ֗יהָ וְהָֽיְתָה֙ לְגוֹיִ֔ם מַלְכֵ֥י עַמִּ֖ים מִמֶּ֥נָּה יִֽהְיֽוּ: [יז] וַיִּפֹּ֧ל אַבְרָהָ֛ם עַל־פָּנָ֖יו וַיִּצְחָ֑ק וַיֹּ֣אמֶר בְּלִבּ֗וֹ הַלְּבֶ֤ן מֵאָֽה־שָׁנָה֙ יִוָּלֵ֔ד וְאִם־שָׂרָ֕ה הֲבַת־תִּשְׁעִ֥ים שָׁנָ֖ה תֵּלֵֽד:

16 And I will bless her, and moreover I will give you a son of her; and I will bless her, and she shall be a mother of nations; kings of peoples will be of her." 17 Then Abraham fell on his face, and laughed, and said in his heart, "Will a child be born to someone who is a hundred years old? And will Sarah, who is ninety years old, give birth?"

Genesis 17:16–17

ELEMENT A₁   Abram is 99 years old

ELEMENT B₁   Abram falls on his face

ELEMENT C₁   Father of nations

CENTER

ELEMENT C₂   Mother of nations

ELEMENT B₂   Abraham falls on his face

ELEMENT A₂   Abraham is 100 years old

What's in a Name?

Now that we've spotted element C, we know where we'd expect to find the next pair. It should come right after A₁, B₁, and C₁ — and right before C₂, B₂, and A₂. So let's look there and see what we can find.

In the top half of this text describing the *brit*, right after elements A₁, B₁, and C₁, we have a name change:

| Genesis 17:5 | וְלֹא־יִקָּרֵא עוֹד אֶת־שִׁמְךָ אַבְרָם וְהָיָה שִׁמְךָ אַבְרָהָם כִּי אַב־הֲמוֹן גּוֹיִם נְתַתִּיךָ: | Your name will no longer be called Abram, but your name will be Abraham; for the father of a multitude of nations have I made you. |

And lo and behold, in the bottom half of the text describing the *brit*, right before elements C₂, B₂, and A₂, there's a name change too:

| Genesis 17:15 | וַיֹּאמֶר אֱלֹקִים אֶל־אַבְרָהָם שָׂרַי אִשְׁתְּךָ לֹא־תִקְרָא אֶת־שְׁמָהּ שָׂרָי כִּי שָׂרָה שְׁמָהּ: | And God said to Abraham, "As for Sarai your wife, you shall not call her name Sarai, but Sarah will her name be." |

Abram's new name reflects his new status as a father of a multitude of nations. Sarai's new name, the chiasm seems to suggest, may well express a similar idea. In Hebrew, שָׂרַי (*Sarai*), her former name, means "my princess." *Sarah*, the new name, means just "princess," without the possessive "my." It is as if God is saying to Abraham: *She's no longer just **your** princess; she belongs to humanity. She is the princess of the world.*

| Genesis 17:1–5 | [א] וַיְהִי אַבְרָם בֶּן־תִּשְׁעִים שָׁנָה וְתֵשַׁע שָׁנִים וַיֵּרָא יְקֹוָה אֶל־אַבְרָם וַיֹּאמֶר אֵלָיו אֲנִי־אֵל שַׁדַּי הִתְהַלֵּךְ לְפָנַי וֶהְיֵה תָמִים: [ב] וְאֶתְּנָה בְרִיתִי בֵּינִי וּבֵינֶךָ וְאַרְבֶּה אוֹתְךָ בִּמְאֹד מְאֹד: [ג] וַיִּפֹּל | 1 And when Abram was ninety-nine years old, the Lord appeared to Abram, and said to him, "I am God Almighty; walk before Me, and be wholehearted. 2 And I will make My covenant between Me and you, and will multiply you exceedingly." 3 And Abram fell on his face; and God |

אַבְרָם עַל־פָּנָיו וַיְדַבֵּר אִתּוֹ
אֱלֹקִים לֵאמֹר: [ד] אֲנִי הִנֵּה
בְרִיתִי אִתָּךְ וְהָיִיתָ לְאַב
הֲמוֹן גּוֹיִם: [ה] וְלֹא־יִקָּרֵא
עוֹד אֶת־שִׁמְךָ אַבְרָם וְהָיָה
שִׁמְךָ אַבְרָהָם כִּי אַב־הֲמוֹן
גּוֹיִם נְתַתִּיךָ:

[טו] וַיֹּאמֶר אֱלֹקִים אֶל־
אַבְרָהָם שָׂרַי אִשְׁתְּךָ לֹא־
תִקְרָא אֶת־שְׁמָהּ שָׂרָי כִּי
שָׂרָה שְׁמָהּ: [טז] וּבֵרַכְתִּי
אֹתָהּ וְגַם נָתַתִּי מִמֶּנָּה לְךָ
בֵּן וּבֵרַכְתִּיהָ וְהָיְתָה לְגוֹיִם
מַלְכֵי עַמִּים מִמֶּנָּה יִהְיוּ:
[יז] וַיִּפֹּל אַבְרָהָם עַל־פָּנָיו
וַיִּצְחָק וַיֹּאמֶר בְּלִבּוֹ הַלְּבֶן
מֵאָה־שָׁנָה יִוָּלֵד וְאִם־שָׂרָה
הֲבַת־תִּשְׁעִים שָׁנָה תֵּלֵד:

talked with him, saying: 4 "As for Me, behold, My covenant is with you, and you will be the father of a multitude of nations. 5 Your name will no longer be called Abram, but your name will be Abraham; for the father of a multitude of nations have I made you.

15 And God said to Abraham, "As for Sarai your wife, you shall not call her name Sarai, but Sarah will her name be. 16 And I will bless her, and moreover I will give you a son of her; and I will bless her, and she shall be a mother of nations; kings of peoples will be of her." 17 Then Abraham fell on his face, and laughed, and said in his heart, "Will a child be born to someone who is a hundred years old? And will Sarah, who is ninety years old, give birth?"

Genesis 17:15–17

ELEMENT A₁   Abram is 99 years old
ELEMENT B₁   Abram falls on his face
ELEMENT C₁   Father of nations
ELEMENT D₁   Name change
CENTER
ELEMENT D₂   Name change
ELEMENT C₂   Mother of nations
ELEMENT B₂   Abraham falls on his face
ELEMENT A₂   Abraham is 100 years old

The chiasm is starting to take shape, with elements A_1, B_1, C_1, and D_1 toward the beginning of the text, and their mirrors at the end of the text. You'll notice, however, that there's a good deal of text yet to be explored in the middle:

Genesis 17:6–14

[ו] וְהִפְרֵתִי אֹתְךָ בִּמְאֹד מְאֹד וּנְתַתִּיךָ לְגוֹיִם וּמְלָכִים מִמְּךָ יֵצֵאוּ: [ז] וַהֲקִמֹתִי אֶת־בְּרִיתִי בֵּינִי וּבֵינֶךָ וּבֵין זַרְעֲךָ אַחֲרֶיךָ לְדֹרֹתָם לִבְרִית עוֹלָם לִהְיוֹת לְךָ לֵאלֹקִים וּלְזַרְעֲךָ אַחֲרֶיךָ: [ח] וְנָתַתִּי לְךָ וּלְזַרְעֲךָ אַחֲרֶיךָ אֵת אֶרֶץ מְגֻרֶיךָ אֵת כָּל־אֶרֶץ כְּנַעַן לַאֲחֻזַּת עוֹלָם וְהָיִיתִי לָהֶם לֵאלֹקִים: [ט] וַיֹּאמֶר אֱלֹקִים אֶל־אַבְרָהָם וְאַתָּה אֶת־בְּרִיתִי תִשְׁמֹר אַתָּה וְזַרְעֲךָ אַחֲרֶיךָ לְדֹרֹתָם: [י] זֹאת בְּרִיתִי אֲשֶׁר תִּשְׁמְרוּ בֵּינִי וּבֵינֵיכֶם וּבֵין זַרְעֲךָ אַחֲרֶיךָ הִמּוֹל לָכֶם כָּל־זָכָר: [יא] וּנְמַלְתֶּם אֵת בְּשַׂר עָרְלַתְכֶם וְהָיָה לְאוֹת בְּרִית בֵּינִי וּבֵינֵיכֶם: [יב] וּבֶן־שְׁמֹנַת יָמִים יִמּוֹל לָכֶם כָּל־זָכָר לְדֹרֹתֵיכֶם יְלִיד בָּיִת וּמִקְנַת־כֶּסֶף מִכֹּל בֶּן־נֵכָר אֲשֶׁר לֹא מִזַּרְעֲךָ הוּא: [יג] הִמּוֹל יִמּוֹל יְלִיד בֵּיתְךָ וּמִקְנַת כַּסְפֶּךָ וְהָיְתָה בְרִיתִי בִּבְשַׂרְכֶם לִבְרִית עוֹלָם: [יד] וְעָרֵל זָכָר אֲשֶׁר לֹא־יִמּוֹל אֶת־בְּשַׂר עָרְלָתוֹ וְנִכְרְתָה הַנֶּפֶשׁ הַהִוא מֵעַמֶּיהָ אֶת־בְּרִיתִי הֵפַר:

6 And I will make you exceedingly fruitful, and I will make nations of you, and kings will come out of you. 7 And I will establish My covenant between Me and you and your seed after you throughout their generations for an everlasting covenant, to be a God to you and to your seed after you. 8 And I will give to you, and to your seed after you, the land of your sojournings, all the land of Canaan, for an everlasting possession; and I will be their God." 9 And God said to Abraham, "And as for you, you shall keep My covenant, you, and your seed after you throughout their generations. 10 This is My covenant, which you shall keep, between Me and you and your seed after you: every male among you shall be circumcised. 11 And you shall be circumcised in the flesh of your foreskin; and it will be a sign of a covenant between Me and you. 12 And he that is eight days old shall be circumcised among you, every male throughout your generations, he that is born in the house, or bought with money of any foreigner, that is not of your seed. 13 He that is born in your house, and he that is bought with your money, needs to be circumcised; and My covenant shall be in your flesh for an everlasting covenant. **14 And the uncircumcised male who is not circumcised in the flesh of his foreskin, that soul shall be cut off from his people; he has broken My covenant."**

Are there pairs yet to be found in that middle?

Of Fruitfulness and Nullification

Look at the very first word in this excerpt and you'll discover something fascinating: it parallels the very last word of the excerpt. On the "top" half of the chiasm, we find:

וְהִפְרֵתִי אֹתְךָ בִּמְאֹד מְאֹד וּנְתַתִּיךָ לְגוֹיִם וּמְלָכִים מִמְּךָ יֵצֵאוּ:	And I will make you exceedingly fruitful, and I will make nations of you, and kings will come out of you.	Genesis 17:6

And on the "bottom" half, we have:

וְעָרֵל זָכָר אֲשֶׁר לֹא־יִמּוֹל אֶת־בְּשַׂר עָרְלָתוֹ וְנִכְרְתָה הַנֶּפֶשׁ הַהִוא מֵעַמֶּיהָ אֶת־בְּרִיתִי הֵפַר:	And the uncircumcised male who is not circumcised in the flesh of his foreskin, that soul shall be cut off from his people; he has broken My covenant.	Genesis 17:14

The three letters at the core of each of these "outlier" words are the same: ה-פ-ר. But fittingly for a chiasm, which is, in essence, a "mirror-image" pattern, the meanings of these two words are themselves mirror images of each other. *Vehifreiti* (וְהִפְרֵתִי), God's promise to Abraham at the top of the chiasm, is a blessing: it means "and I will make you fruitful." *Heifar* (הֵפַר), at the bottom of the chiasm, describes someone breaking Abraham's covenant and, as a result, being "cut off from his people"— the very opposite of having children. *Vehifreiti* is about having a legacy that survives you; *heifar* denotes nullification, coming to zero.

So they're mirror images, these two versions of ה-פ-ר. It's a fascinating bit of wordplay. It's as if God is saying to Abraham: *I want to "heifer" you* [make you fruitful], *so don't do the mirror image of that to Me — don't "heifar," don't cast that covenant away, so that it amounts to nothing.*

A Multi-Layered Pair

There's a certain elegance to this particular pair we've just seen. It's not just a pair at the linguistic level; it operates at a thematic level too. These two verses involving ה-פ-ר really seem to be in conversation with each other. I'll show you what I mean. Go to the top half of the chiasm, and you'll see that the verse we've been looking at breaks down into three distinct ideas:

Genesis 17:6

> וְהִפְרֵתִי אֹתְךָ בִּמְאֹד מְאֹד
> וּנְתַתִּיךָ לְגוֹיִם וּמְלָכִים
> מִמְּךָ יֵצֵאוּ:

And I will make you exceedingly fruitful, and I will make nations of you, and kings will come out of you.

Essentially, God is telling Abraham:

1	You are going to have lots of *children*
2	Those children will coalesce into a *nation*
3	That nation will be governed by *kings*

There is a progression here, a progression crucial to the concept of nationhood itself. The three elements express greater and greater *cohesion*. Abraham is promised a lot of kids — but a lot of people milling around in a given area does not a nation make. So God then says: *Those kids, they're going to coalesce into a nation.* And finally, God tells him about the crowning (pardon the pun) jewel of nationhood, the political institution that will organize the individuals into a single autonomous body: kings. *Kings will come out of you.*

Now look at the bottom half of the chiasm. Is there anything in the corresponding verse (17:14) that speaks to these themes? Here's that verse again:

Genesis 17:14

> וְעָרֵל זָכָר אֲשֶׁר לֹא־יִמּוֹל
> אֶת־בְּשַׂר עָרְלָתוֹ וְנִכְרְתָה
> הַנֶּפֶשׁ הַהִוא מֵעַמֶּיהָ
> אֶת־בְּרִיתִי הֵפַר:

And the uncircumcised male who is not circumcised in the flesh of his foreskin, that soul shall be cut off from his people; he has broken My covenant.

Anybody who doesn't observe the covenant, any male who is not circumcised — what will happen to him? *He'll be cut off from the nation.* In other words, he'll revert from being a part of the nation to being a mere lone *individual*, outside of the cohesive whole. It's the mirror image of verse 6.

Let's call that element **E**. At the top of the chiasm, individuals coalesce into a nation ... and at the bottom, those who were once part of a nation revert to being mere individuals.

Genesis
17:1–6

[א] וַיְהִי אַבְרָם בֶּן־תִּשְׁעִים שָׁנָה וְתֵשַׁע שָׁנִים וַיֵּרָא יְקֹוָק אֶל־אַבְרָם וַיֹּאמֶר אֵלָיו אֲנִי־אֵל שַׁדַּי הִתְהַלֵּךְ לְפָנַי וֶהְיֵה תָמִים: [ב] וְאֶתְּנָה בְרִיתִי בֵּינִי וּבֵינֶךָ וְאַרְבֶּה אוֹתְךָ בִּמְאֹד מְאֹד: [ג] וַיִּפֹּל אַבְרָם עַל־פָּנָיו וַיְדַבֵּר אִתּוֹ אֱלֹקִים לֵאמֹר: [ד] אֲנִי הִנֵּה בְרִיתִי אִתָּךְ וְהָיִיתָ לְאַב הֲמוֹן גּוֹיִם: [ה] וְלֹא־יִקָּרֵא עוֹד אֶת־שִׁמְךָ אַבְרָם וְהָיָה שִׁמְךָ אַבְרָהָם כִּי אַב־הֲמוֹן גּוֹיִם נְתַתִּיךָ: [ו] וְהִפְרֵתִי אֹתְךָ בִּמְאֹד מְאֹד וּנְתַתִּיךָ לְגוֹיִם וּמְלָכִים מִמְּךָ יֵצֵאוּ:

1 And when Abram was ninety-nine years old, the Lord appeared to Abram, and said to him, "I am God Almighty; walk before Me, and be wholehearted. 2 And I will make My covenant between Me and you, and will multiply you exceedingly." 3 And Abram fell on his face; and God talked with him, saying: 4 "As for Me, behold, My covenant is with you, and you will be the father of a multitude of nations. 5 Your name will no longer be called Abram, but your name will be Abraham; for the father of a multitude of nations have I made you. 6 And I will make you exceedingly fruitful, and I will make nations of you, and kings will come out of you."

Genesis
17:14–17

[יד] וְעָרֵל זָכָר אֲשֶׁר לֹא־יִמּוֹל אֶת־בְּשַׂר עָרְלָתוֹ וְנִכְרְתָה הַנֶּפֶשׁ הַהִוא מֵעַמֶּיהָ אֶת־בְּרִיתִי הֵפַר: [טו] וַיֹּאמֶר אֱלֹקִים אֶל־אַבְרָהָם שָׂרַי אִשְׁתְּךָ לֹא־תִקְרָא אֶת־שְׁמָהּ שָׂרָי כִּי שָׂרָה שְׁמָהּ: [טז] וּבֵרַכְתִּי אֹתָהּ וְגַם נָתַתִּי מִמֶּנָּה לְךָ בֵּן וּבֵרַכְתִּיהָ וְהָיְתָה לְגוֹיִם מַלְכֵי עַמִּים מִמֶּנָּה יִהְיוּ: [יז] וַיִּפֹּל אַבְרָהָם עַל־פָּנָיו וַיִּצְחָק וַיֹּאמֶר בְּלִבּוֹ הַלְבֶן מֵאָה־שָׁנָה יִוָּלֵד וְאִם־שָׂרָה הֲבַת־תִּשְׁעִים שָׁנָה תֵּלֵד:

14 And the uncircumcised male who is not circumcised in the flesh of his foreskin, that soul shall be cut off from his people; he has broken My covenant." 15 And God said to Abraham, "As for Sarai your wife, you shall not call her name Sarai, but Sarah will her name be. 16 And I will bless her, and moreover I will give you a son of her; and I will bless her, and she shall be a mother of nations; kings of peoples will be of her." 17 Then Abraham fell on his face, and laughed, and said in his heart, "Will a child be born to someone who is a hundred years old? And will Sarah, who is ninety years old, give birth?"

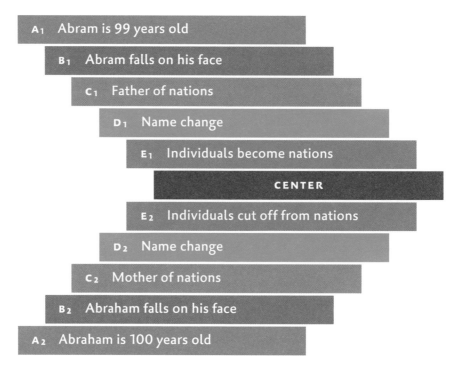

Establishing Permanence

Let's keep moving and see if we can find yet another pair. We'll continue looking at this passage that describes the covenant, at the ever-shrinking middle area of text, and see if we can find another pair. In bold are the two verses in which we might expect to find some kind of pair:

Genesis
17:7–13

[ז] וַהֲקִמֹתִי אֶת־בְּרִיתִי בֵּינִי וּבֵינֶךָ וּבֵין זַרְעֲךָ אַחֲרֶיךָ לְדֹרֹתָם לִבְרִית עוֹלָם לִהְיוֹת לְךָ לֵאלֹקִים וּלְזַרְעֲךָ אַחֲרֶיךָ: [ח] וְנָתַתִּי לְךָ וּלְזַרְעֲךָ אַחֲרֶיךָ אֵת אֶרֶץ מְגֻרֶיךָ אֵת כָּל־אֶרֶץ כְּנַעַן לַאֲחֻזַּת עוֹלָם וְהָיִיתִי לָהֶם לֵאלֹקִים: [ט] וַיֹּאמֶר אֱלֹקִים אֶל־אַבְרָהָם וְאַתָּה אֶת־בְּרִיתִי תִשְׁמֹר אַתָּה וְזַרְעֲךָ אַחֲרֶיךָ לְדֹרֹתָם: [י] זֹאת בְּרִיתִי אֲשֶׁר תִּשְׁמְרוּ בֵּינִי וּבֵינֵיכֶם

7 And I will establish My covenant between Me and you and your seed after you throughout their generations for an everlasting covenant, to be a God to you and to your seed after you. 8 And I will give to you, and to your seed after you, the land of your sojournings, all the land of Canaan, for an everlasting possession; and I will be their God." 9 And God said to Abraham, "And as for you, you shall keep My covenant, you, and your seed after you throughout their generations. **10** This is My covenant, which you shall keep, between Me

וּבֶין זַרְעֲךָ אַחֲרֶיךָ
הִמּוֹל לָכֶם כָּל־זָכָר:
[יא] וּנְמַלְתֶּם אֵת בְּשַׂר
עָרְלַתְכֶם וְהָיָה לְאוֹת
בְּרִית בֵּינִי וּבֵינֵיכֶם:
[יב] וּבֶן־שְׁמֹנַת יָמִים יִמּוֹל
לָכֶם כָּל־זָכָר לְדֹרֹתֵיכֶם
יְלִיד בָּיִת וּמִקְנַת־כֶּסֶף
מִכֹּל בֶּן־נֵכָר אֲשֶׁר לֹא
מִזַּרְעֲךָ הוּא: [יג] הִמּוֹל
יִמּוֹל יְלִיד בֵּיתְךָ וּמִקְנַת
כַּסְפֶּךָ וְהָיְתָה בְרִיתִי
בִּבְשַׂרְכֶם לִבְרִית עוֹלָם:

and you and your seed after you: every male among you shall be circumcised. **11** And you shall be circumcised in the flesh of your foreskin; and it will be a sign of a covenant between Me and you. **12** And he that is eight days old shall be circumcised among you, every male throughout your generations, he that is born in the house, or bought with money of any foreigner, that is not of your seed. **13 He that is born in your house, and he that is bought with your money, needs to be circumcised; and My covenant shall be in your flesh for an everlasting covenant.**

What do you say? Where are the connections here?

Well, each of these verses at the edges combines two phrases: בְּרִיתִי, "My covenant," followed by לִבְרִית עוֹלָם, "an everlasting covenant." From a language standpoint, then, the two verses go together. But they also share a larger *idea*: together, this pair of verses seems to speak of how this "everlasting covenant" becomes *real*, how it translates from mere theory into actuality. A covenant, by definition, is an agreement between two parties — in this case, God and Abraham. God's end of the covenant is set out in the "top" half of the chiasm, and Abraham's is in the "bottom" half.

God, for His part, makes "My covenant" into something permanent and real — an "everlasting covenant," if you will — when He keeps His word: when, over time, He delivers to Abraham's descendants the multitudes of progeny and the land that He has promised them. That's what the verse at the "top" half of the chiasm is driving at. As for *you*, Abraham, says God, I need you too, to take "My covenant" and make it into something permanent, an "everlasting covenant." How? By etching a permanent sign of it into your own flesh, and the flesh of your descendants, through the practice known as circumcision. And that's the point of the corresponding verse at the "bottom" of the chiasm.

Let's stop here to ponder the implications of this. I think what we're seeing here are two expressions of what it *means* for something to be "everlasting": there's God's kind of everlasting, and there's a human kind of everlasting. When God establishes an "everlasting covenant," He's talking about eternity. He's granting us everlasting nationhood, a nation that will endure for all time. That's forever, from God's perspective. But individual human beings don't operate on that timescale; we are only around for a human lifetime, so what constitutes "forever" from man's perspective is something that lasts for a lifetime — a change to the human body, for example, like circumcision. This, then, is the covenant: God gives us the gift of His "forever," and asks us to reciprocate at our own scale, making an irrevocable physical change to our bodies, gifting our own "forever" back to God. So here's where we are now:

Genesis 17:1–8

[א] וַיְהִי אַבְרָם בֶּן־תִּשְׁעִים שָׁנָה וְתֵשַׁע שָׁנִים וַיֵּרָא יְקֹוָק אֶל־אַבְרָם וַיֹּאמֶר אֵלָיו אֲנִי־קֵל שַׁדַּי הִתְהַלֵּךְ לְפָנַי וֶהְיֵה תָמִים: [ב] וְאֶתְּנָה בְרִיתִי בֵּינִי וּבֵינֶךָ וְאַרְבֶּה אוֹתְךָ בִּמְאֹד מְאֹד: [ג] וַיִּפֹּל אַבְרָם עַל־פָּנָיו וַיְדַבֵּר אִתּוֹ אֱלֹקִים לֵאמֹר: [ד] אֲנִי הִנֵּה בְרִיתִי אִתָּךְ וְהָיִיתָ לְאַב הֲמוֹן גּוֹיִם: [ה] וְלֹא־יִקָּרֵא עוֹד אֶת־שִׁמְךָ אַבְרָם וְהָיָה שִׁמְךָ אַבְרָהָם כִּי אַב־הֲמוֹן גּוֹיִם נְתַתִּיךָ: [ו] וְהִפְרֵתִי אֹתְךָ בִּמְאֹד מְאֹד וּנְתַתִּיךָ לְגוֹיִם וּמְלָכִים מִמְּךָ יֵצֵאוּ: [ז] וַהֲקִמֹתִי אֶת־בְּרִיתִי בֵּינִי וּבֵינֶךָ וּבֵין זַרְעֲךָ אַחֲרֶיךָ לְדֹרֹתָם לִבְרִית עוֹלָם לִהְיוֹת לְךָ לֵאלֹקִים וּלְזַרְעֲךָ אַחֲרֶיךָ:

1 And when Abram was ninety-nine years old, the Lord appeared to Abram, and said to him, "I am God Almighty; walk before Me, and be wholehearted. 2 And I will make My covenant between Me and you, and will multiply you exceedingly." 3 And Abram fell on his face; and God talked with him, saying: 4 "As for Me, behold, My covenant is with you, and you will be the father of a multitude of nations. 5 Your name will no longer be called Abram, but your name will be Abraham; for the father of a multitude of nations have I made you. 6 And I will make you exceedingly fruitful, and I will make nations of you, and kings will come out of you. 7 And I will establish My covenant between Me and you and your seed after you throughout their generations for an everlasting covenant, to be a God to you and to your seed after you.

. . . .

[יג] הִמּוֹל יִמּוֹל יְלִיד בֵּיתְךָ וּמִקְנַת כַּסְפֶּךָ וְהָיְתָה בְרִיתִי בִּבְשַׂרְכֶם לִבְרִית עוֹלָם: [יד] וְעָרֵל זָכָר אֲשֶׁר לֹא־ יִמּוֹל אֶת־בְּשַׂר עָרְלָתוֹ וְנִכְרְתָה הַנֶּפֶשׁ הַהִוא

13 He that is born in your house, and he that is bought with your money, needs to be circumcised; and My covenant shall be in your flesh for an everlasting covenant. 14 And the uncircumcised male who is not circumcised in the flesh of his foreskin,

מֵעַמֶּיהָ אֶת־בְּרִיתִי הֵפַר: [טו] וַיֹּאמֶר אֱלֹקִים אֶל־אַבְרָהָם שָׂרַי אִשְׁתְּךָ לֹא־תִקְרָא אֶת־שְׁמָהּ שָׂרָי כִּי שָׂרָה שְׁמָהּ: [טז] וּבֵרַכְתִּי אֹתָהּ וְגַם נָתַתִּי מִמֶּנָּה לְךָ בֵּן וּבֵרַכְתִּיהָ וְהָיְתָה לְגוֹיִם מַלְכֵי עַמִּים מִמֶּנָּה יִהְיוּ: [יז] וַיִּפֹּל אַבְרָהָם עַל־פָּנָיו וַיִּצְחָק וַיֹּאמֶר בְּלִבּוֹ הַלְּבֶן מֵאָה־שָׁנָה יִוָּלֵד וְאִם־שָׂרָה הֲבַת־תִּשְׁעִים שָׁנָה תֵּלֵד:

that soul shall be cut off from his people; he has broken My covenant." 15 And God said to Abraham, "As for Sarai your wife, you shall not call her name Sarai, but Sarah will her name be. 16 And I will bless her, and moreover I will give you a son of her; and I will bless her, and she shall be a mother of nations; kings of peoples will be of her." 17 Then Abraham fell on his face, and laughed, and said in his heart, "Will a child be born to someone who is a hundred years old? And will Sarah, who is ninety years old, give birth?"

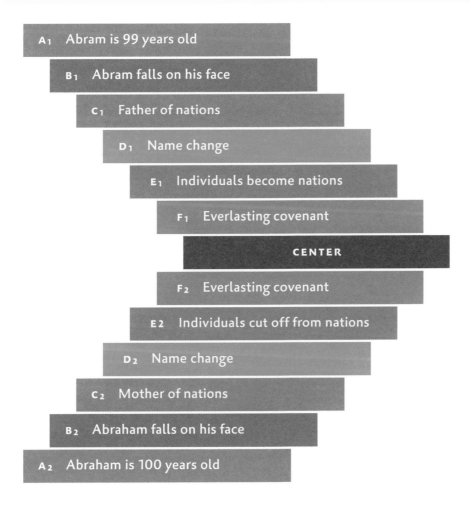

A₁ Abram is 99 years old

B₁ Abram falls on his face

C₁ Father of nations

D₁ Name change

E₁ Individuals become nations

F₁ Everlasting covenant

CENTER

F₂ Everlasting covenant

E₂ Individuals cut off from nations

D₂ Name change

C₂ Mother of nations

B₂ Abraham falls on his face

A₂ Abraham is 100 years old

The Terms of the Covenant

As you can see, we're getting closer and closer to the center of this text. And as we do, I think we can identify another parallel emerging between the top and bottom halves of our remaining text.

Take a look at the two passages in bold:

Genesis
17:7–12

לִהְיוֹת לְךָ לֵאלֹקִים וּלְזַרְעֲךָ
אַחֲרֶיךָ: [ח] וְנָתַתִּי לְךָ
וּלְזַרְעֲךָ אַחֲרֶיךָ אֵת אֶרֶץ
מְגֻרֶיךָ אֵת כָּל־אֶרֶץ כְּנַעַן
לַאֲחֻזַּת עוֹלָם וְהָיִיתִי
לָהֶם לֵאלֹקִים: [ט] וַיֹּאמֶר
אֱלֹקִים אֶל־אַבְרָהָם וְאַתָּה
אֶת־בְּרִיתִי תִשְׁמֹר אַתָּה
וְזַרְעֲךָ אַחֲרֶיךָ לְדֹרֹתָם:
[י] זֹאת בְּרִיתִי אֲשֶׁר
תִּשְׁמְרוּ בֵּינִי וּבֵינֵיכֶם וּבֵין
זַרְעֲךָ אַחֲרֶיךָ הִמּוֹל לָכֶם
כָּל־זָכָר: [יא] וּנְמַלְתֶּם
אֵת בְּשַׂר עָרְלַתְכֶם וְהָיָה
לְאוֹת בְּרִית בֵּינִי וּבֵינֵיכֶם:
[יב] וּבֶן־שְׁמֹנַת יָמִים יִמּוֹל
לָכֶם כָּל־זָכָר לְדֹרֹתֵיכֶם
יְלִיד בָּיִת וּמִקְנַת־כֶּסֶף
מִכֹּל בֶּן־נֵכָר אֲשֶׁר לֹא
מִזַּרְעֲךָ הוּא:

...to be a God to you and to your seed after you. **8** And I will give to you, and to your seed after you, the land of your sojournings, all the land of Canaan, for an everlasting possession; and I will be their God." **9** And God said to Abraham, "And as for you, you shall keep My covenant, you, and your seed after you throughout their generations. **10** This is My covenant, which you shall keep, between Me and you and your seed after you: every male among you shall be circumcised. **11 And you shall be circumcised in the flesh of your foreskin; and it will be a sign of a covenant between Me and you. 12 And he that is eight days old shall be circumcised among you, every male throughout your generations, he that is born in the house, or bought with money of any foreigner, that is not of your seed.**

At first, it isn't clear what one section might have to do with the other: at the top, the promise of Canaan as an inheritance, and at the bottom, a command to circumcise all males in Abraham's household, two themes that seem unrelated. But put aside the *meaning* of these verses for just a moment (don't worry—we'll come back to the verses' interconnectedness of meaning in just a moment); at the structural level, you'll discover an elegant commonality. Read the two passages. Don't both of them strike you as just a bit repetitive? Well, your mind isn't playing tricks on you. As it turns out, in each case, you are looking at — make sure you're sitting down for this — a chiasm *within* a chiasm.

I kid you not. There are two short and sweet A-B-A patterns here. Let's take a look at the first one, in verses 7–8:

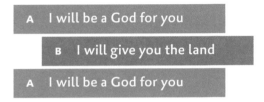

And sure enough, we find the very same pattern in verses 11–12:

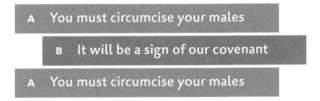

So that's the first clue that there is, in fact, a mirror to be found here. Within our larger chiasm, these passages are "paired" with each other in at least one way: each one is a chiasm in and of itself!

But their connection goes deeper than this. The parallels in their construction (A-B-A; A-B-A) clue us in to the connection in meaning between the verses. Take a look at the "center" of each of these mini-chiasms:

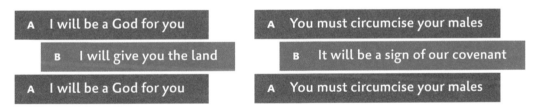

It turns out, wondrously enough, that these centers play off each other. Look and see: the first center affirms that God will give us the land, and the second center declares circumcision a sign of the covenant. The parallel structure suggests that the two ideas are connected — that, in truth, *one is inconceivable without the other*. Yes, the Almighty is promising you the land of Canaan (the first center), but that promise is contingent upon your keeping the sign of the covenant: circumcision (the second center).

In other words, what God *promises* us and what God *asks* of us are tied together: God promises us land ("top" center), and He asks that we keep the covenant ("bottom" center). The two are inextricable.

And this makes a lot of sense, doesn't it? We've seen this hold true for another element of God's promise to Abraham. After all, broadly speaking, what *does* God say He is giving Abraham in this covenant? Bottom line, it's two things: (1) children, who will coalesce into a nation, and (2) a land in which that nation can dwell. Now, when it came to children, we found earlier that the promise of children coalescing into a nation was contingent on the rite of circumcision. That was the point of element E: no circumcision, no nation — in the sense that any person who didn't observe the covenant would be cut off from the nation:

Genesis 17:14	וְעָרֵל זָכָר אֲשֶׁר לֹא־יִמּוֹל אֶת־בְּשַׂר עָרְלָתוֹ וְנִכְרְתָה הַנֶּפֶשׁ הַהִוא מֵעַמֶּיהָ אֶת־בְּרִיתִי הֵפַר:	And the uncircumcised male who is not circumcised in the flesh of his foreskin, that soul shall be cut off from his people; he has broken My covenant.

And what do we see now? That the same applies to the second of God's gifts to Abraham: land. No circumcision, no land. Both of God's great promises are tied up in His covenant.[7]

Genesis 17:1–8	[א] וַיְהִי אַבְרָם בֶּן־תִּשְׁעִים שָׁנָה וְתֵשַׁע שָׁנִים וַיֵּרָא יְקֹוָה אֶל־אַבְרָם וַיֹּאמֶר אֵלָיו אֲנִי־אֵל שַׁדַּי הִתְהַלֵּךְ לְפָנַי וֶהְיֵה תָמִים: [ב] וְאֶתְּנָה בְרִיתִי בֵּינִי וּבֵינֶךָ וְאַרְבֶּה אוֹתְךָ בִּמְאֹד מְאֹד: [ג] וַיִּפֹּל אַבְרָם עַל־פָּנָיו וַיְדַבֵּר אִתּוֹ אֱלֹקִים לֵאמֹר: [ד] אֲנִי הִנֵּה בְרִיתִי אִתָּךְ וְהָיִיתָ לְאַב הֲמוֹן גּוֹיִם: [ה] וְלֹא־יִקָּרֵא עוֹד אֶת־שִׁמְךָ אַבְרָם וְהָיָה שִׁמְךָ אַבְרָהָם כִּי אַב־הֲמוֹן גּוֹיִם נְתַתִּיךָ: [ו] וְהִפְרֵתִי אֹתְךָ בִּמְאֹד מְאֹד וּנְתַתִּיךָ לְגוֹיִם וּמְלָכִים מִמְּךָ יֵצֵאוּ: [ז] וַהֲקִמֹתִי אֶת־	1 And when Abram was ninety-nine years old, the Lord appeared to Abram, and said to him, "I am God Almighty; walk before Me, and be wholehearted. 2 And I will make My covenant between Me and you, and will multiply you exceedingly." 3 And Abram fell on his face; and God talked with him, saying: 4 "As for Me, behold, My covenant is with you, and you will be the father of a multitude of nations. 5 Your name will no longer be called Abram, but your name will be Abraham; for the father of a multitude of nations have I made you. 6 And I will make you exceedingly

---

7   See the concluding section of this essay, **How We Are Different** (page 59), for a fascinating corroboration of this idea in Joshua 5:2–9.

fruitful, and I will make nations of you, and kings will come out of you. 7 And I will establish My covenant between Me and you and your seed after you throughout their generations for an everlasting covenant, to be a God to you and to your seed after you. 8 And I will give to you, and to your seed after you, the land of your sojournings, all the land of Canaan, for an everlasting possession; and I will be their God."

בְּרִיתִי בֵּינִי וּבֵינֶךָ וּבֵין זַרְעֲךָ אַחֲרֶיךָ לְדֹרֹתָם לִבְרִית עוֹלָם לִהְיוֹת לְךָ לֵאלֹקִים וּלְזַרְעֲךָ אַחֲרֶיךָ: [ח] לִהְיוֹת לְךָ לֵאלֹקִים וּלְזַרְעֲךָ אַחֲרֶיךָ: וְנָתַתִּי לְךָ וּלְזַרְעֲךָ אַחֲרֶיךָ אֵת אֶרֶץ מְגֻרֶיךָ אֵת כָּל־אֶרֶץ כְּנַעַן לַאֲחֻזַּת עוֹלָם וְהָיִיתִי לָהֶם לֵאלֹקִים:

---

11 And you shall be circumcised in the flesh of your foreskin; and it will be a sign of a covenant between Me and you. 12 And he that is eight days old shall be circumcised among you, every male throughout your generations, he that is born in the house, or bought with money of any foreigner, that is not of your seed. 13 He that is born in your house, and he that is bought with your money, needs to be circumcised; and My covenant shall be in your flesh for an everlasting covenant. 14 And the uncircumcised male who is not circumcised in the flesh of his foreskin, that soul shall be cut off from his people; he has broken My covenant." 15 And God said to Abraham, "As for Sarai your wife, you shall not call her name Sarai, but Sarah will her name be. 16 And I will bless her, and moreover I will give you a son of her; and I will bless her, and she shall be a mother of nations; kings of peoples will be of her." 17 Then Abraham fell on his face, and laughed, and said in his heart, "Will a child be born to someone who is a hundred years old? And will Sarah, who is ninety years old, give birth?"

[יא] וּנְמַלְתֶּם אֵת בְּשַׂר עָרְלַתְכֶם וְהָיָה לְאוֹת בְּרִית בֵּינִי וּבֵינֵיכֶם: [יב] וּבֶן־שְׁמֹנַת יָמִים יִמּוֹל לָכֶם כָּל־זָכָר לְדֹרֹתֵיכֶם יְלִיד בָּיִת וּמִקְנַת־כֶּסֶף מִכֹּל בֶּן־נֵכָר אֲשֶׁר לֹא מִזַּרְעֲךָ הוּא: [יג] הִמּוֹל יִמּוֹל יְלִיד בֵּיתְךָ וּמִקְנַת כַּסְפֶּךָ וְהָיְתָה בְרִיתִי בִּבְשַׂרְכֶם לִבְרִית עוֹלָם: [יד] וְעָרֵל זָכָר אֲשֶׁר לֹא־יִמּוֹל אֶת־בְּשַׂר עָרְלָתוֹ וְנִכְרְתָה הַנֶּפֶשׁ הַהִוא מֵעַמֶּיהָ אֶת־בְּרִיתִי הֵפַר: [טו] וַיֹּאמֶר אֱלֹקִים אֶל־אַבְרָהָם שָׂרַי אִשְׁתְּךָ לֹא־תִקְרָא אֶת־שְׁמָהּ שָׂרָי כִּי שָׂרָה שְׁמָהּ: [טז] וּבֵרַכְתִּי אֹתָהּ וְגַם נָתַתִּי מִמֶּנָּה לְךָ בֵּן וּבֵרַכְתִּיהָ וְהָיְתָה לְגוֹיִם מַלְכֵי עַמִּים מִמֶּנָּה יִהְיוּ: [יז] וַיִּפֹּל אַבְרָהָם עַל־פָּנָיו וַיִּצְחָק וַיֹּאמֶר בְּלִבּוֹ הַלְּבֶן מֵאָה־שָׁנָה יִוָּלֵד וְאִם־שָׂרָה הֲבַת־תִּשְׁעִים שָׁנָה תֵּלֵד:

Genesis
17:11–17

A₁   Abram is 99 years old

B₁   Abram falls on his face

C₁   Father of nations

D₁   Name change

E₁   Individuals become nations

F₁   Everlasting covenant

G₁   Promise of land

CENTER

G₂   Circumcision

F₂   Everlasting covenant

E₂   Individuals cut off from nations

D₂   Name change

C₂   Mother of nations

B₂   Abraham falls on his face

A₂   Abraham is 100 years old

Bull's-Eye

And now, finally, we've arrived at what seems to be the center of our chiasm:

Genesis
17:9–10

[ט] וַיֹּאמֶר אֱלֹקִים אֶל־אַבְרָהָם
וְאַתָּה אֶת־בְּרִיתִי תִשְׁמֹר אַתָּה
וְזַרְעֲךָ אַחֲרֶיךָ לְדֹרֹתָם: [י] זֹאת
בְּרִיתִי אֲשֶׁר תִּשְׁמְרוּ בֵּינִי
וּבֵינֵיכֶם וּבֵין זַרְעֲךָ אַחֲרֶיךָ
הִמּוֹל לָכֶם כָּל־זָכָר:

9 And God said to Abraham, "And as for you, you shall keep My covenant, you, and your seed after you throughout their generations. **10** This is My covenant, which you shall keep, between Me and you and your seed after you: every male among you shall be circumcised.

You must keep the covenant. This is the core idea, the center of gravity around which the entire chapter revolves. This covenant — God's obligations to us and our reciprocal obligations to Him — inaugurates our existence as a nation. But look carefully, and you'll find that this core idea consists of two elements:

וְאַתָּה אֶת־בְּרִיתִי תִשְׁמֹר אַתָּה וְזַרְעֲךָ אַחֲרֶיךָ לְדֹרֹתָם: זֹאת בְּרִיתִי אֲשֶׁר תִּשְׁמְרוּ בֵּינִי וּבֵינֵיכֶם וּבֵין זַרְעֲךָ אַחֲרֶיךָ: הִמּוֹל לָכֶם כָּל־זָכָר:	And as for you, you shall keep My covenant, you, and your seed after you throughout their generations. This is My covenant, which you shall keep, between Me and you and your seed after you: every male among you shall be circumcised.	Genesis 17:9–10

So there's actually a double center here: the center itself is a chiastic pair. The connection between the verses is indicated by the repeated verb *tishmor/tishmeru* (תִשְׁמֹר/תִּשְׁמְרוּ), "you shall keep," which is the key idea of both verses: the need to guard the covenant. But the two verses employ slightly different grammatical forms of the verb, and in these two forms, you can see how the two verses play off each other.

Think about the contrast between *tishmor* and *tishmeru*; what's the difference between them? The distinction lies in whom God is addressing. In the first verse, the singular form of the verb *tishmor* makes it clear that God is speaking to Abraham. True, later in that verse, God will mention Abraham's progeny, but it seems tacked on, almost an afterthought: You, Abraham, **אַתָּה** אֶת־בְּרִיתִי תִשְׁמֹר — *you* are to keep this covenant; and when you have children, at some point in the future, what applies to you will apply to them too. In the second verse, on the other hand, God directly addresses *all* Abraham's progeny, throughout the generations: *tishmeru* is plural, as if to say to the entire people, "You *all* shall keep it!"

Step back and consider this; Abraham's generations, whom God seems to address directly in that second verse, don't *exist* yet! They aren't there to hear the command, so how could God be talking to them? Think back, however, to the nature of the covenant, as God has defined it here. It is a *brit olam*, an "eternal covenant." We talked earlier about the divine "forever" being different from *our* "forever." God is timeless, and the "forever" that He promises us is a nation that will endure throughout all time. So here, at the center of the chiasm, we are overhearing the timeless God speaking directly to His eternal nation … a nation that, from our perspective, didn't exist yet — but from His timeless perspective, it did. It's all laid out, right there in front of Him.

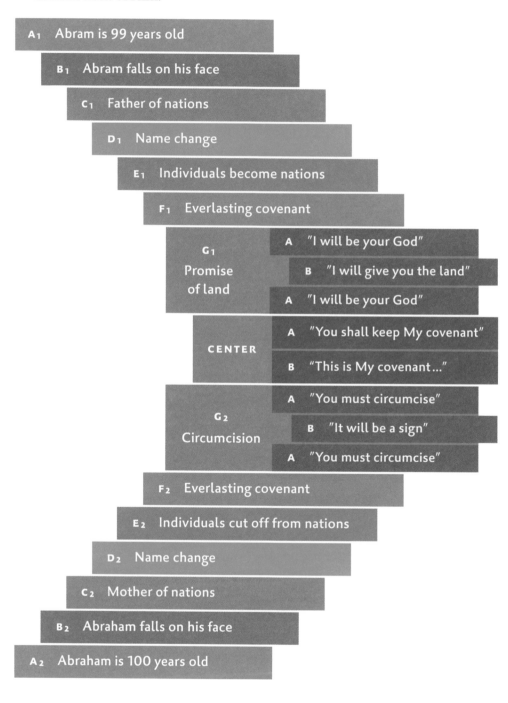

How We Are Different

What does all this mean? What does this elegant *atbash* structure teach us? Many things, I would suggest. One overarching theme, though, seems to shine through from the center — and for that matter, from a number of the chiastic pairs on the way to the center: the covenant is primary. Everything depends on it. There is no promise of land without the covenant. The future descendants of Abraham will become a nation only by virtue of the covenant; should any "child" of Israel disassociate himself from the covenant, he is "cut off" from the nation.[8]

We see this play out in history, in the book of Joshua. What do the Israelites do immediately upon entering the Land of Israel? Before the conquest of Jericho, everyone stops in order to circumcise all those who had been born in the wilderness and were not yet circumcised.° If you think about it from the standpoint of military preparedness, that decision was the height of insanity. Why subject your entire male population of soldiers to a sensitive act of surgery (without anesthesia or antibiotics, mind you) days before their inaugural battle to conquer their land? No commander would order such a thing. But that's exactly what Joshua does. Why? It all comes back to what God told Abraham: *If you want to inherit the land, to dwell in it, then you must keep the circumcision covenant.* That covenant supersedes everything.[9]

Joshua 5:2–9

The primacy of the covenant speaks to the special nature of Israel's nationhood. Crack open any history book and read up on how nations come to be. A strongman, a military leader, manages to aggregate a group of warriors around him, and they conquer a plot of land. The warriors take up farming on the side, build an economy to go with their army, and voilà! A nation is born, and the chief strongman is its king. But that's not how it worked with us. There is no conquering warrior to whom we owe our nationhood — or at least, no human warrior. We were a nomadic family that descended into wretched slavery in a land not our own. We were taken

---

8   See Deuteronomy 29:9–20, and particularly verse 20, which makes this point explicit.

9   This association between covenant and land becomes codified in Jewish law in the obligation to mention *brit milah* (circumcision) in *birkat ha'aretz*, the blessing on the land, as part of *Birkat HaMazon* (grace after meals)." See Tosefta Berachot 3:9, Berachot 49a.

out with signs and miracles by … the Master of the Universe Himself, and brought into the land of Canaan. We owe our nationhood to no human leader, only to the Divine Master of All.[10]

And now, of course, Joshua's decision makes sense: if Joshua is the great conqueror, then of course, surgery on the eve of battle is out of the question. But if Joshua *isn't* the great conqueror, if *God* is, then reaffirming our commitment to the covenant — well, that's exactly what the doctor ordered.

The covenant that our Divine Master establishes with us — that's the soul of our nationhood.

The Torah Really *Does* Comment on Itself

So there it was, all along, hiding in plain sight: an extensive *atbash* pattern lurking just underneath the surface of the text in **Parshat Lech Lecha**. I speculated with you about what some of it might mean. And certainly, you may see some of its meaning differently than I did. But for me, above and beyond the question of meaning, the most amazing thing about this pattern is … the fact that it's there in the first place.

Let me assure you, this is not an outlier. *Atbash* patterns like this abound in the Torah, and invariably, they are windows into magnificent layers of hidden meaning. Speaking personally, the feeling that I get when I stumble upon one of them — there's nothing like it. Here's this ordinary, somewhat repetitive section of text, and all of a sudden, it's not so ordinary anymore. At least for me, it's a real "Toto, I've a feeling we're not in Kansas anymore" moment. At the end of the day, it's one thing to believe that the Torah is deep, an utterly remarkable and unique document—but it's quite another to see it with your very own eyes.

As you come to see other hidden structures in the Torah's text, I hope you never let the thrill grow old. Indeed, the human capacity for awe is a precious thing. What better way to use it than in appreciation of the Almighty's very own book?

---

10 This point is implied by the chiasm here in **Parshat Lech Lecha** — but is made explicit later, in Deuteronomy 4:32–34. See also Ramban to Leviticus 18:25.

What Kind of Test Was the *Akeidah*?

וַיֹּאמֶר יִצְחָק
אֶל־אַבְרָהָם אָבִיו
וַיֹּאמֶר אָבִי וַיֹּאמֶר
הִנֶּנִּי בְנִי וַיֹּאמֶר
הִנֵּה הָאֵשׁ וְהָעֵצִים
וְאַיֵּה הַשֶּׂה לְעֹלָה:
וַיֹּאמֶר אַבְרָהָם
אֱלֹקִים יִרְאֶה־לּוֹ
הַשֶּׂה לְעֹלָה בְּנִי

And Isaac said to Abraham his father, and he said, "My father." And he said, "Here I am, my son." And he said, "Behold the fire and the wood; but where is the lamb for a burnt-offering?" And Abraham said, "God will provide Himself the lamb for a burnt-offering, my son."

GENESIS 22:7–8

What Kind of Test Was the *Akeidah*?

THE BINDING OF ISAAC (or in Hebrew, the *Akeidah*) is one of the more difficult stories in the Torah. Abraham seems to be portrayed as a hero by the text for being willing to offer up his son at the top of a mountain, as God asks. But the reader's mind is left whirling: Can it be right to take the life of one's child? Was God asking Abraham to do something "wrong"? And even if we could resolve the moral issues that puzzle us about the *Akeidah*, what's the point of it all? Why would God arrange for such a "test"?

These are puzzling questions, and we will not answer all of them in the space of a single essay. We will content ourselves here to deal with the second issue we raised: What's the point? Given that the *Akeidah* was a kind of "test" of Abraham — the text tells us as much — what, exactly, was the point of that test? What, if anything, did God mean to test?

We tend to think of the *Akeidah* as a classic test of faith. God comes to Abraham and commands him to offer up his son Isaac. Will Abraham be steadfast in his devotion to God, or will he be overcome by his emotions and lack the strength to do the deed? Sure enough, Abraham is loyal to God; he passes the test. God stays Abraham's hand at the last minute, Abraham and Isaac come down the mountain together, and everyone lives happily ever after.

What, then, are we meant to learn from all this? Perhaps we're meant to learn that faith in God trumps all else, that we're meant to surrender completely to God, no matter the command, no matter the cost.

That's one way to read it, but I think it misses something significant. I want to argue that the *Akeidah* is more than a test of Abraham's loyalty to God. Far more.

A Pattern Just beneath the Surface of the Text

It turns out that there is a marvelous textual pattern hidden in the text of the *Akeidah* — and this pattern, I want to argue, may well help us decipher something of the *Akeidah*'s deeper meaning.

What kind of pattern am I talking about? The kind we encountered just a few pages ago in the essay on **Parshat Lech Lecha**. There we discovered a remarkable chiasm,[1] or *atbash* pattern, within the passage that describes God's circumcision covenant with Abraham. Well, there's a chiasm in **Parshat Vayeira** too — hiding in plain sight, in the episode of the Binding of Isaac.[2] If we can discern that pattern, we may find ourselves holding a key to a richer understanding of the test of the *Akeidah*.

How Do You Find a Chiasm?

How do you go about discovering a chiasm lurking in a text? The road to discovery usually begins when a pair of elements "jumps out" at you: you're looking at a text and notice some striking phrase or idea — and then this very same phrase or idea just happens to show up again in another

---

1   As we discussed in our essay on **Parshat Lech Lecha**, a chiasm, also known as אתב״ש (*atbash*), is a textual structure that looks like this:

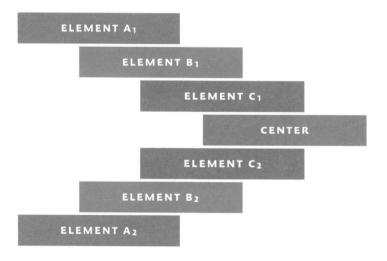

For a more detailed introduction to chiasms, turn back to **Parshat Lech Lecha: Covenant with God** (page 33).

2   A number of elements of the chiasm I'll be describing in this essay were found by Yehuda Radday, who was professor emeritus of Jewish Studies and Hebrew at the Israel Institute of Technology. See Yehuda T. Radday, "Chiasmus in Hebrew Biblical Narrative," in *Chiasmus in Antiquity: Structures, Analyses, Exegesis*, ed. John W. Welch (Provo, Utah: Research Press, 1999), 107–9.

verse, a little ways down, in the very same narrative. When that happens, you may have just stumbled upon part of a larger pattern, a chiasm.

Take a look at the *Akeidah* and you can see how this process of discovery might work. Read through this section of the story; is there a striking phrase or theme that appears twice?

Genesis 22:6–8

[ו] וַיִּקַּח אַבְרָהָם אֶת־עֲצֵי הָעֹלָה וַיָּשֶׂם עַל־יִצְחָק בְּנוֹ וַיִּקַּח בְּיָדוֹ אֶת־הָאֵשׁ וְאֶת־הַמַּאֲכֶלֶת וַיֵּלְכוּ שְׁנֵיהֶם יַחְדָּו: [ז] וַיֹּאמֶר יִצְחָק אֶל־אַבְרָהָם אָבִיו וַיֹּאמֶר אָבִי וַיֹּאמֶר הִנֶּנִּי בְנִי וַיֹּאמֶר הִנֵּה הָאֵשׁ וְהָעֵצִים וְאַיֵּה הַשֶּׂה לְעֹלָה: [ח] וַיֹּאמֶר אַבְרָהָם אֱלֹקִים יִרְאֶה־לּוֹ הַשֶּׂה לְעֹלָה בְּנִי וַיֵּלְכוּ שְׁנֵיהֶם יַחְדָּו:

6 And Abraham took the wood of the burnt-offering, and laid it upon Isaac his son; and he took in his hand the fire and the knife; **and they went, both of them, together.** 7 And Isaac said to Abraham his father, and he said, "My father." And he said, "Here I am, my son." And he said, "Behold the fire and the wood; but where is the lamb for a burnt-offering?" 8 And Abraham said, "God will provide Himself the lamb for a burnt-offering, my son." **And they went, both of them, together.**

The repetition is pretty conspicuous. In verse 6, we hear that Abraham and Isaac are heading to the mountain, walking together. But just two verses later, we hear precisely the same thing: they are walking together. Exactly the same Hebrew words.

Why does the Torah bother to tell us this again? Later, we'll try to find an answer to that question; for now, let's just recognize that we seem to have stumbled upon a repeated phrase in the *Akeidah* narrative; the two instances of "and they went, both of them, together" are a pair. Now we need to ask: Is this an isolated curiosity, or is this part of a larger pattern? Are there other such pairs in the *Akeidah*?

Look Outward

If we're really looking at a chiasm here, we might want to explore the text that appears right before the first וַיֵּלְכוּ שְׁנֵיהֶם יַחְדָּו (*vayeilchu shneihem yachdav*, "and they went, both of them, together") and see if it matches up with anything that appears right after the second וַיֵּלְכוּ שְׁנֵיהֶם יַחְדָּו. Let's look at the "before" and "after" text and see if we can find another pair.

Genesis 22:6–8

[ו] וַיִּקַּח אַבְרָהָם אֶת־עֲצֵי
הָעֹלָה וַיָּשֶׂם עַל־יִצְחָק
בְּנוֹ וַיִּקַּח בְּיָדוֹ אֶת־הָאֵשׁ
וְאֶת־הַמַּאֲכֶלֶת וַיֵּלְכוּ
שְׁנֵיהֶם יַחְדָּו: [ז] וַיֹּאמֶר
יִצְחָק אֶל־אַבְרָהָם אָבִיו
וַיֹּאמֶר אָבִי וַיֹּאמֶר הִנֶּנִּי
בְנִי וַיֹּאמֶר הִנֵּה הָאֵשׁ
וְהָעֵצִים וְאַיֵּה הַשֶּׂה לְעֹלָה:
[ח] וַיֹּאמֶר אַבְרָהָם אֱלֹקִים
יִרְאֶה־לּוֹ הַשֶּׂה לְעֹלָה
בְּנִי וַיֵּלְכוּ שְׁנֵיהֶם יַחְדָּו:
[ט] וַיָּבֹאוּ אֶל־הַמָּקוֹם אֲשֶׁר
אָמַר־לוֹ הָאֱלֹקִים וַיִּבֶן שָׁם
אַבְרָהָם אֶת־הַמִּזְבֵּחַ וַיַּעֲרֹךְ
אֶת־הָעֵצִים וַיַּעֲקֹד אֶת־יִצְחָק
בְּנוֹ וַיָּשֶׂם אֹתוֹ עַל־הַמִּזְבֵּחַ
מִמַּעַל לָעֵצִים:

6 And Abraham took the wood of the burnt-offering, and laid it upon Isaac his son; and he took in his hand the fire and the knife; and they went, both of them, together. **7 And Isaac said to Abraham his father, and he said, "My father." And he said, "Here I am, my son." And he said, "Behold the fire and the wood; but where is the lamb for a burnt-offering?" 8 And Abraham said, "God will provide Himself the lamb for a burnt-offering, my son."** And they went, both of them, together. **9 And they came to the place which God had told him of; and Abraham built the altar there, and laid the wood in order, and bound Isaac his son, and laid him on the altar, upon the wood.**

At first blush, the passages don't seem to match up at all. The first narrates Abraham and Isaac's walk up the mountain, carrying all the things they'll need for the offering at the summit, and the second describes Isaac being tied up and readied for sacrifice. Apples and oranges, right? But upon closer examination, commonalities do begin to emerge. Think, for example, about the appearance of wood in each verse. In verse 6, Abraham is carrying wood, and in verse 8, the wood makes a reappearance: Isaac is bound and placed atop the wood.

The parallel, actually, is even sharper than this. Look more carefully at the first appearance of wood. Abraham takes the branches and puts them on Isaac's back so that Isaac can carry them up the mountain. Stop and take a snapshot, in your mind's eye, of that scene: What would it look like? If you actually wanted Isaac to carry these logs up, what would you have to do to make sure they didn't just slip off his back and go rolling down the mountain? *You'd have to tie them together, and tie the bundle onto Isaac's back.*

Now do you see the parallel? First, Abraham places *tied-up wood on top of Isaac*. Later, Abraham places *tied-up Isaac on top of wood*. We've found our second parallel.

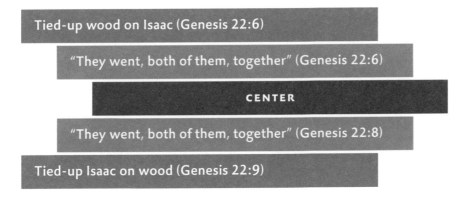

A Third Pair

If we keep on searching, we may find a third pair.

Let's look beyond the edges we've defined: *Before* Isaac takes that bundled wood up the mountain, and *after* Abraham lays Isaac on top of that bundled-up wood, are there any elements that seem to parallel one another?

That question brings us to the very first event of the *Akeidah* story, and to the very last one. How does the *Akeidah* begin? God suddenly addresses Abraham:

וַיֹּאמֶר אֵלָיו אַבְרָהָם   And [God] said to him, "Abraham,"   Genesis 22:1
וַיֹּאמֶר הִנֵּנִי: and he said, "Here I am."

Now think about how the *Akeidah* ends: Abraham is poised to offer up his son to God, but an angel stops him, calling out to him from heaven at the very last minute:

וַיֹּאמֶר אַבְרָהָם אַבְרָהָם   And [the angel] said, "Abraham, Abraham."   Genesis 22:11
וַיֹּאמֶר הִנֵּנִי: And [Abraham] said, "Here I am."

The *Akeidah* seems to end almost exactly as it begins, with Abraham saying, "Here I am"— our third element. A chiasm *does* appear to be unfolding before us, a once-invisible structure slowly coming into focus. At the outer edges, Abraham says, "Here I am." Between these two bookends, there are those two instances involving Isaac, Abraham, and that bundle of wood. And inside that, we have the two times Abraham and Isaac are described as walking together.

Genesis 22:1	וַיְהִי אַחַר הַדְּבָרִים הָאֵלֶּה וְהָאֱלֹקִים נִסָּה אֶת־אַבְרָהָם וַיֹּאמֶר אֵלָיו אַבְרָהָם וַיֹּאמֶר הִנֵּנִי:	And it came to pass after these things, that God tested Abraham, and said to him, "Abraham," and he said, **"Here I am."**
Genesis 22:6–9	[ו] וַיִּקַּח אַבְרָהָם אֶת־עֲצֵי הָעֹלָה וַיָּשֶׂם עַל־יִצְחָק בְּנוֹ וַיִּקַּח בְּיָדוֹ אֶת־הָאֵשׁ וְאֶת־הַמַּאֲכֶלֶת וַיֵּלְכוּ שְׁנֵיהֶם יַחְדָּו: [ז] וַיֹּאמֶר יִצְחָק אֶל־אַבְרָהָם אָבִיו וַיֹּאמֶר אָבִי וַיֹּאמֶר הִנֶּנִּי בְנִי וַיֹּאמֶר הִנֵּה הָאֵשׁ וְהָעֵצִים וְאַיֵּה הַשֶּׂה לְעֹלָה: [ח] וַיֹּאמֶר אַבְרָהָם אֱלֹקִים יִרְאֶה־לּוֹ הַשֶּׂה לְעֹלָה בְּנִי וַיֵּלְכוּ שְׁנֵיהֶם יַחְדָּו: [ט] וַיָּבֹאוּ אֶל־הַמָּקוֹם אֲשֶׁר אָמַר־לוֹ הָאֱלֹקִים וַיִּבֶן שָׁם אַבְרָהָם אֶת־הַמִּזְבֵּחַ וַיַּעֲרֹךְ אֶת־הָעֵצִים וַיַּעֲקֹד אֶת־יִצְחָק בְּנוֹ וַיָּשֶׂם אֹתוֹ עַל־הַמִּזְבֵּחַ מִמַּעַל לָעֵצִים:	6 And Abraham took the wood of the burnt-offering, and laid it upon Isaac his son; and he took in his hand the fire and the knife; and they went, both of them, together. 7 And Isaac said to Abraham his father, and he said, "My father." And he said, "Here I am, my son." And he said, "Behold the fire and the wood; but where is the lamb for a burnt-offering?" 8 And Abraham said, "God will provide Himself the lamb for a burnt-offering, my son." And they went, both of them, together. 9 And they came to the place which God had told him of; and Abraham built the altar there, and laid the wood in order, and bound Isaac his son, and laid him on the altar, upon the wood.
Genesis 22:11	וַיִּקְרָא אֵלָיו מַלְאַךְ יְקֹוָה מִן־הַשָּׁמַיִם וַיֹּאמֶר אַבְרָהָם אַבְרָהָם וַיֹּאמֶר הִנֵּנִי:	And the angel of the Lord called to him out of heaven, and said, "Abraham, Abraham." And he said, **"Here I am."**

Perhaps there are other pairs to be found in this chiasm. But for now, let's concentrate on another question: What's in the middle?

The Middle

Every chiasm, by definition, has a center. The unfolding pairs converge upon some sort of central point, drawing your attention toward it. At that center, you'd expect to find something key, some "center of gravity" around which the story revolves. So the question is: What is the center of this *Akeidah* chiasm?

The elements at the center are surprising because at first glance, they seem so mundane. At the center is what appears to be an entirely unremarkable conversation between Abraham and Isaac:

וַיֹּאמֶר יִצְחָק אֶל־אַבְרָהָם אָבִיו וַיֹּאמֶר אָבִי וַיֹּאמֶר הִנֶּנִּי בְנִי וַיֹּאמֶר הִנֵּה הָאֵשׁ וְהָעֵצִים וְאַיֵּה הַשֶּׂה לְעֹלָה: וַיֹּאמֶר אַבְרָהָם אֱלֹקִים יִרְאֶה־לּוֹ הַשֶּׂה לְעֹלָה בְּנִי	And Isaac said to Abraham his father, and he said, "My father." And he said, "Here I am, my son." And he said, "Behold the fire and the wood; but where is the lamb for a burnt-offering?" And Abraham said, "God will provide Himself the lamb for a burnt-offering, my son."	Genesis 22:7–8

It's a discussion between father and son about the technicalities of an offering: *Here's the fire, here's the wood.* Why is this so important? It's a conversation that might strike you as entirely trivial — until you realize that it's the only conversation the Torah ever records between Abraham and Isaac.

Think about that remarkable fact: we know of *no other thing* that these two men, father and son, ever told each other — other than *this.* Surely they must have talked to each other, but the Torah doesn't bother recording any of those other conversations, as interesting as they might have been. It is only *this* conversation that the Torah deems worthy of preserving for us, and for all generations throughout time.

It must have been a pretty important conversation. Indeed, its import is so great that it is the center of gravity for the entire *Akeidah* episode. The story, as a whole, seems to revolve around *this.* Why? Let's read the conversation carefully, and we'll see.

Small Talk

Isaac is the first to speak:

Genesis 22:7

וַיֹּאמֶר יִצְחָק אֶל־אַבְרָהָם   And Isaac said to Abraham his father,
אָבִיו וַיֹּאמֶר אָבִי   and he said, "My father."

A couple of things are puzzling here. First off, the Torah's insistence on reminding us that Abraham is Isaac's father: "And Isaac said to Abraham his father . . ." The text could easily have saved a word here and left out אָבִיו , "his father." After all, if you've gotten this far in the Abraham saga and you still don't know that Abraham is Isaac's father . . . well, you just haven't been paying attention.

This verse is odd for a second reason: it features an annoying redundancy. The word וַיֹּאמֶר (vayomer, "and he said") appears twice:

Genesis 22:7

וַיֹּאמֶר יִצְחָק אֶל־אַבְרָהָם   And Isaac **said** to Abraham his
אָבִיו וַיֹּאמֶר אָבִי   father, and he **said**, "My father."

The Torah could have made things simpler for us by saying "Isaac said to Abraham his father" only *once*, and then telling us what Isaac, in fact, said. There was no need to stop and add a second "and he said." But actually, it's worse than that. There's more than redundancy at work here: upon closer inspection, what the verse is saying doesn't even make sense.

A Matter of "Spoke" and "Said"

You see, there's a grammatical problem here. It's easy to miss if you're reading quickly, so let me try and spell it out clearly.

Biblical Hebrew has two different words for speaking: וַיְדַבֵּר (vayedaber, "and he spoke") and וַיֹּאמֶר (vayomer, "and he said"). The two might sound like they amount to the same thing, but there's a difference: the former is generally an intransitive verb, and the latter is always transitive. If your high-school grammar escapes you, that's just a fancy way of saying that if I tell you that "I spoke to someone," that phrase makes sense in and of itself. You don't need to know *what* I said for that statement to work. If, on the other hand, I tell you that "I said to someone . . ."— I can't just leave that sentence hanging. It doesn't make sense unless I tell you the *content* of what I said.

All of which makes for problems in the *Akeidah*'s conversation between Isaac and Abraham. The Torah doesn't tell us that Isaac "spoke" to Abraham and said to him: "My father." It uses *vayomer* instead, telling us that Isaac *said* to his father and said to him: "My father." And that doesn't make any sense at all. What did he say to Abraham the first time, before he said "My father"? [3]

The Intentional Use of a Nongrammatical *Vayomer*

I have a theory I'd like to share with you. It's based on an insight related to me by a great teacher of mine, Rabbi Yaakov Weinberg, *z"l*. He suggested that the Torah intentionally employs a grammatically incorrect *vayomer*—a "said," without telling us *what* Isaac said—in order to suggest an interrupted conversation.[4] In other words, Isaac and Abraham were going up the mountain, talking about something—maybe the weather, who knows?—and Isaac opened his mouth to say something, but stopped. He abandoned what he was *going* to say, and said something else instead.[5] And that "something else" was one word: אָבִי (*avi*, "my father").

The Very Last Thing You Want to Hear

Avi. It's really the last word that Abraham wants to hear right now. It's the one word he would do anything to hide from. A father's obligation, at its core, is to protect his son. God has asked him to do the opposite, to

---

3   See also Rabbeinu Bachye and Alshich (Genesis 22:7), who likewise question the need for this extra *vayomer*.

4   In fact, R. Weinberg saw this as something of a general principle. He observed that there are other times in the Torah — as, for example, in the story of the Tower of Babel (Genesis 11:3–4) and in the story of Hagar (Genesis 16:9–11) — when we encounter this kind of unexpected doubled *vayomer*. When this happens, R. Weinberg posited, the Torah is telling the reader, in effect, *You thought there was one speech or declaration here? You're wrong. You're looking at two separate declarations. Now go and figure out why.*

5   Hence the double *vayomer*: the first, nongrammatical one signifies an interrupted thought, and the second introduces what was actually said instead.

do away with his son: to offer him up on the mountaintop, back to God. If you are Abraham, every fiber of your being wants to run away when you hear your son say "My father." You want to run right back down the mountain. Or if you aren't going to run away physically, you want, at the very least, to run away emotionally. At that moment, he would have given anything to change the subject — to talk about something else, anything else, rather than respond authentically to Isaac's one-word query: אָבִי (*avi*), "My father!"

But Abraham, at that moment, doesn't run. He knows what's going to come next. Why, after all, would Isaac stop mid-sentence and say "My father"? Something has changed for Isaac; he has a question, a painful, difficult question, as the truth is beginning to dawn on him. Isaac is going to ask that question. But Abraham doesn't run. He tells Isaac:

Genesis 22:7	הִנֶּנִּי בְנִי Here I am, my son

It's the very opposite of running away. *I know who I am: I am your father. I know who you are: you are my son. I'm present. I'm listening. Ask what you want to ask.*

Eifoh and *Ayeh*

So Isaac does. Here's what he says:

Genesis 22:7	וַיֹּאמֶר הִנֵּה הָאֵשׁ וְהָעֵצִים And he said, "Behold the fire and the wood; וְאַיֵּה הַשֶּׂה לְעֹלָה: but where is the lamb for a burnt-offering?"

To really understand Isaac's question, you need to go back to the Hebrew and translate it carefully. Isaac asks אַיֵּה (*ayeh*, "where") the lamb for the offering is — but that doesn't quite capture it. There are, in fact, two words in Hebrew for "where": אֵיפֹה (*eifoh*) and אַיֵּה (*ayeh*). The first, *eifoh*, is a garden-variety "where," a simple request for something's location. So, for example, when Naomi asks Ruth *eifoh*, "Where did you collect grain today?" (אֵיפֹה לִקַּטְתְּ הַיּוֹם),° she really wants to know which field Ruth was collecting in; which field-owner was so generous to her? But *ayeh* has a different connotation. When God asks Adam where he is after eating the forbidden fruit,° God doesn't ask *eifoh*, He asks *ayeh*. God isn't asking Adam for his location; an omniscient God knows where Adam is. He's asking, instead, "Where did you go?" *How come you aren't here, where I expected you to be?*

Ayeh is a question you ask when you expect something to be there, but it's not.[6] Which, of course, changes everything in terms of what Isaac is really asking his father. He's *not* asking, "So where's the lamb? Is it by the woodshed, or maybe behind those bushes?" That would be an *eifoh* question. Instead, he is asking *ayeh*, "Where did the lamb go?" In other words: *Father, I see the wood. I see the knife. But there's no lamb! Father, how come there's no lamb?*

Well, that's a different question entirely, isn't it? Perhaps now we can understand why this is the one and only conversation the Torah ever records between Abraham and Isaac. This is when Isaac figures it out. He's asking, in essence, "Am I the lamb?"

This is the moment that the truth begins to dawn on Isaac about what his fate might be on the top of that mountain. And it's not just the moment that Isaac finally knows the truth. It's also the moment that Abraham *knows* that Isaac knows. So how does Abraham answer his son's question?

All in a Comma

וַיֹּאמֶר אַבְרָהָם אֱלֹקִים
יִרְאֶה־לוֹ הַשֶּׂה לְעֹלָה בְּנִי
וַיֵּלְכוּ שְׁנֵיהֶם יַחְדָּו:

And Abraham said, "God will provide Himself the lamb for a burnt-offering, my son." And they went, both of them, together.

Genesis 22:8

On the face of it, his response is somewhat ambiguous. There are two ways of interpreting Abraham's statement, and the difference between the two boils down to punctuation. Is there an implied comma there, or a colon?

---

6   See *HaKtav VehaKabalah* to Genesis 3:9. See also *Kli Yakar* to Genesis 18:9.

Ruth 2:19

Genesis 3:9

On the one hand, you can read Abraham's response this way:

God will provide Himself the lamb for a burnt-offering, my son.

That's one way to read it. Read with a comma, the statement seems rather innocuous. It's as if Abraham is saying: *Nothing to worry about, my boy! That missing lamb? Don't fret. God will find us a lamb!* But there's a darker possibility, too — one Rashi alludes to — when the statement is read with a colon:

God will provide Himself the lamb for a burnt-offering: my son.

Maybe "my son" is the offering. Maybe "my son" is the lamb.[7]

Intentional Ambiguity

So, which is the true meaning of Abraham's response? If Abraham means one of the two, why doesn't he just say what he means to say, clearly? Why is he being so ambiguous here?

Maybe Abraham's ambiguity is not an attempt at evasion, but an attempt at radical truth-telling. After all, things really *are* ambiguous. Put yourself in Abraham's shoes here, and ask yourself: *What do you really know?* The truth is, you *don't know* what's going to happen at the top of this mountain. On the one hand, God has promised you that a great nation will come through Isaac. And yet He has also told you that you are to give Isaac back to Him at the top of the mountain! *None of this makes any sense.* It seems absolutely absurd.

Abraham *can't* make sense of it, and he doesn't try. The truth is radically uncertain, which is exactly what he is telling Isaac with that purposeful ambiguity. It's as if Abraham is saying to Isaac:

*I don't know what the offering is. Maybe God will find a lamb, my son. Maybe you, my son, are the lamb. That's up to God. But there's something that **is** up to me…*

What is up to Abraham here? He may desperately want to control the identity of the lamb, but he can't. What *can* he control?

Bull's-Eye

To find out, let us return to our *atbash* pattern. We've seen that this conversation between Abraham and Isaac occupies the center of the chiastic

---

7   See Pirkei de-Rabbi Eliezer 31 and Midrash Aggadah 22:8.

structure in the *Akeidah*. But this conversation — the center point of the chiasm — *itself* has a center. And that center is perhaps the most crucial single word in the entire story.

What is the center of Abraham's conversation with Isaac? Well, here's a way to think about it: their conversation is made up of a number of separate verbal declarations, each delineated by the word וַיֹּאמֶר (*vayomer*, "and he said"). If you count them, you'll find five separate instances of *vayomer* in the conversation. That means that the third *vayomer* is the middle one. Zoom in on that third *vayomer* and you'll find something fascinating:

The middle *vayomer* is Abraham's response to Isaac: הִנֶּנִּי בְנִי, "Here I am, my son." That, truly, is the center. Not just the center of this particular conversation, but the center of the entire *Akeidah* narrative.

Why is that one phrase spoken by Abraham so very important? What was Abraham really saying to Isaac?

וַיֹּאמֶר יִצְחָק אֶל־אַבְרָהָם אָבִיו

And Isaac **said** to Abraham his father,

וַיֹּאמֶר אָבִי

and he **said**, "My father."

וַיֹּאמֶר הִנֶּנִּי בְנִי

And he **said**, "Here I am, my son."

וַיֹּאמֶר הִנֵּה הָאֵשׁ וְהָעֵצִים וְאַיֵּה הַשֶּׂה לְעֹלָה:

And he **said**, "Behold the fire and the wood;
but where is the lamb for a burnt-offering?"

וַיֹּאמֶר אַבְרָהָם אֱלֹקִים יִרְאֶה־לּוֹ הַשֶּׂה לְעֹלָה בְּנִי

And Abraham **said**, "God will provide Himself the lamb
for a burnt-offering, my son."

He was saying: *Right when I most want to run away, I will not. I am here, my son. I know who you are: you are my son, and I am your father. I will not evade that hard truth. I will be fully present with you, truthful with you, even when it seems maddeningly impossible. I am not hiding from you. Now ask your question.*

And it worked. The relationship between these two men, father and son, survived. Think back to the very first chiastic pair that we uncovered, the repeated phrase וַיֵּלְכוּ שְׁנֵיהֶם יַחְדָּו, "And they went, both of them, together." Rashi offers a fascinating interpretation of the second of these phrases: *that Abraham and Isaac were united in spirit and purpose.* Now, it's one thing for Isaac to walk harmoniously together with his father when Abraham knows about God's command and Isaac doesn't. But it's another thing entirely to walk harmoniously together *after* Isaac has asked his question, and *after* Abraham has answered it. Now Isaac knows the truth. Consider this: What could possibly introduce more dissonance into a relationship between a father and son than the father turning to his child and saying, "The Lord appeared to me last night and said I have to kill you"? Yet this is what Abraham and Isaac must somehow confront, this most difficult of all possible conversations. Somehow, after the conversation, they continue to walk together, as Rashi suggests, in the same shared spirit in which they walked earlier, before Isaac was in the know.[8] Their relationship endures. Indeed, it is perhaps even stronger for it.

Abraham's greatness was that he didn't run away, not physically and not emotionally. *What's going to happen on the top of the mountain? I have no idea. But whatever happens, I am your father, and I am here for you. I can't control who the lamb is. That's up to God. But I can control how I relate to you. I will not distance myself from you. I am present for you, in love, always. Even now.*

Balance

What is the *Akeidah* really about? I want to argue that it's about an exquisite, almost impossible, balancing act. We've found that the center of the *Akeidah* is the word *hineini* that Abraham speaks to his son. But the *Akeidah* begins with the word *hineini* too: God calls out and says, "Abraham, Abraham," and Abraham answers God, "Here I am." And, as we've already pointed out, the *Akeidah* also ends with the word *hineini*: the angel of God calls out to Abraham from heaven to stay his hand, at the last moment — and Abraham answers, "Here I am."

8　The idea that is implicit in Rashi here is more explicit in Rabbeinu Bachye to Genesis 22:7, in explanation of Bereishit Rabbah 56:4.

The edges of the chiasm mirror its center, conveying to us — pithily, but powerfully — the essential nature of Abraham's test.

I want to argue that the *Akeidah* was not just a test of Abraham's loyalty to God. It was a far more difficult test than that. It was a test of his loyalty to God and to Isaac at the very same time, even when these dueling imperatives seemed impossible to balance.

It's one thing to say "Here I am" to God when He asks you to give back your son; in your single-minded devotion to the Almighty, suddenly that becomes the only imperative that matters: you turn yourself off emotionally to your son and walk numbly up the mountain, focusing only on your devotion to God. Or you could imagine the opposite: in Abraham's shoes, you might reject allegiance to God entirely, saying, "God, I'll have nothing to do with You; this is crazy. My allegiance is to Isaac." But Abraham? His greatness is that he is "here" for both of them.

How can he be there for God *and* for Isaac? That's impossible, you say; it makes no sense! True, but it doesn't matter. God has asked something of Abraham that seems absurd, and Abraham responds in kind. It makes no sense, but it's true anyway: *I will not turn my back on God, and I will not turn my back on Isaac.* Abraham, going up that mountain, is like a horseman riding two steeds at once, with one foot in one stirrup of each horse. Suddenly, the two horses, who had been galloping together, begin to diverge. He will stand there, with a foot on each, and not abandon either: *I will be loyal to God and to Isaac. I will be there for both of them.*

But Abraham, we want to ask, what will you do at the top of the mountain? The horses are going separate ways! His answer: *What happens at the top of the mountain — who the lamb is — God will have to figure that out. Until then, I am here, and not just for God; I am here for my son too.*[9]

Abraham preserves his fealty to his two most important relationships, even when it seems absurd, even when these two worlds are about to diverge. His loyalty, to his Creator and to his son, is uncompromising — all the way to the unknowable end.

---

9   See Rambam (*Moreh Nevuchim* 3:24), Radak, and Rabbeinu Bachye (the latter two to Genesis 22:1), who discuss the tension Abraham must have felt between his love for God and his love for Isaac. Many commentators take the position that Abraham's love for God "wins out," as it were, but the Netziv, notably, reads Genesis 22:7 — the center of our chiasm — as evidence for Abraham's continued loyalty to and love for Isaac (See *Ha'amek Davar* ad loc.).

What Makes for an Extraordinary Life?

וַיִּהְיוּ חַיֵּי שָׂרָה מֵאָה
שָׁנָה וְעֶשְׂרִים שָׁנָה
וְשֶׁבַע שָׁנִים שְׁנֵי
חַיֵּי שָׂרָה:

And the life of Sarah was one hundred years and twenty years and seven years; [these were] the years of the life of Sarah.

GENESIS 23:1

What Makes for an Extraordinary Life?

THE PASSAGE OF TIME can seem cruel. Aging, even in the best-case scenario, means accommodating ourselves to certain basic frailties of the human condition: we aren't as strong or as mobile as we used to be, as independent as we used to be. But every once in a while, we meet someone getting on in years who seems ... different. By different, I don't mean that they have been granted a free pass from the inevitable process of aging. They might suffer the same outward maladies as the next person, but there is something *extraordinary* about them: they exude a certain richness of being that makes them an absolute pleasure to be around. Their life seems enviable, somehow.

I had a grandmother like that. She died a while ago, but her palpable joy in life, her infectious enthusiasm, seemed undiminished, even enhanced, by the passage of time. "That's how I want to be when I get to be her age," my wife always said. What secret do people like this possess? What is it that makes them so extraordinary? What are they doing right? And is there a way we can learn to do it too?

Sarah

I think we get some guidance in these issues from the very first verse of **Parshat Chayei Sarah** — and from Rashi's interpretation of that verse.

The opening verses of the parsha tell us that Abraham gave a eulogy for his wife, Sarah. Now, we don't really know much about that eulogy. The text simply tells us:

וַיָּבֹא אַבְרָהָם לִסְפֹּד לְשָׂרָה וְלִבְכֹּתָהּ: And Abraham came to eulogize Sarah and to cry for her.

Genesis 23:2

We don't hear what Abraham said about her, but we do know what the Torah says about her. Indeed, the verse describing the death of Sarah can also be read as a eulogy of sorts, delivered by the Torah itself:

Genesis 23:1

וַיִּהְיוּ חַיֵּי שָׂרָה מֵאָה שָׁנָה
וְעֶשְׂרִים שָׁנָה וְשֶׁבַע שָׁנִים
שְׁנֵי חַיֵּי שָׂרָה:

And the life of Sarah was one hundred years and twenty years and seven years; [these were] the years of the life of Sarah.

That verse, and its unusual phraseology, is the basis for one of the most famous comments made by Rashi in all of his commentary on the book of Genesis. Rashi notes that the verse doesn't merely declare that Sarah died when she was 127 years old. Instead, it breaks up the numbers, saying that the years of her life were a hundred years, twenty years, and seven years. Rashi is bothered by this: Why break the years into three groups like that, making us do the addition ourselves? Why insert the word "years" between each of the figures? It's almost like the text is saying that yes, there were 127 years in total, if you want to do the math, but that's not the whole truth of the matter. Really, there were a hundred years, twenty years, and seven years.

Rashi argues that this is exactly the intent of the verse: there were three groups of years, each connected to the other. When Sarah was a hundred, Rashi says, she was as guiltless, as free from sin as she was when she was merely twenty.[1] And when she was twenty, she was as beautiful, as innocent-looking, as when she was seven.

What is Rashi trying to tell us with this cryptic series of comments? Is there a larger meaning here?

I want to suggest that Rashi is getting at something deep about what it means to live an extraordinary life. But to see the full implications of Rashi's comment, I want to take a moment to introduce you to another vision of Sarah, a complementary vision of her, articulated by another rabbinic great, someone who lived many years before Rashi. I'm thinking now of Rabbi Akiva.

1   In halachah, one is not liable until the age of twenty for certain particularly severe crimes that call for divine punishment (see Shabbat 89b, Talmud Yerushalmi Bikkurim 2:1 and Sanhedrin 11:5).

Rabbi Akiva's Riddle

The Talmudic sage Rabbi Akiva also famously references Sarah's 127 years, in a riddle he crafted for his students:

רַבִּי עֲקִיבָא הָיָה יוֹשֵׁב
וְדוֹרֵשׁ וְהַצִּבּוּר מִתְנַמְנֵם
בִּקֵּשׁ לְעוֹרְרָן אָמַר מָה
רָאֲתָה אֶסְתֵּר שֶׁתִּמְלֹךְ עַל
שֶׁבַע וְעֶשְׂרִים וּמֵאָה מְדִינָה,
אֶלָּא תָּבוֹא אֶסְתֵּר שֶׁהָיְתָה
בַּת בִּתָּהּ שֶׁל שָׂרָה שֶׁחָיְתָה
מֵאָה וְעֶשְׂרִים וָשֶׁבַע
וְתִמְלֹךְ עַל מֵאָה וְעֶשְׂרִים
וְשֶׁבַע מְדִינוֹת.

Rabbi Akiva was once sitting and lecturing, and [his students] were falling asleep. To rouse them, he said, "What occasioned Esther's rule over 127 provinces? It came about because Esther was a descendant of Sarah, who lived to 127; [therefore] let Esther come and rule over 127 provinces!"

Bereishit Rabbah 58:3

Why does the Midrash bother to tell us of Rabbi Akiva's playful stunt with his sleepy students? *Was* it just a playful stunt? Does Queen Esther, heroine of the Purim saga, *really* have anything to do with Sarah, Abraham's wife — other than an admittedly remarkable coincidence regarding numbers associated with each? Was Rabbi Akiva just joking here, or did his little joke conceal a hidden meaning that his students, and we, might harvest from it? I believe that these two sages — first, Rabbi Akiva, and later, Rashi — might have been getting at remarkably similar ideas.

Queenship

What do Sarah and Esther have in common? Yes, they are notable figures of the Bible. But so are many other women: Miriam, Deborah, Yael, and Ruth, to name just a few. And yet, in Rabbi Akiva's mind, there was something particular about Sarah and Esther that bound together their respective "hundred-and-twenty-sevens." What was that quality?

It was queenship. Consider, for example, Sarah's name and how she got it. Her name was originally Sarai,° which can be translated as "my princess," almost as if it were a term of endearment that Abraham, her husband, used for her. But one day, God changed her name. He told Abraham that from here on out, she was to be known as Sarah:

Genesis 11:29

וַיֹּאמֶר אֱלֹקִים אֶל־אַבְרָהָם
שָׂרַי אִשְׁתְּךָ לֹא־תִקְרָא
אֶת־שְׁמָהּ שָׂרָי כִּי שָׂרָה
שְׁמָהּ ... מַלְכֵי עַמִּים
מִמֶּנָּה יִהְיוּ:

And God said to Abraham, "As for
Sarai your wife, you shall not call her
name Sarai, but Sarah will her name
be ... Rulers of nations will come
from her."

Sarah. Not "my princess," just "princess." It was as if God was saying to
Abraham: *She is not merely **your** princess. She is more universal than that.
Rulers of nations will come from her. She is to be a princess of the world. She
belongs to humanity itself.*

But listen carefully to those words of the verse: "Rulers of nations will
come from her." Yes, "rulers of nations" indeed. Historically, when *did* a descendant of Sarah live to become not just a queen over a particular nation,
but a ruler of many nations — an empress, as it were?

It happened at the dawn of the age of empires, in the days of Achashvei-
rosh, when Esther became queen over Persia's 127 provinces. The woman
who ruled over 127 territories was the scion of the woman who had lived
to 127 years. Years and territories. Time and space. Might Esther, who
ruled over space, have had an ancestress — Sarah — who ruled similarly
over ... time?

Rabbi Soloveitchik on Sarah's Life

We're getting closer to the meaning of Rabbi Akiva's words, but to truly
fathom what his riddle is trying to teach us about Sarah and Esther, I
think we need to come back to that comment of Rashi that we looked at
earlier. Let's reexamine those three units of time that Rashi noted in the
Torah's account of Sarah's years. What was his point in calling our attention to them?

Rabbi Yosef Dov Soloveitchik offers an intriguing interpretation.[2] Part
of what it means to be human, R. Soloveitchik suggests, is passing through
different stages in life. To be sure, every person experiences these stages in

---

2   R. Joseph B. Soloveitchik, *Abraham's Journey: Reflections on the Life of the Founding
Patriarch* (Jersey City, NJ: Ktav, 2008), 184–193.

their own unique way, but still, some generalizations can be made. Earliest youth is a time of innocence, exuberance, and curiosity. We discover ourselves and our world: *This is an arm; look what it can do! I wonder what would happen if I put it in my mouth? This is a glass. I wonder what would happen if I dropped it?* When we become adolescents, different priorities begin to take hold. We prize independence: *Who am I? I'm not just the product of my parents' world. How will I be different from them?* A bit later in life, still different goals and values emerge: *I'd like to settle down, get married one day. I'll need a job soon. What should I do about my career?* Then, let's say you do get married. Other priorities begin to loom large: *I'm raising my kids. How shall I instruct them? What values do I want to pass on to them?* Gradually, adulthood gives way to middle age, and middle age gives way to our sunset years. Each comes with new priorities, new vistas, new ways of looking at our lives and at the world.

So let's accept, as a given, that life passes through different stages. We may experience them differently, but we all traverse some version of them. What R. Soloveitchik argues, though, is that some of us traverse these stages in an ordinary way, while others do so in an extraordinary way.

How so?

Ordinary and Extraordinary Living

One way to go through the stages of life is to experience them in succession, to live each stage for what it is, and then to leave it behind and experience the next one. That's the ordinary way to go through life. But there's another way to go through life, an extraordinary way. It's the way Sarah did it, R. Soloveitchik argues — and it's what Rashi was getting at with his cryptic comment. The way Sarah did it, you don't just passively travel through life's stages, discarding the past for the more pressing priorities of the present. No, you build as you go: you take each stage with you as you encounter the next one.

What does that look like? You're seven, wide-eyed and innocent. And soon enough, you're not seven anymore, you're growing up. But as the years pass and you approach twenty, you don't *exchange* that innocence for independence and self-discovery. You don't say: *Exuberance and innocence? That's kid's stuff. I'm ready to move on. I'm ready to find myself!* No. You *keep* the innocence, exuberance, and curiosity you had when you were seven, and you build on it. You take it with you. You find a way to channel your wide-eyed curiosity about life, and merge it somehow into your new, teenage self, complete with new values and desires.

As you progress further, toward adulthood, you accrue responsibilities, and in dealing with those newfound responsibilities, you accumulate life experience. You attain a bit of wisdom. But as you do, you don't leave the teenage passion for independence behind; you take it with you. You don't leave childhood's innocence, exuberance, and curiosity behind. You take all that with you too. All these qualities inform your newfound wisdom, leavening it. So you're an adult and you pay your bills on time; you've been around the block and you're smart enough to smell a scam. But you're able to pause sometimes, as you eat lunch outdoors, to examine a lady-bug perched on a blade of grass and be overcome with childlike wonder. You put your kids to bed on time, yes. But occasionally, you get swept up in a wild pillow fight with your children, and to their delight (and yours), allow yourself to forget, if only for the moment, that it's way past bedtime.

You progress to later stages of life. As the end of life begins to twinkle, ever so vaguely, on the horizon, you begin to consider: *What lasting impact might I have, in even a small way, on this world of ours?* But instead of experiencing that question solely as a crisis — and instead of distracting yourself from that crisis by buying a shiny red sports car — you surprise yourself by finding the courage, optimism, and will to directly confront the question. How do you do that? You call on the reservoirs of innocence, exuberance, and curiosity that you've brought with you from childhood. You call on the wisdom, the life experience, and the clarity of principle that you earned when you and your wife wrestled with how you would educate your kids. You bring all your earlier selves with you as you confront the new challenges of middle age.

As you make your way toward the last stage of life, when the prospect of death starts to become more real, that growing awareness of life's end doesn't leave you feeling empty inside; fear of that inevitable end doesn't become your sole, obsessive focus. Why? Perhaps because the way that you've *lived* life prepares you to *leave* life. You've lived without leaving your earlier selves behind. And maybe that gives you the confidence to see death itself as just another stage that will give way into yet another, an ultimate stage whose mystery you ready yourself, in your entirety, to embrace. Paradoxically, when you confront death *that* way, you feel more able to surrender your life — when that day finally arrives — to the One who created it. Maybe that's what it means to live an extraordinary life.

In the Image of God

There is something almost "divine" about living this way. The Torah declares that man is created in the image of God, but that declaration is full of mystery. What does it mean to be created in God's likeness? How do we live as God "lives"? One answer to that question, perhaps, has to do with one of the only things we know about God: His name. In the Torah, God is referred to as י-ה-ו-ה (YHVH), a four-letter name that seems suspiciously close to three Hebrew words that denote states of being: היה (*hayah*), to exist in the past; הוה (*hoveh*), to exist in the present; and יהיה (*yihyeh*), to exist in the future. And yet it is none of these. Or, more precisely, it is all of these: if you take the letters ה-י-ה, overlay them with ה-ו-ה, and overlay that combination with י-ה-י-ה, the result is י-ה-ו-ה (YHVH).

Some would see in this evidence that God is eternal. But "eternal" doesn't quite get at the depth of the meaning here. If I'm eternal, I exist forever — but still, my past is past and is now gone; the future is not yet here; for now, I just exist in the present. But God's name YHVH seems to indicate that God exists in a very special, concentrated way: He is past, present, and future existence, all at once. There is something extraordinarily powerful about this mode of existence. The past is not lost in the mists of time; the future isn't unreal. All God ever was or will be, as it were, is here *now*, in an existence far richer than we can imagine.

Humans don't exist that way; we exist in time. Our past leaves us and is gone. We live in the fragile present, a mere hairbreadth of time, constantly on the move. But perhaps we, as humans, can experience some pale shadow of God's mode of existence when we move through life in a way that aggregates the stages we go through, when we find ways to merge our past selves with our present reality. R. Soloveitchik's model of extraordinary existence, the kind of life he asserts that Sarah lived, stands as a model, perhaps, for how we can bring a sliver of the divine into our own being.

Sarah and Esther

We may now be in a position to perceive more clearly what Rabbi Akiva was trying to tell those sleepy students when he said, "Esther was a descendant of Sarah, who lived to 127; [therefore] let Esther come and rule over 127 provinces!" Earlier, we suggested that Rabbi Akiva sees a certain commonality between Sarah and Esther: both ruled over 127 units. But what does it really mean to be a ruler, a queen?

Rashi's remarks about Sarah offer an explanation. You see, a queen is not merely someone who makes the rules for a certain territory, or decides the fate of her subjects in that territory. A queen does do all that, but if she is successful, her tenure as monarch is of greater moment: by uniting her subjects in some way, she transforms a mere territory into a *nation*. The people that comprise a nation are not just individuals living in proximity to one another. They have some sort of common cause, and the monarch is a living symbol of that cause, and, hopefully, works proactively to advance it.

How does a king or queen advance that cause? At their best, monarchs find ways to join individual talents to form a larger whole. Bob is a blacksmith, Phil is a farmer, Carol is a shepherdess, Beryl is a tailor — and the monarch? The monarch lays out a vision and helps to structure society in a way that incorporates the energies of Bob, Phil, Carol, and Beryl. A king or queen unites unique individuals and inflects their talents toward service of the nation's cause.

Esther played such a role on the world stage, uniting peoples across far-flung provinces.[3] She was a ruler of territory, of *space*. But in doing this, Rabbi Akiva argues, she was living out a vision first formulated by her ancestor Sarah — an empress of *time*. Esther had a teacher, as it were. What Esther did for individual *people*, Sarah, long before her, did for individual *moments*. She was a ruler of years.[4]

Of Xylophones and Symphonies

Sarah lived her years in an extraordinary way. To summarize her mastery of those years, in the Torah's "eulogy" for her, we might draw an analogy

---

3   For further elaboration of this idea, see my book *The Queen You Thought You Knew*, pt. 1, ch. 3.

4   Rashi's notion, as elaborated by R. Soloveitchik — that the Torah's eulogy for Sarah expressed her "mastery over time" — is perhaps hinted at in the biblical text itself. Sarah becomes the woman who, to her own astonishment, gives birth at the age of ninety. While her ability to do this is obviously the product of a divine miracle, perhaps this miracle was, in fact, little more than an external expression of an internal state that Sarah herself had cultivated: she lived life in a way that was timeless.

from the world of music. Think of each stage we experience in life as a discrete musical note. You could strike one note at a time, leaving each note behind, as you seek out yet another to play. But that's kind of like playing a Fisher-Price toy xylophone. The sound you end up making is simple, one-dimensional. It's ordinary. How do you begin to create great music? You take one note and integrate it into the next. When you do that, you are playing *chords*; you are developing *harmony*. Whether the song you ultimately play will be beautiful or haunting, fast or slow, upbeat or melancholy — that is yet to be determined. But if you play this way, you have the building blocks for a richer song; you have the stuff of which symphonies are made.

That's what it means to live an extraordinary life, to seem timeless, as we get on in years. In the words of Rashi, when you are twenty years old, you still have seven; and when you are a hundred, you still have both twenty and seven. This is the Torah's eulogy for Sarah. It is, as R. Soloveitchik explained it, what made Sarah's life special.

Not all of us can be emperors over space. We don't have to be. But we can be emperors of time. Indeed, Esther is not the only one who can learn from Sarah; Sarah's example can help us, her descendants, find ways to become maestros of our moments too.

If You Were Rebecca's Lawyer

THE JACOB SAGA, PART I

אוּלַי יְמֻשֵּׁנִי אָבִי
וְהָיִיתִי בְעֵינָיו
כִּמְתַעְתֵּעַ

Maybe my father will feel my skin, and in his eyes, I'll seem like a trickster

GENESIS 27:12

If You Were Rebecca's Lawyer

THE JACOB SAGA, PART I

IT'S NOT AN EASY STORY to come to grips with: an elderly and nearly-blind Isaac calls to his firstborn son, Esau, and tells him he wishes to bestow a blessing upon him before his death. To this end, Esau should go out, hunt game, and prepare delicacies for his father; Isaac will partake of them and bless him. That's the plan. But it's not what happens: Rebecca overhears the discussion between father and son, and goes to Jacob — the son *she* loves, as we've been told° — and instructs *him* to go to his father instead. Jacob ends up going to Isaac, dressed in the clothes of his brother, Esau, and impersonates the hunter long enough to make off with his brother's blessing.

Genesis 25:28

When Esau returns from the hunt and finds out what happened, he is at first heartbroken, and then infuriated. He pledges to kill Jacob. At that point, Rebecca suggests to Jacob, somewhat optimistically, that Jacob should run away to her brother's house until things blow over; she will call for him when Esau's anger subsides and it's safe to come home.° But twenty years elapse, and she never calls for him. Evidently, it was never safe enough for her to summon her beloved child back home. Even after decades, seemingly, Esau's anger has not subsided.

Genesis 27:42–45

You don't have to be a rocket scientist to perceive the questions this story puts to the reader — basic, plain vanilla questions: Jacob's supposed to be a good guy, right? So how can he commit this premeditated act of deception upon his father, leaving his brother to cry bitter tears? And Rebecca — she's supposed to be good too. So how does she put her son up to this?

Now, you might respond that Esau was a bad guy and he deserved to get hoodwinked. When the chips were down, Jacob did what he had to do. But the text doesn't seem to lead us in that direction: it emphasizes Esau's tears, not his depravity. Does the Torah really want us to conclude that, when push comes to shove, the ends justify the means? And, to push the envelope a little further, is that a conclusion we're comfortable sharing with our kids?

I'll delve into these possibilities soon, but first I want to give you a road map of where I'm going. I'll be spending the next three essays — on **Toldot**, **Vayeitzei**, and **Vayishlach** — examining this story of the deception of Isaac and its aftermath. In this essay, I want to start us off by suggesting an alternative way of understanding our story, sharing with you an approach suggested to me by Rabbi Simcha Cook, a teacher of mine at the Ner Israel yeshiva. This approach, I think, puts some of the moral quandaries of our story in a different and unexpected light. I'll focus on a narrow aspect of this story: what Rebecca might be thinking in making the choices she does. Seeing Rebecca and her role differently will lead us, I think, to view *everyone's* actions differently, allowing us to see some of the ethical dimensions of our story in new and surprising ways.[1]

1   WHAT WAS SHE THINKING?

Why start with Rebecca? Because, when you think about it, she was the architect of the deception. It wasn't Jacob who came up with the idea of deceiving his father. She instructed him to do it; she was the one who heard the conversation between Isaac and Esau, and she was the one who told Jacob to go to his father. But understanding *why* she acted as she did is difficult.

Say you're Rebecca, and you're convinced, for whatever reason, that your husband, Isaac, is about to bless the wrong child. You believe Jacob deserves that blessing instead. What do you do? Maybe you'd talk to Isaac about it, try to win him over, explain to him your point of view. But Rebecca doesn't do that; she elects for Jacob to play dress-up instead. Why?

To get a handle on this, I thought it might be helpful to engage in a bit of role-playing: if the Heavenly Court were trying Rebecca for her role in our tale of deception, and you were her lawyer, what — if anything — would you say in her defense?

If You Were Rebecca's Lawyer...

As Rebecca's newly hired attorney, here's one line of defense you might advance on behalf of your client: Rebecca was not at fault for her untoward

---

1   Over the generations, many have struggled with these questions — and some, indeed, have looked at Rebecca's role closely, seeing in her actions a key to the story as a whole. See Bereishit Rabbah 65:5–6 and Ramban to Genesis 27:4, as well as R. Samson Raphael Hirsch and Malbim.

actions because, really, she was doing nothing more than actualizing a prophecy.[2] Back when she was pregnant with her twins, Jacob and Esau, God spoke to her of the destiny of the two children she was carrying:

שְׁנֵי גוֹיִם בְּבִטְנֵךְ וּשְׁנֵי	Two nations are in your womb; two	Genesis 25:23
לְאֻמִּים מִמֵּעַיִךְ יִפָּרֵדוּ	separate peoples shall issue from your body.	
וּלְאֹם מִלְאֹם יֶאֱמָץ	One people shall struggle with the other;[3]	
וְרַב יַעֲבֹד צָעִיר׃	and the greater shall serve the younger.	

Case closed, then — she's off the hook, right? God had told her that Jacob, "the younger," was meant to be preeminent over the "greater" (older) child, and all she did was bring this prophecy to fruition. Rebecca has this prophecy about Jacob's rightful place in history, but one fateful day, her husband decides it's time to pass on the mantle of Abraham's heritage to one of his children — and he chooses Esau. She overhears him tell Esau to go hunt game, come back with meat, and then receive this momentous blessing.° Rebecca knows there's a problem here: *Isaac is choosing the wrong son.*

Genesis 27:1–5

When Rebecca hears this, she wants to make sure history doesn't go off the rails. She feels she needs to do *something* to set things right, to make the divine prophecy happen. Everything, she feels, rides on what she does — or doesn't do — right now. It is up to her to fulfill God's will — even if she has to resort to deception.

And maybe that line of thinking justifies everything.

Was the "Prophecy" Really So Clear?

So … does this lawyerly logic work? It would certainly be convenient to find an "out" for Rebecca this easily, but I want to suggest that the logic here is flawed, and that it fails as a defense for at least two reasons.

First, if you go back and look at what God actually tells Rebecca when she's pregnant, you'll find that the meaning of the words spoken to her isn't so plain and clear. Chizkuni, for example, argues that, in Rebecca's prophecy,

---

2 See Ramban to Genesis 27:4 for one version of this theory.

3 Our translation of וּלְאֹם מִלְאֹם יֶאֱמָץ follows *Ha'amek Davar.*

Genesis 31:41

וְרַב יַעֲבֹד צָעִיר may *not* mean "the greater shall serve the younger." [4] Instead, it could mean something like "a great deal [of time] shall the younger child serve," a version of the prophecy that *does* come true: Jacob is later pressed into service in his father-in-law's house for a great deal of time.°
And there are still other interpretations of Rebecca's prophecy to be found among the commentators.[5] All in all, it seems more like a mysterious premonition than a prophecy that could plausibly force Rebecca's hand in real time — clear, perhaps, in *retrospect*, but in the moment, too vague to justify such irrevocable actions.

Second, an even more serious objection against the notion that the prophecy justifies Rebecca's actions: even if you were to argue that her prophecy constituted an ironclad revelation that Jacob was destined to be "the chosen one," it's still hard to see how this, in and of itself, would justify her actions. There's a basic question of *responsibility* that must be settled: Whose responsibility is it to make sure that this prophecy is fulfilled? Is it Rebecca's? Let me show you what I mean.

A Divinely Ordained Campaign

Imagine you go to sleep one night and you have a prophetic dream (I know we don't have prophecy nowadays — at least not in the way our forefathers and foremothers did back in biblical times — but let's suspend disbelief and pretend for a moment). The Lord comes to you in this dream and says He has a mission for you: your destiny is to become the next congressperson for your district.

Until now, politics has been the furthest thing from your mind. You've been just a humble lawyer (or speech therapist, or soccer mom), tending to your garden, minding your own business. But all of a sudden, that changes.

---

4   See his comment to Genesis 25:23.

5   See, for example, *Ha'amek Davar*, who offers another possible way of understanding God's words to Rebecca. According to his reading, the word רַב (*rav*) does refer to the older child, and the verse is indeed saying that one brother will end up serving the other — but *who* shall serve *whom* is not made clear. Moreover, *Ha'amek Davar* adds that the Torah doesn't make this clear *on purpose*: the inherent ambiguity of the verse means that the older *could* serve the younger — but on the other hand, the older might be the one to press the younger into his service. Things could go either way. History — not divine predestination — will ultimately decide how the relationship between the brothers develops.

God Himself reveals that you have a grand future on the national stage. You are going to be a congressperson, the Lord tells you in this dream. And just to prove it, says the Almighty in the dream's final scene, He is giving you $530,000 to start your campaign.

You wake up, and your first instinct is to dismiss the dream as nonsense. But then you look under your pillow, and — wonder of wonders — you spot a check made out to your election committee for $530,000. The check is drawn on the First Heavenly Bank of God. You can't believe it, but you deposit the check in your account . . . *and it clears.*

So the dream was real. God Himself has spoken to you. What do you do now?

Well, you declare your candidacy, of course. And you begin to reorient your life: you read up on politics and legislation. You go out and make some speeches. Slowly, your name recognition builds. Before you know it, you're neck and neck with your opponent. It looks like it might really happen. You might really win.

Five days before the election, Bob, your chief of staff, calls and tells you he has bad news: internal polling says you're going to lose by 5 to 7 points. It'll be close, but you're going to lose. Just as the crushing news starts to set in, though, Bob speaks up: "Sir, there *is* one last thing we can do."

It turns out Bob has an old friend, Phil, who administers the computer systems at the state election board. Bob thinks that if you slip Phil a little something — *I don't know, $530,000 or so* — Phil might just be able to make that 5- to 7-point deficit go away.

Bob hangs up, leaving you alone with your thoughts.

So *what do you do?* Do you slip the money to Phil? After all, you *did* have that prophecy. *God Himself* told you that you were destined to win. And here's your chance to make it happen!

What's Your Responsibility—and What's God's?

I think the answer is that you *don't* slip the money to Phil. You can't just sit on your couch and do nothing, waiting for God's prophecy to materialize; you *should* actively take some steps to realize the prophecy. You should, for example, start a campaign and try hard to prevail. But that doesn't mean you can and should do *anything* to win. It doesn't mean you should do something *unethical* to win.

Why not? Isn't it your responsibility to fulfill the prophecy? No, the responsibility to make the prophecy come true doesn't fall exclusively on your shoulders; God can act to influence the course of events too. So at some point, you've got to say something like, "God, we're partners here. I've fulfilled my end of the bargain. I've done everything I can do — legally and ethically — to win. Now, Lord, the ball is in Your court. If You want me to win, You've got your ways. It's up to You now."

Has Rebecca's Lawyer Reached the End of the Road?

Bottom line, then: if you're Rebecca's lawyer, defending her actions solely on the basis of the prophecy seems to fall short — it doesn't let her off the hook.

I want to propose an entirely different theory about Rebecca's intentions, but first I need to lay some groundwork: I want to show you three important clues in our text that, when combined, suggest that something strange is afoot in this story of Rebecca instructing her son Jacob to deceive Isaac. Let's go back to the text, and I'll try to show you what I'm talking about.

2   THREE CLUES

Reading without the End in Mind

One of the difficulties we sometimes encounter when we read the Torah is that we know its stories too well. We know, for example, how every story *ends*, so we can easily fall prey to the illusion that the story *had* to end the way it does. But it didn't, of course: the people in these stories had free will. They *could* have chosen differently. In real time, as events were actually unfolding, all sorts of "endings" were possible.

Our familiarity with the Torah also affects our view of the *middle* of a story: we already know what's going to happen, so we can fail to notice a plot twist. We can fail to be surprised by a truly astonishing turn that a story takes because we're already expecting it.

As readers of the Torah, how can we avoid being misled by this false sense of inevitability? We need to make a conscious effort to read "without the end in mind." In other words, you need to stop every once in a while, mid-story, and ask yourself, "If I didn't know what happened next, what would I expect to happen right now?" And if what *does* happen next is far afield of what you expected, you need to wonder, "What am I missing here?"

Let's try this out now: let's go through the Torah's description of the events that immediately precede, and immediately follow, Jacob impersonating Esau and getting the blessing from Isaac. As we look at that text, I want us to focus on three crucial moments when Rebecca and Jacob, mother and child, discuss things with one another. In those moments, do things proceed as we might expect, or in surprising ways?

Did Jacob Just Get Thrown under the Bus?

Let's start at the end: after the deception is complete, after Jacob successfully manages to wrest that coveted blessing from his father, Esau comes back home and discovers what's happened. Then Rebecca summons Jacob for an urgent consultation. She tells her son that Esau is furious and intends to kill him. Jacob must run away from home, she says, and take shelter with her brother, Lavan, in the land of Charan. He should stay there until his brother's fury subsides:

וְשָׁכַח אֵת אֲשֶׁר־עָשִׂיתָ לּוֹ   until he forgets what you have done to him   Genesis 27:45

Now, pay close attention to the way she puts this, and you should be able to see just how surprising it is. If you don't immediately see the problem, try listening as if you were her son Jacob, hearing what she's telling you. You might be more than a little upset to hear your mother characterize things this way; you might think, "I should stay away until Esau forgets what *I* did to him? Mom, *you* were the one who came up with the whole deception, from beginning to end. The least you could have said was "until he forgets what *we* did to him." You can't pin this all on me, as if you had nothing to do with it!"

Indeed, in the lead-up to the deception, Rebecca not only suggests but *commands* Jacob to listen to her. She's the one who insists he go to his father while Esau is away hunting:

וְעַתָּה בְנִי שְׁמַע בְּקֹלִי   Now, my son, listen to my voice,   Genesis 27:8
לַאֲשֶׁר אֲנִי מְצַוָּה אֹתָךְ:   to that which I command you to do.

Seemingly, then, this plot is *all on her*. Why, then, when it's all over and things have gone badly — Esau wants to kill Jacob, and Jacob must run away—why, at that moment, would she cast this as somehow having been *Jacob's* idea? She's his mother; why throw him under the bus like that?

Unless somehow, in her mind, she *genuinely believes* she didn't really put him up to this—and in a matter-of-fact way, she's telling the truth as she sees it: *You did this to Esau.* Now, I understand how preposterous that sounds: How can she take such a view when she was the mastermind behind the deception in the first place? But for now, let's just call this our first clue as to how Rebecca might perceive the events of our story—and we'll move on to clue number two.

What Are the Odds?

Our second clue is a curious moment earlier in the story.

When Rebecca is trying to convince Jacob to go to Isaac and get that blessing, Jacob pushes back on the plan: *I have smooth arms*, he tells her. *Father may be blind, but he hasn't lost his sense of touch. He'll feel my arms and know it's me.*° Jacob concludes his protestations by telling Rebecca that he's worried that, in the end, his father might hold him guilty for deceiving him, and curse him instead of blessing him. In response, Rebecca says:

Genesis 27:11–12

Genesis 27:13

עָלַי קִלְלָתְךָ בְּנִי   Upon me shall your curse be,
אַךְ שְׁמַע בְּקֹלִי   my son! Just do as I say

Let's step back and consider the import of what she's just said—what an incredible risk she's taking. Presumably, Rebecca doesn't take lightly the significance of a curse uttered by Isaac. After all, she's angling for Jacob to get her husband's blessing; she evidently takes quite seriously any blessing or curse that Isaac might bestow. In light of that, aren't her words rather astonishing? Here she is, blithely accepting the curse of her husband in the event of failure.

Perhaps she's just confident the ruse will succeed. But how can she be so confident? Put yourself in her shoes: What would you say the odds are that her hastily improvised plan will succeed? Sure, in the end, the plan *does* work—Isaac is deceived—but reading without the end in mind, what are the odds?

Any rational person would have to put those odds at close to zero.

IF YOU WERE REBECCA'S LAWYER 101

Jacob is to dress up in his smartest, most fashionable Esau-style clothes and do his level best to impersonate his brother. He'll have to approximate Esau's voice: its pitch, its timber, its cadence — the whole nine yards. Remember: Isaac is blind, but he isn't deaf.[6] To succeed, Jacob will have to fool his father, who has lived for decades with his two sons; it seems highly improbable that Jacob will somehow manage to pull this off.

Which, again, makes Rebecca's words astounding. The fear Jacob is expressing seems well-founded: *What if Dad discovers my ruse, and ends up cursing me instead of blessing me?* Reading without the end in mind, that's not just a remote possibility; I think everyone would agree it's the expected, most likely, outcome.[7] But Rebecca doesn't even seem to give it a second thought: *No problem, Son. I'll take your curse!* Why does she so casually assume such a terrible risk?

That's clue number two.

To Seem as a Deceiver

We'll find a third clue if we take a closer look at the rest of this little exchange between Rebecca and Jacob. We've focused on Rebecca's response to Jacob, her willingness to take Isaac's curse upon herself — but look at what Jacob tells her right before that. He tells her his worry: his own skin is smooth, he says, while Esau's is covered with hair. *If Father touches me…*

וְהָיִיתִי בְעֵינָיו כִּמְתַעְתֵּעַ וְהֵבֵאתִי עָלַי קְלָלָה וְלֹא בְרָכָה:	In his eyes, I'll seem like a trickster — and I'll bring upon myself a curse and not a blessing.	Genesis 27:12

If you read his words carefully, he doesn't quite say what you'd expect to hear from someone who's worried that his ruse will be discovered. He doesn't say, "Mom, I'm worried Father will *discover* I'm a trickster." He says he's worried he'll *seem* like a trickster in his father's eyes — implying

---

6   If anything, those who are blind are said to experience a sharpening of their other senses — a better-than-average ability to distinguish nuances in sounds, for example — making Jacob's ability to pull off the ruse all the more improbable.

7   See Ramban to Genesis 27:12.

that no trick is *really* being played here, that at most, his father will "get the wrong idea" about him. Why does he pull his punch like that? He's talking to his mother, the one who hatched this whole deception plot; he's got nothing to hide from her. On the contrary, it's in his interest to tell it like it is — after all, he's trying to convince her that her plan is too dangerous, and should be abandoned.

Why, then, is Jacob being so unnecessarily evasive? [8]

I want to suggest to you that Jacob *isn't* being evasive, that he — and, for that matter, his mother — never planned on deceiving Isaac at all. Isaac *was*, in the end, deceived; that much is true. But they hadn't actually *planned* this. The deception occurred because their plan went off the rails.

To show you how that might be the case, I want to take you through the conversations between Rebecca and Jacob in slow motion. But first, I want to put those conversations in context. And to do that, I need to take you back to the beginning, the very beginning: the moment Jacob and Esau first came into being.

3   WHAT DOES IT TAKE TO UNDO A NAME?

Rebecca's newborn twins are named Jacob and Esau. How did they get those names?

At face value, the answer might seem obvious: Isaac and Rebecca named them, just after each came into the world. But look closer, and you'll see that something ever-so-slightly different happened:

Genesis 25:25–26

וַיֵּצֵא הָרִאשׁוֹן אַדְמוֹנִי כֻּלּוֹ כְּאַדֶּרֶת שֵׂעָר וַיִּקְרְאוּ שְׁמוֹ עֵשָׂו: וְאַחֲרֵי־כֵן יָצָא אָחִיו וְיָדוֹ אֹחֶזֶת בַּעֲקֵב עֵשָׂו וַיִּקְרָא שְׁמוֹ יַעֲקֹב

The first one emerged red, like a cloak of hair all over; and **they called** him Esau. Then his brother emerged, holding on to the heel of Esau; and **he called** him Jacob.

When Esau, the first to emerge from the womb, is named, the text uses the plural וַיִּקְרְאוּ (*vayikre'u*, "and they called") to denote, implicitly, who

---

8   Cf. R. Samson Raphael Hirsch to Genesis 27:12.

is doing the naming: וַיִּקְרְאוּ שְׁמוֹ עֵשָׂו, "and **they called** him Esau." "They" would seem to indicate that *both* parents, Isaac and Rebecca, named him Esau.[9] But now, consider the naming of Jacob: here, the verb "call" appears in singular form, *vayikra*: וַיִּקְרָא שְׁמוֹ יַעֲקֹב, "and **he called** him Jacob," which means only one parent, evidently, called him Jacob.[10] Moreover, since the verb takes the *masculine* singular form, we know that parent was a "he." Meaning ... it had to be Isaac.

Add it all up, and here's what we get: *both* parents called their first child Esau. They arrived at his name together. But only *one* parent, Isaac, decided to call the second-born child Jacob. Rebecca, for some reason, declined to join Isaac in bestowing that name upon this second child. The question, of course, is *why*.

Names to Grow into; Names to Grow out Of

The meanings of the names may provide us with our answer. Why, after all, was Esau such an obviously appropriate name for the first child? The name seems to derive from the verb עָשָׂה (*asa*), "do." Esau, then, would mean "the done one," or maybe "the doer"[11]— a singularly fitting name for this child, really, for the Torah tells us that, in some ways, he was born an "already-made" man. He comes out of the womb looking like a mature adult; he's ruddy, vigorous, and already covered in hair. And, lo and behold, as Esau grows up, he becomes a person who gets things "done." The text tells us that he develops into a hunter, a man of the field. But hunting is not the only thing he can "do." Recall, after all, what Isaac asks of Esau before he'll bless him: *Go hunt me some game and prepare it as a delicacy, just the way I like it.* Esau is a jack-of-all-trades. Not only can he hunt; he can prepare the meat, cook it, and make it into "delicacies"; he can present the food with grace and flair. He is, quite literally, a "doer," just as his name suggests. And Rebecca and Isaac agree on this name.

But now look at Jacob's name: it's related to the word עָקֵב (*akeiv*), "heel," and the idea behind Jacob's name seems to be prompted by the way this baby emerges from the womb: grasping Esau's *heel*. It's as if this second child had wanted to come out first ... but Esau, the doer, beat him to it.

---

9   Cf. Rashi to 25:25, from Targum Yonatan.

10 Cf. Midrash Tanchuma to Exodus 4, Rashi to Genesis 25:26.

11 See Rashi and Targum Yonatan to Genesis 25:25.; cf. Midrash Lekach Tov ad loc..

"Heel" also suggests something else: a sense of being "roundabout," not straightforward, inasmuch as a heel looks that way: it curves sharply; it isn't straight. Certainly, Esau would come to see Jacob's name in precisely this fashion when, years later, he discovers that his brother has taken his blessing. He exclaims:

Genesis 27:36

הֲכִי קָרָא שְׁמוֹ יַעֲקֹב   That's why he's called Jacob—
וַיַּעְקְבֵנִי זֶה פַעֲמַיִם   because he "heeled" me twice!

As Rebecca gives birth to these children, Isaac stares at this child who emerged second, this baby grasping the heel of his brother, and he sees in this child someone who was beaten out, someone who will always come in second unless he does something "roundabout." And Isaac named him Jacob, evoking the heel to which he clung.

And maybe this tells us something about why Rebecca was silent, why she didn't join her husband in bequeathing this name. Maybe it's not such a nice name. *Jacob, "heel": the child who came in second, who won the prize for trying hard. The child who would need to be roundabout, indirect.*

Isaac named him Jacob. But Rebecca didn't. And, as if to let us know why she demurred, the Torah — just after telling us about the children's names — also makes sure to tell us about Rebecca's feelings for Jacob:

Genesis 25:28

וְרִבְקָה אֹהֶבֶת אֶת־יַעֲקֹב: And Rebecca loved Jacob.

Her love, perhaps, led her to believe in a different destiny for him. She wanted him to be more than a "roundabout" man: he should be able to be direct, straightforward. She would not lend her own voice to that name. It was a name whose connotations she rejected — a name, I want to suggest, that Rebecca would in due time seek to *undo*.

Two Decisions

We don't know much about Rebecca, but right here, at the moment her children are born, we hear of a significant choice she makes. It's a quiet choice, this rejection of a name — a choice she makes by doing nothing more than remaining silent. And for a long stretch of time, the Torah tells us little more about her. Isaac lives his life — goes to Gerar, skirmishes with the Philistines, digs wells, makes treaties with Avimelech — and all the while, the Torah is more or less silent about Rebecca's activities. Finally, though, as Isaac grows old, the Torah tells us of one more choice Rebecca makes. If her first choice was a refusal to go along with that name, Jacob, I want to suggest that her second choice was an attempt to, in effect, banish the implications of that name once and for all.

Upon hearing that her husband wishes to bless Esau, not Jacob, she calls to her younger son and delivers instructions to him:

[ו] הִנֵּה שָׁמַעְתִּי אֶת־אָבִיךָ מְדַבֵּר אֶל־עֵשָׂו אָחִיךָ לֵאמֹר: [ז] הָבִיאָה לִּי צַיִד וַעֲשֵׂה־לִי מַטְעַמִּים וְאֹכֵלָה וַאֲבָרֶכְכָה לִפְנֵי יְהֹוָה לִפְנֵי מוֹתִי: [ח] וְעַתָּה בְנִי שְׁמַע בְּקֹלִי לַאֲשֶׁר אֲנִי מְצַוָּה אֹתָךְ: [ט] לֶךְ־נָא אֶל־הַצֹּאן וְקַח־לִי מִשָּׁם שְׁנֵי גְּדָיֵי עִזִּים טֹבִים וְאֶעֱשֶׂה אֹתָם מַטְעַמִּים לְאָבִיךָ כַּאֲשֶׁר אָהֵב: [י] וְהֵבֵאתָ לְאָבִיךָ וְאָכָל בַּעֲבֻר אֲשֶׁר יְבָרֶכְךָ לִפְנֵי מוֹתוֹ:	**6** I overheard your father speaking to your brother Esau, saying, **7** "Bring me some game and prepare delicacies for me to eat, that I may bless you, before God, before I die." **8** Now, my son, listen carefully as I instruct you. **9** Go to the flock and fetch me two choice young goats, and I will make of them delicacies for your father, such as he likes. **10** Then take them to your father to eat, in order that he may bless you before he dies.	Genesis 27:6–10

We're so used to assuming that Rebecca was the architect of a plan to steal the blessings that we casually take for granted that she was instructing her son to go in and trick Isaac into thinking he was Esau. But read carefully the words she actually says here, and see if you think that's really what she's saying to her son. Does she really have deception in mind? I mentioned before that the approach I'm sharing with you came, originally, from a teacher of mine, R. Simcha Cook; he was the one who pointed out to me that, in her opening speech to Jacob, Rebecca never actually mentions deception at all.

Remember what we said earlier about not reading with the end in mind. Don't allow yourself to be prejudiced by the fact that, in the end, Jacob *does* deceive his father. Think only about what Rebecca is saying right now, at *this* point in the story. What she seems to be saying is something like this:

> *Yes, your father wants Esau, your brother, to come back with delicacies, so he can bless him before he dies. But you don't have to take that lying down. You go approach him with delicacies, so you can get a blessing from him too, before he dies.*[12]

And, of course, there's a certain logic to this. After all, what does Father really want to see in Esau? Why, before blessing him, does he dispatch Esau to go hunting, of all things, and bring him delicacies? What do hunting and food preparation have to do with Isaac's ability to bless him? Apparently, Isaac wants to see Esau display the quality he's always prized in him — his ability to get things *done*[13] — and in so doing, provide the inspiration for

---

12 Rebecca never tells Jacob to go get himself a blessing *instead of* Esau, or to go *take* Esau's blessing. All she tells him is to make sure his father blesses him before he dies (Genesis 27:10). She doesn't appear to be suggesting that Jacob take Esau's blessing and dispossess him. For all she knows, Esau can have his blessing ... and if Jacob impresses Isaac, Jacob can have one too. The fact that this blessing is a zero-sum game, as Isaac later reveals, is something the reader — and for that matter, Rebecca — doesn't know at this stage.

13 Why does Isaac prize being a "doer" so much? The Torah doesn't tell us, so we can only speculate. But if we put ourselves in Isaac's shoes, perhaps it's not so mysterious. Isaac seems to believe it falls to him to bestow his legacy, the legacy of his forefathers, on one of his two children. He needs to pick one who will carry the torch of the nation God had promised to him forward into history. He doesn't know when he will die. Before leaving this world, he wants to put on its strongest legs the incipient nation he was meant to father.

   Which child would you trust to do that? Jacob's a nice enough fellow, this man of the tents, but does he have the strength and initiative? Esau, on the other hand, maybe he's a little rough around the edges — he eats, shoots, and leaves — but he has staying power in this world. He can make things happen. He's a doer.

   Here's one thing Isaac knows for sure: the nation God promised his father, Abraham, would suffer pain and hardship in spades. It would have to endure hundreds of years of civilization-crushing oppression, and then some. So, which of your children would you pick to head up this endeavor? It doesn't seem so foolish to have your eye on the doer.

the blessing he is to bestow. But Rebecca's point to Jacob is this: *You don't need to be left behind. You can show Father that you can be a doer too.*

And in a way, she's right about that: if Jacob presents himself to his father with delicacies of his own, he really *will* have shown himself to be a doer. And not just because he's demonstrated that he's a good chef — he's done more than that. Just by approaching his father and arguing that he too should be blessed, he would, in effect, be making a claim: he too can be direct, straightforward, and forceful. He's someone to be reckoned with. He's a doer too.

If the plan works, Rebecca surmises, Jacob will undo, for all intents and purposes, his wretched name. No, an angel won't necessarily come out of heaven to change his name, but Jacob will show his father that he can be *more* than his name. He is more than Mr. Roundabout Man, more than the brother who always comes in second, consigned to perpetually clutch the heel of Esau. Father will come to understand that the circumstances of Jacob's birth would not forever define who he is.[14]

A Hidden Flaw

Now, if we're right about this, Rebecca's plan seems fairly noble. If anything, she's advocating for honesty: *Just be who you are.* But if this is her plan, there's a flaw in it. For even if we imagine Jacob doing *exactly* what his mother asks of him here, we can still ask, in all fairness: Would Jacob *really* be demonstrating that he's the "doer" she wants him to portray?

To some extent, maybe — but not entirely. After all, it's not like she's telling him to go out and hunt game, as Esau has been asked to do, or even to prepare delicacies for his father, as Esau has been asked to do. No. She's offering to do it *for him.*° It's like she knows he's no hunter … and maybe not even much of a chef. She's not certain he can do all this himself, so she's doing part of it for him. From a certain perspective, you might say she's helping her son take the first step. But from another perspective, you might say she's undermining the very argument she's trying to make: he's not yet the doer she wants him to be.

° Genesis 27:9

---

14 Could Rebecca have taken Isaac aside instead and said, "Look, I think you've underestimated Jacob; he's more of a doer than you think"? Yes, but those are just words. Evidently, she wants Isaac not just to hear an argument she might make for Jacob, but to actually *experience* Jacob differently — as someone who can advocate for himself in a forthright way.

Jacob Demurs

Let's go on and examine how Jacob responds to his mother's proposal. He says:

Genesis
27:11–12

הֵן עֵשָׂו אָחִי אִישׁ שָׂעִר
וְאָנֹכִי אִישׁ חָלָק: אוּלַי
יְמֻשֵּׁנִי אָבִי וְהָיִיתִי
בְעֵינָיו כִּמְתַעְתֵּעַ

Esau is hairy-skinned, and I am smooth-skinned. Maybe my father will feel my skin, and in his eyes, I'll seem like a trickster

With these words, Jacob expresses doubt that the whole thing will work. As we noted before, Jacob speaks only about *seeming* like a trickster in his father's eyes; he doesn't tell his mother that he's worried Father will *discover* that he's tricking him. And the reason why should now be evident: neither he nor his mother think that what she's proposing is actually deceitful. Jacob's worry, then, is confined to appearances: he's worried about *seeming* to deceive Isaac, about seeming . . . *inauthentic*, somehow. He's standing there with this food for his father, but his hands . . . his hands betray him. For Jacob, his doubts concentrate themselves in a worry about his own skin: the feel of his hands, he frets, will put the lie to his words:

Genesis 27:12

אוּלַי יְמֻשֵּׁנִי אָבִי וְהָיִיתִי
בְעֵינָיו כִּמְתַעְתֵּעַ

Maybe my father will feel my skin, and I will seem in his eyes as if I'm tricking him

His father will reach out and feel his hands, and suddenly Jacob's whole argument to his father will seem ridiculous:

You show up once, bring me food, and you expect me to think that all of a sudden you've changed? All of a sudden you're a doer? Look at these hands of yours, Son! Smooth, from never having done a day of hard labor. No blisters from arrows or a hoe, no scars from a spear or sickle. Your hands show who you really are; why bother pretending otherwise?

Jacob fears his hands will speak louder about him than a momentary act of initiative. Father will regard him as the same tent-dweller he's always been and reject him out of hand. He'll end up receiving a curse from his father rather than a blessing.

Rebecca's Response

It is at this point that Rebecca responds:

עָלַי קִלְלָתְךָ בְּנִי   Upon me shall your curse be,   Genesis 27:13
אַךְ שְׁמַע בְּקֹלִי   my son! Just do as I say

We asked before why Rebecca would accept upon herself any curse that
might come from Isaac, given that the likelihood of Jacob pulling off a real
heist of the blessing seems close to zero. But remember, a heist of the blessing was *not* what anyone, at this point, was planning. Had Rebecca been
suggesting some reckless plot to do something truly underhanded — to
stand there and brazenly impersonate Esau, to simply *lie* to his father about
who he is — then yes, that would be both unethical and radically unlikely
to succeed. But that's not what she's suggesting. What she's doing is en-
couraging her child to defy his father's expectations for him. She's trying to
bring out the best in Jacob, and she's willing to stand by her child, urging
him to take this risk. In effect, she's saying: *I don't think Father will scorn
you and curse you as you fear, my son. But if he does, it's on me.*

Once again, her stance seems noble. She's not being reckless; she's
being compassionate. And yet, there's another way to look at this: once
again, she's subtly undercutting her own argument on Jacob's behalf. After
all, what does it really *mean* to be a doer? Part of being a doer is incurring
risk, acting decisively in unsure circumstances. To succeed, Jacob needs
to *do* this: in this case, he needs to stand up in front of Isaac and make his
case, come what may. At the end of the day, his willingness to take the risk
of being cursed is part of what's supposed to impress his father. Except
now… *his mother assumes that risk for him.*

The argument Rebecca is asking Jacob to make is getting thinner and
thinner. First she's going to make the delicacies for him … and now she's
promising to take upon herself any curse that should come his way.

Clothes Make the Man

After assuring Jacob that she will assume Isaac's curse, should it come,
Rebecca goes and finds some of Esau's clothes and dresses Jacob in them.
She puts goat skins on his hands and the smooth parts of his neck. Why,
exactly, does she do this?

The way we've always read the story, the answer is easy: she's trying to — quite literally — pull the wool over her husband's eyes. She wants Jacob to pretend he is Esau and deceive her husband. But there's a problem with that theory: As we've already observed, Rebecca has *never told Jacob that he should go and deceive his father.* And that is singularly strange. If that really *is* her intent, you'd think that, at some point, she'd have to tell Jacob the game plan. But she never does this. She just silently dresses him in Esau's clothes.

Why would she do that? If deception isn't her intent, what is?

Well, what was the last thing Jacob said to her? He told her about a fear: If Isaac were to feel him, the smoothness of his skin would make a mockery of his words. Now, whether Jacob is right or wrong about that, one thing's for sure: he's worried about it. And, left unaddressed, that worry could easily ruin everything: *He'll never be able to present himself confidently to Isaac if he's preoccupied about his skin.* So she comes up with an idea, a way she can help.

She's cooked the food for him. She's accepted the possible curse of his father for him. And now, she'll do one last thing for him: she'll help him with that preoccupation about his smooth hands. *You're worried you don't seem, on the outside, like a doer? Put on these clothes, then. Maybe if you wear the clothes of a doer, you'll feel more like a doer.*

After all, the clothes make the man.

The clothes Rebecca asks Jacob to wear aren't meant to be instruments to deceive his father. They're just another bit of motherly scaffolding to help Jacob approach his father in a frame of mind that won't be self-defeating. Even if the clothes don't yet express who he is *now*, perhaps this is his mother's way of telling him she believes he can get there, that this is something he can grow into. It's as if she is insisting to him:

> *Your smooth hands don't tell the whole truth about you, my son. They tell of the person you've been. But these clothes tell of what you have the potential to become. You can become every bit the doer Esau is.*

So, Who Are You?

And so, bearing the food his mother gives him, the assurance about the curse his mother provides him, and the clothes she places upon him, Jacob finally, reluctantly, accedes to his mother's directive and comes before Isaac. And as he does, Father greets him with a very simple, but piercing, question:

מִי אַתָּה בְּנִי: Who are you, my son?   Genesis 27:18

It is a very good question indeed. Given all that's transpired between Rebecca and Jacob in the lead-up to this moment, Isaac's question goes to the core of what mother and child have been struggling with: *Who, really, is this child standing before Isaac?* Rebecca certainly has her opinion: *she* wants him to be the doer. But does *he* think he's the doer?

Look at him in this situation: he doesn't want to be there. He's told his mother he thinks the whole thing isn't going to work. Nevertheless, she's commanded him to go in. So he goes, wearing clothes that aren't his own, bearing food he hasn't cooked, on a mission to tell his father he's someone that, truthfully, he doesn't feel himself to be.

Given all this, what's the real answer to Isaac's question?

Under normal circumstances, when you try on some new and different clothes, at best, they help express an aspiring sense of self within you — *I feel like spring this morning; I'll wear that new linen suit* — but they don't make you into something you're not. You are who you are, and you express yourself a bit differently with your various changes of clothes. But when your sense of self is uncertain or wanting, radically different clothes can overwhelm you. You can feel ... hollow inside, as if there's virtually nothing left of the real you.

The outside can drown out the inside.

Perhaps this is the crisis confronting Jacob right now. His father has asked him who he is. *What, really, is the answer to that?* The answer is ... in flux. Can he be who his mother wants him to be? Is that really him? The answer is a big question mark. So Jacob looks at himself, and the only certain thing he sees about this man standing before Isaac ... are those clothes he's wearing. Suddenly, the clothes engulf the man wearing them, and despite himself, all he can say to his father is, "I am Esau, your firstborn." *The clothes define me, because right now... I don't know what else does.*

Catastrophe

Once those words slip out of Jacob's mouth, all bets are off. Against all odds, Isaac actually accepts at face value what he's just been told: that the person standing in front of him really *is* Esau. Which means Jacob is just going to have to ad-lib. And so, with barely a moment to think, he tells his father:

Genesis 27:19

עָשִׂיתִי כַּאֲשֶׁר דִּבַּרְתָּ אֵלָי
קוּם־נָא שְׁבָה וְאָכְלָה מִצֵּידִי
בַּעֲבוּר תְּבָרֲכַנִּי נַפְשֶׁךָ:

I've done what you've asked of me. Get up now; sit; eat from my hunted game, so that your soul will bless me.

In the split second that he says this, Rebecca's plan goes spectacularly to pieces. All of a sudden, Jacob really *is* deceiving his father. This isn't what Rebecca had planned. It's not even what *Jacob* had planned. Jacob is standing in front of his father without a script, without a plan. From here on in, he's just winging it ... and by hook or by crook, he manages to get out of his father's tent with a blessing.

You can imagine what it might have been like to be Rebecca, listening from the kitchen, hearing her son, Jacob, say those words to Isaac: "I am Esau, your firstborn." She'd be astonished and cringing, all at the same time: *What? How could he have said that?* Indeed, later, when it's all over, she tells Jacob that Esau is seeking to kill him because of "what *you* have Genesis 27:45 done to him."° Earlier, we asked why she would throw him under the bus like that. But she's not throwing him under the bus; she's just telling it to Jacob like it is: *What you said in there wasn't part of my plan. It probably wasn't part of your plan either. But one way or the other, it was something you did. Still, I'll do whatever I can to keep you safe.*

In the end, a terrible act of deception takes place. Esau is hoodwinked. So is Isaac. But neither mother nor child ever actually ... *planned* it. Neither ever imagined it would happen.

A Series of Unfortunate Events

If you are Rebecca's lawyer, then, this would be her defense. She didn't mean to trick anyone; she was just trying to help her son step into himself. Jacob, for that matter, didn't mean to trick anyone either — at least, he hadn't *planned* to. He was just trying to do what his mother wanted from him, to once and for all rise above the implications of that unfortunate name, "heel," or "Mr. Roundabout Man." But benign intentions don't always lead to good outcomes. In the end, despite all Rebecca's encouragement, all her scaffolding, Jacob wasn't yet ready to do what she asked. And her plan came crashing down.

The great tragedy is that Rebecca's plan didn't just fail; it backfired. Instead of comporting himself before his father in a way that would show he was more than "Mr. Roundabout Man," Jacob, if anything, did the reverse: he reconfirmed that unfortunate perception. At the end of the story, a sobbing Esau, realizing he's been tricked, declares to his father:

הֲכִי קָרָא שְׁמוֹ יַעֲקֹב
וַיַּעְקְבֵנִי זֶה פַעֲמַיִם
אֶת־בְּכֹרָתִי לָקָח וְהִנֵּה
עַתָּה לָקַח בִּרְכָתִי

Was he, then, named Jacob that he might "go around me" these two times? First he took away my birthright, and now he has taken away my blessing!

Genesis 27:36

And What about the Judge?

Up to this point, we've adopted the perspective of Rebecca's lawyer — and implicitly, Jacob's lawyer too. And in essence, this is what the defense amounts to: *Your Honor, I see the unsavory outcome here, but this wasn't what my client planned.* But here's the question: How far does this get you in the eyes of the judge?

And make no mistake about it: the judge, in this case, isn't really me and you. We're just the readers of the story. The judge is ... the Master of the Universe, who, as it happens, is very much a part of this story. Indeed, the Almighty shows up in the very next scene.

Right after Jacob takes the blessing meant for Esau, his mother sends him away to Charan to escape the wrath of his brother. But along the way, he stops for the night, and God speaks to him in a dream. Now, just play this out with me: if you were the Lord, and you were upset with what Jacob had just done, you might imagine that you'd confront him about it. You'd signify your displeasure in some way. But the really remarkable thing about God's speech to Jacob in that dream is that He seems to do nothing of the sort: He reassures Jacob. He lets him know He is giving him this land, and that He will protect him until he returns to his father's house.

Why is the Almighty so silent concerning Jacob's actions? Does the Judge, in fact, have nothing to say?

This is the question that we'll try to address now. Come join me as we begin our look at **Parshat Vayeitzei**.

Jacob Meets Rachel—and Cries?

THE JACOB SAGA, PART II

וַיִּשַּׁק יַעֲקֹב לְרָחֵל
וַיִּשָּׂא אֶת־קֹלוֹ וַיֵּבְךְּ:

And Jacob kissed Rachel and he
lifted up his voice and he cried.

GENESIS 29:11

Jacob Meets Rachel— and Cries?

THE JACOB SAGA, PART II

IN PARSHAT VAYEITZEI, we meet Jacob on the lam, running away from home, seeking to escape the wrath of his brother, Esau. When Jacob stops for the night, God appears to him in a dream, and what is particularly interesting about that dream is what God *doesn't* say. God speaks reassuringly to Jacob, but says nothing to him about the deception that just transpired. As I suggested at the close of the last essay, it leads one to wonder: What is the Lord's perspective on all that's happened? God neither rebukes Jacob for taking the blessings nor congratulates him for it; He is just silent. What are we to make of that? Is God indifferent as to the circumstances under which Jacob procured the blessing? Does the Almighty think it was "all good"? Is He simply choosing not to get involved?

I want to suggest that, at least in the view of the rabbis of the Midrash, God's silence does not indicate indifference at all. The divine response is more subtle; it plays out over the long arc of history.

Mysterious Tears

One midrashic teaching that makes this point is cited by Rashi, who seems to be bothered by something that happens when Jacob first lays eyes on Rachel. The Torah tells us that when Jacob sees her, he is immediately overcome with emotion:

וַיִּשָּׂא אֶת־קֹלוֹ וַיֵּבְךְּ׃   And he lifted up his voice and he cried.   Genesis 29:11

Why does he cry? One might perhaps argue that Jacob is crying out of joy: here he is, lonely and forlorn, running away from home, and he encounters this wonderful damsel. He falls in love with her and, overwhelmed with joy at the thought that she might become his wife, he cries. But that is decidedly *not* how the Sages understood those tears. Rashi offers two reasons, both grounded in Midrash,[1] why Jacob might have cried. And both are a far cry — you'll pardon the pun — from any feeling of joy.

| Rashi to Genesis 29:11 | לְפִי שֶׁצָּפָה בְרוּחַ הַקֹּדֶשׁ שֶׁאֵינָהּ נִכְנֶסֶת עִמּוֹ לִקְבוּרָה. | [Jacob cried] because he had a prophetic premonition that [Rachel] would not be buried with him. |

We'll unpack this explanation soon, but let's continue reading what Rashi has to say:

| Rashi to Genesis 29:11 | דָּבָר אַחֵר: לְפִי שֶׁבָּא בְּיָדַיִם רֵקָנִיּוֹת... | Another interpretation [as to why Jacob cried]: because he came [to meet Rachel] with empty hands... |

Here, Rashi cites a second midrashic interpretation for Jacob's tears, and at first glance, this second interpretation has nothing to do with the first. This new interpretation asserts that Jacob cries because he realizes that he has shown up in Charan empty-handed. Here he is, seeking to marry this woman before him, Rachel, and he has nothing of value to give her. In the story the Midrash tells, Jacob contemplates this and says to himself:

| Rashi to Genesis 29:11 | אֱלִיעֶזֶר עֶבֶד אָבִי אַבָּא הָיוּ בְיָדָיו נְזָמִים וּצְמִידִים וּמִגְדָּנוֹת וַאֲנִי אֵין בְּיָדִי כְלוּם | When Eliezer, my grandfather's servant [sought my mother's hand in marriage], he came with all sorts of bracelets, rings, and jewels—and me, I have nothing! |

The Midrash continues, explaining why Jacob has nothing with him:

---

1 Bereishit Rabbah 70:12; see also Devarim Rabbah 2:20.

לְפִי שֶׁרָדַף אֱלִיפַז   [After Jacob deceived Esau], Eliphaz, son of   Rashi to

בֶּן עֵשָׂו בְּמִצְוַת   Esau, pursued [Jacob] at the behest of his father,   Genesis 29:11

אָבִיו אַחֲרָיו לְהָרְגוֹ   seeking to kill him [in revenge]. [Eliphaz] caught

וְהִשִּׂיגוֹ וּלְפִי שֶׁגָּדַל   up with Jacob, but because Eliphaz had been

אֱלִיפַז בְּחֵיקוֹ שֶׁל   brought up on Isaac's lap, he pulled back his

יִצְחָק, מָשַׁךְ יָדָיו.   hand [at the last moment].

So Eliphaz spares Jacob. But this choice leaves him in a quandary — and he shares his dilemma with Jacob:

אָמַר לוֹ מָה   Eliphaz said to Jacob: But what shall I do about   Rashi to

אֶעֱשֶׂה לַצִּוּוּי   my father's command [to kill you]? Jacob   Genesis 29:11

שֶׁל אַבָּא? אָמַר   answered him, "Take [the money and jewels] in

לוֹ יַעֲקֹב טוֹל מַה   my hands [and then I will be a poor man]. A poor

שֶׁבְּיָדִי, וְהֶעָנִי   person is as good as dead [so you can justifiably

חָשׁוּב כַּמֵּת.   tell your father you've done away with me]." [2]

What a strange story this midrash tells. It feels almost fantastical, woven out of thin air. Why tell us all this? Was it so important for us to hear Jacob's thoughts on the equivalence of death and poverty? Why do we care how many bracelets Jacob had with him, or didn't have with him, or why he lost them? It's all very entertaining, but where is the midrash getting it from?

Why, moreover, does Rashi feel a need to cite for us two wildly different interpretations as to why Jacob cried? Jacob intuited that he wouldn't be buried with Rachel . . . or he was sorry he came penniless. The two explanations couldn't be further apart. What is the reader to make of them?

To Lift Up One's Voice and Cry

I want to argue that Rashi's two interpretations are not as different as they may seem. In fact, they are two sides of a single coin.

To see how, look carefully at the verse the Sages are interpreting:

---

2 See Nedarim 64b.

Genesis 29:11

וַיִּשָּׂא אֶת־קֹלוֹ וַיֵּבְךְּ׃   And he lifted up his voice and he cried.

If you trace the occurrence of that phrase throughout the Hebrew Bible, you'll find that it has a very particular connotation: generally speaking, it seems to convey the sense that something is being lost irrevocably. Something precious is slipping through your fingers, and there is nothing you can do but watch it happen.

A good example comes from the first time the expression is used — in the narrative of Hagar and Ishmael. Hagar goes off into the desert with her young child Ishmael, and when the water in their canteen is used up, the child appears to be dying of thirst. It is then that:

Genesis 21:16

וַתִּשָּׂא אֶת־קֹלָהּ וַתֵּבְךְּ׃   She lifted up her voice and she cried.

Something precious and irreplaceable is being lost — her son. And seemingly, there is nothing she can do about it.[3]

The Sages seem to be ascribing a similar kind of mindset to Jacob when he first meets Rachel. In this case, the precious one being lost is none other than Rachel, the woman of Jacob's dreams. When Jacob first meets her, the Sages are saying, he has a premonition that, no matter how hard he tries, she will slip away from him. But *how* will she slip away? The Sages' two explanations are really just allusions to two ways in which Rachel will evade his grasp.

One way Jacob loses her is in her death: Rachel dies young, before him. Years after he first meets Rachel, when Jacob is finally en route back home from Charan, Rachel dies giving birth to her second child, Benjamin, forcing Jacob to bury her by the roadside. When Jacob first met her, according to the Midrash, he had a prophetic vision of this moment, and it caused him to cry. Knowing you'll be buried with your soul mate can bring a measure of peace, but that kind of peace, that connection to Rachel in death, would elude Jacob.

---

3 Of course, in Hagar's case, it wasn't true: she simply couldn't see the lifesaving well that would allow Ishmael to live — perhaps because she was so overcome with emotion.

But Rachel would elude Jacob in life, too — and that is what the Sages are getting at in the second explanation Rashi cites. What, in Jacob's life, becomes the greatest obstacle he faces in achieving union with Rachel? It is that famous switch of sisters under the chuppah: after Jacob works seven years in order to "earn" Rachel for a wife, his father-in-law-to-be substitutes a veiled Leah for Rachel on their wedding night.° Suddenly, Rachel eludes his grasp. Ask yourself, though: Why did it happen? *Why* was Lavan able to take advantage of Jacob so thoroughly? That's what the Rabbis are getting at in the second explanation Rashi quotes: Lavan was able to take advantage of Jacob, the Rabbis are saying, because when Jacob met Rachel, *he had come with empty hands.*

Genesis 29:20–25

To see what the Rabbis mean, just consider the alternative: What if Jacob had not come to meet Rachel with empty hands? What if, like Eliezer before him, he had shown up in Charan with massive wealth, with sacks of gold and jewels? Then he would have been able to dazzle the damsel's family, just as Eliezer had done. Remember, Eliezer had negotiated with Lavan, Rebecca's brother, and now Jacob was negotiating with that same Lavan in order to marry Rachel.

Of course, Lavan made no attempt to beguile Eliezer or play games with him. Eliezer's copious wealth had given Lavan the sense that Eliezer was a man of substance, and was not to be trifled with. The same *could* have been true, the Sages are saying — *should* have been true — for Jacob. But something went wrong: he lost his money on the way, and when he did meet Lavan, all the penniless Jacob had to give for Rachel was his own hard labor. Lavan regarded him as a pauper and took advantage of him. Jacob lost Rachel for those seven years, the Sages are saying, because he came to Lavan empty-handed.[4]

Understanding the Eliphaz Story

Now we can see that the two interpretations Rashi offers are really variations on a single theme: Jacob's loss of Rachel. Fair enough. Still, we

---

4   When Jacob tells Eliphaz that a poor person is considered the same as a dead person, he seems to be suggesting that the poor and the dead alike are at the mercy of others. Just as a dead person has "interests" in the world he leaves behind, but no power to see to those interests, a destitute person is virtually powerless to achieve his aims in this world. Little does Jacob know when he reasons along these lines with Eliphaz that he is soon to taste the bitter fruits of this powerlessness in his own interactions with Lavan.

might ask, where do the Sages get these interpretations from? The first interpretation, at least, is actually grounded in the text, which explicitly tells us just a few chapters later that Jacob and Rachel weren't buried together. But the second story, this fanciful tale about Eliphaz, seems to come out of nowhere. Did the Rabbis just haphazardly pluck this story right out of their collective imagination?

The answer is no. The Rabbis are actually reading the biblical text quite closely. They pick up on something in the language that propels them in the direction of their interpretation. What did they notice, exactly? It all comes back to וַיִּשָּׂא אֶת־קֹלוֹ וַיֵּבְךְּ (*vayisa et kolo vayeivk*, "and he lifted up his voice and he cried").

Our Sages, with their "fanciful" story, are actually drawing a line between *this* use of *vayisa et kolo vayeivk* (when Jacob meets Rachel) and the *previous* time the Torah used that phrase.

When was the last time someone cried that way? It happened when Jacob took the blessings from Esau:

Genesis 27:38   וַיִּשָּׂא עֵשָׂו קֹלוֹ וַיֵּבְךְּ:   And Esau lifted up his voice and he cried.

It's as if the Rabbis are saying to us: *You want to understand why, when Jacob met Rachel, he lifted up his voice and cried? Just look at the last time someone lifted up his voice and cried.* For Esau had cried that very same way when his brother, Jacob, deceived him. Esau experienced that terrible, sinking feeling that something precious was slipping through his fingers: the blessing his father had intended for him. Now it would be forever lost to him, taken with guile by Jacob. Recognizing that bitter reality, Esau had cried.

Drawing the Line

Why is it that Jacob ends up crying hopelessly when he meets Rachel? The Sages conclude that Esau's tears led, through a natural train of consequences, to Jacob's. In other words, the Sages' story of the encounter with Eliphaz is just their way of "reconstructing" that train of consequences.

It begins when Rebecca sends Jacob away to protect him from his brother's wrath. But Esau's vengeance, the Rabbis reason, would not be so easily foiled. He would dispatch his son Eliphaz to pursue Jacob and hunt him down.

And yet Jacob survives this manhunt. How? By means of a ruse, say the Sages. Jacob had a helpful suggestion for his pursuer: *Deceive your father, Eliphaz, as I deceived mine! Here, take my money; now you can just go tell him I am dead.*

That ruse is the next point in the line the Sages are drawing to connect Esau's tears with Jacob's. On one level, the ruse works. Jacob escapes with his life; he survives the threat of Eliphaz. But that escape comes at a terrible hidden cost. By parting with his money, the Sages tell us, by giving it to Eliphaz, Jacob finds that he has nothing left just when it matters most. He tells Eliphaz that a poor man is as good as dead. But now, when Jacob meets Lavan, he finds that this white lie he asked Eliphaz to tell his father has now become all too true. Jacob is a pauper, and Lavan treats him with utter disregard. He takes advantage of Jacob's weakened stature by switching Rachel for Leah under the chuppah. The line the Sages are drawing has now reached its endpoint: *Jacob had provoked his brrother's anguished tears; now Jacob will shed his own tears of anguish when he first meets his beloved Rachel.*[5] He perceives at that moment that she will slip away from him.

The justice seems apparent: Jacob can't escape the effects of his own earlier actions. The tears Jacob caused his brother to shed when he substituted himself for Esau, replacing an older child with a younger one, are now repaid with the tears Jacob sheds when his father-in-law, Lavan, replaces a *younger* child (Rachel) with an *older* one (Leah). The deceiver has become the deceived.[6]

---

5   Another textual resonance between the two stories serves to further buttress the Rabbis' case: any doubts we might have had that Esau's and Jacob's tears are in fact connected are put to rest by the sly words Lavan uses to justify his trickery. Pressed by Jacob to explain his actions, Lavan answers him: לֹא־יֵעָשֶׂה כֵן בִּמְקוֹמֵנוּ לָתֵת הַצְּעִירָה לִפְנֵי הַבְּכִירָה׃, "We don't do it that way in our place, to give the younger before the firstborn." What does he mean when he says "we don't do it that way in our place"? There's a little dig there: *Maybe where you come from, Jacob, you do things that way. Yes, I hear that back in Canaan, the younger can precede the older. But that's not the way we do it around here.*

6   The parallels are, in fact, even sharper than this: Jacob substitutes himself for Esau when Isaac is old and cannot see. Lavan then substitutes Leah for Rachel when Jacob cannot see. Moreover, in the story of the blessings, there are two siblings, one of whom is more beloved by their father, Isaac, who expects to bless that more beloved child. Jacob, though, sees fit to replace the more beloved one (Esau) with the less beloved one (himself). And so it would happen with Lavan: there are two

The Longer Arc of History

So that's the story of *vayisa et kolo vayeivk*, as the Rabbis would have it. But there's one more midrash about Jacob and Esau that I'd like to introduce you to, one that adds a remarkable new dimension to the ideas we've begun to uncover here. This new midrash looks at a different phrase the Torah uses to describe Esau's anguish. It focuses on this expression:

Genesis 27:34	כִּשְׁמֹעַ עֵשָׂו אֶת־דִּבְרֵי אָבִיו וַיִּצְעַק צְעָקָה גְּדֹלָה וּמָרָה עַד־מְאֹד וַיֹּאמֶר לְאָבִיו בָּרְכֵנִי גַם־אָנִי אָבִי׃	When Esau heard his father's words, he **let out a great and bitter cry**. He said to his father, "Bless me too, Father!"

Now, it turns out that this phrase —"a great and bitter cry"— is very unusual. It appears only *one* other time in the entire Hebrew Bible. The Sages picked up on that, and "drew a line," as it were, connecting the two events.

Where else do we find this phrase? In the book of Esther, of all places, just after Mordechai hears word of Haman's genocidal decree:

Esther 4:1	וּמָרְדֳּכַי יָדַע אֶת־כָּל־אֲשֶׁר נַעֲשָׂה וַיִּקְרַע מָרְדֳּכַי אֶת־בְּגָדָיו וַיִּלְבַּשׁ שַׂק וָאֵפֶר וַיֵּצֵא בְּתוֹךְ הָעִיר וַיִּזְעַק זְעָקָה גְדֹלָה וּמָרָה׃	When Mordechai learned all that had happened, Mordechai tore his clothes and put on sackcloth and ashes. He went through the city, and **let out a great and bitter cry**.[7]

These two "great and bitter cries," separated by many centuries, are in fact connected, suggest the Sages. And to understand their point, you just need a bit of history.

---

siblings, one of whom is more beloved to Jacob, and Jacob expects to wed that more beloved child (Rachel). Lavan, though, sees fit to replace the more beloved one (Rachel) with the less beloved one (Leah).

7   The two expressions of grief are very nearly identical, differing only by a single letter: the צְעָקָה (*tze'akah*) of Esau becomes the זְעָקָה (*ze'akah*) of Mordechai. These roots are closely related etymologically, their sound is nearly identical, and the essence of their meaning is the same. .

Haman, the great villain of the Purim story, is described by the book of Esther as an Agagite.° That makes him a descendant of Agag, a king who ruled the nation of Amalek in the time of Saul, as we are told by the book of Samuel.° Now go back a little further: Where does Amalek, in turn, hail from? Long before it was a nation, Amalek was a person — a person named in one of the genealogies of the book of Genesis. And who was he? Amalek was the child of — wait for it — *Eliphaz*.

Esther 3:1

1 Samuel 15;
Megillah 13a.

וַתֵּלֶד לֶאֱלִיפַז אֶת־עֲמָלֵק   And she bore Amalek to Eliphaz

Genesis 36:12

Smoldering Vengeance

Remember what the Rabbis told us about Eliphaz, child of Esau, and his failed bid to kill Jacob? Esau had dispatched Eliphaz to pursue and kill Jacob, but Jacob managed to convince Eliphaz to spare his life and to deceive his father instead. Jacob emerged unharmed, and Esau's plot to avenge Jacob's deception slipped into dormancy.

It was dormant, the Sages tell us, but it didn't die. It smoldered through the centuries . . . *until the days of Haman*. Haman, descendant of Eliphaz, would eventually arrive to finish the job his ancestor left undone. Except now, after all these years, carrying out the vengeance of Esau would not be so simple. It wouldn't mean killing just a single man, as it would have in the times of Eliphaz or Esau. No, to destroy Jacob now, in the days of Mordechai and Esther, would be to destroy an entire *nation*. To destroy Jacob now, every last person would have to go — man, woman, and child:

וְנִשְׁלוֹחַ סְפָרִים בְּיַד הָרָצִים
אֶל־כָּל־מְדִינוֹת הַמֶּלֶךְ
לְהַשְׁמִיד לַהֲרֹג וּלְאַבֵּד אֶת־
כָּל־הַיְּהוּדִים מִנַּעַר וְעַד־זָקֵן
טַף וְנָשִׁים בְּיוֹם אֶחָד

Written instructions were dispatched by couriers to all the king's provinces—to destroy, massacre, and exterminate all the Jews, young and old, children and women, on a single day

Esther 3:13

Haman, the scion of Eliphaz, was determined to wipe out every last remnant of Jacob. When his genocidal decree was promulgated as law, Mordechai cried. And in those tears, the Sages saw a glint of divine justice:

Bereishit
Rabbah 67:4

אָמַר רַבִּי חֲנִינָא כָּל מִי
שֶׁהוּא אוֹמֵר שֶׁהַקָּדוֹשׁ
בָּרוּךְ הוּא וַתְּרָן הוּא
יִתְוַתְּרוּן בְּנֵי מְעוֹהִי, אֶלָּא
מַאֲרִיךְ אַפֵּיהּ וְגָבֵי דִילֵיהּ,
זְעָקָה אַחַת הִזְעִיק יַעֲקֹב
לְעֵשָׂו, דִּכְתִיב: כִּשְׁמוֹעַ
עֵשָׂו אֶת דִּבְרֵי אָבִיו וַיִּזְעַק
זְעָקָה, וְהֵיכָן נִפְרַע לוֹ
בְּשׁוּשַׁן הַבִּירָה, שֶׁנֶּאֱמַר
(אסתר ד, א): וַיִּזְעַק זְעָקָה
גְדוֹלָה וּמָרָה עַד מְאֹד.

Rabbi Chanina said: Anyone who says that God just lets things slide—let him forfeit his own insides! Instead, He delays His anger, but will eventually collect what is rightly His. For it was a single scream that Jacob caused Esau to let out, as it is written, "When Esau heard his father's words, he let out a great and bitter cry." And when did [Jacob] pay for that? [Centuries later], in Shushan the capital city, as it says (Esther 4:1), "And [Mordechai] let out a great and bitter cry."

As when Jacob met Rachel, one man's tears had led to another's. But this time, the chain of causation doesn't end with Jacob's own life; instead, it persists for generations.

Justice Delayed Is Not Justice Denied

Let's return to a question we asked earlier: What are we to make of God's silence in the aftermath of Jacob's deception of his brother? Evidently, the Almighty is silent — but He is not indifferent. There would be a divine response to the episode involving Jacob, Esau, and the blessings, but it would not take the form of words; it was more subtle than that. It was to come in the form of events, playing out over years, decades, even centuries. First, Jacob would cry for Rachel. And ultimately, Mordechai would cry for a nation. Both, the Rabbis insist, were echoes of the tears of Esau.

I want to conclude by leaving you with a little cliffhanger of a question: If the point this last midrash is making is really true — if, as the Rabbis suggest, Mordechai's cry *really* harks back to, and is repayment for, a similar cry once let out by Esau — then why did we survive Haman's plot?

Remember: the Jewish people are *not*, of course, exterminated in the time of Haman. Instead, there is a miraculous salvation: The king has a sleepless night; when Haman comes to the king to ask for Mordechai's head, the king instead asks him how to reward Mordechai. Haman leads

Mordechai through the streets in a triumphant parade. Esther approaches the king and wins her people the right to defend themselves. It all works out. Haman's plot is foiled.

So let me ask you: According to the Sages, whose side was God on? If the Sages are right that the Heavenly Court, in recognition of Esau's tears, allowed Haman's plot to advance, why were we saved from that plot?

Sit tight. We'll take it up in the very next essay, on **Parshat Vayishlach**.

Jacob, Esther & the Hypotenuse of Hope

THE JACOB SAGA, PART III

וַיָּ֤רׇץ עֵשָׂו֙ לִקְרָאתוֹ
וַֽיְחַבְּקֵ֔הוּ וַיִּפֹּ֥ל עַל־צַוָּארָ֖ו
וַׄיִּשָּׁקֵ֑הוּ וַיִּבְכּֽוּ׃

Esau ran to greet him, and he
hugged him; he fell on his neck,
kissed him—and they cried.

GENESIS 33:4

129

Jacob, Esther & the Hypotenuse of Hope

THE JACOB SAGA, PART III

PARSHAT VAYISHLACH catalogs a new encounter between Jacob and Esau. Jacob, finally on his way home from the house of Lavan, sends messengers to Esau, the brother he hasn't seen in twenty years. The messengers return with word that Esau is coming to greet him with four hundred men. Jacob immediately senses the peril. Long before, he had fled to Charan to escape his brother's wrath — as his mother put it, "until he forgets what you have done to him." ° But after all these years, it seems that Esau has forgotten nothing. His enmity toward Jacob is apparently as fresh as it was on day one.

Genesis 27:45

What happens next between Jacob and Esau constitutes the opening story in **Parshat Vayishlach**. But the ramifications of this story will not be confined to the immediate present, as it plays out in the book of Genesis. No, this story will echo for many years hence. To see how, let's pick up where we left off at the end of our last essay, on **Parshat Vayeitzei**.

Back to the Future

At the close of that essay, we saw that the Sages perceive in the book of Esther an echo of the original Jacob and Esau story. When Mordechai let out a "great and bitter cry" upon hearing of Haman's genocidal decree, that was a sort of repayment in kind, the Sages say, for Esau's "great and bitter cry"— the tears Esau shed, centuries earlier, when he first discovered that Jacob had taken the blessing meant for him. God doesn't let things slide, the Sages declare. Sometimes it takes centuries, but unrequited pain and anguish will eventually be redeemed.

In suggesting this connection, the Sages seem to be addressing an implicit theological problem in the Purim story. A single man, Haman, plots death and destruction for the entire Jewish people and he very nearly succeeds. How did that happen? Where was God?

The Midrash suggests the beginnings of an answer. As difficult as it is for us to understand, God was "involved" in the decree leveled against the Jewish people in the days of Mordechai and Esther. That is not to say that God was actively prosecuting the case against the Jews, as it were. But God wasn't "silent," either; He wasn't absent when Haman cast his lots. Haman did what he did — and God's involvement was in *allowing* Haman's plot to go forward, to get off the ground, at least. The tears of Esau had not yet been repaid. The vengeance of Esau would have to be allowed its last stand.°

Cf. Megillah 12a

But I left you, at the end of the last essay, to ponder a question: If, as the Rabbis suggest, Mordechai's cry harks back to, and is repayment for, a similar cry once let out by Esau, how did the Jewish people survive Haman's onslaught? If the Heavenly Court allowed Haman's plot to be formulated because, on some level, Eliphaz's descendants had a moral leg to stand on, why did the Jewish people escape with their lives through the miracles of Purim?

Mordechai's Confidence

The truth is, the question is even starker than this. The Jews didn't just *somehow* manage, in the end, to survive Haman's onslaught. No, long before their final victory, Mordechai *knew* they would survive — or at least, so he said. In the Jews' darkest hour, when things looked like they couldn't possibly turn around — when Haman was ascendant, and Esther was vacillating, unsure whether the king would even be willing to grant her an audience — even then, Mordechai expressed supreme confidence that Haman's plot would be foiled. Here, in fact, is what he told Esther at that moment:

Esther 4:13–14

אַל־תְּדַמִּי בְנַפְשֵׁךְ לְהִמָּלֵט בֵּית־הַמֶּלֶךְ מִכָּל־הַיְּהוּדִים: כִּי אִם־הַחֲרֵשׁ תַּחֲרִישִׁי בָּעֵת הַזֹּאת רֶוַח וְהַצָּלָה יַעֲמוֹד לַיְּהוּדִים מִמָּקוֹם אַחֵר וְאַתְּ וּבֵית־אָבִיךְ תֹּאבֵדוּ

Do not imagine that you, of all the Jews, will escape with your life by being in the king's palace. If you keep silent at this moment, relief and deliverance will come to the Jews from some other place—while you and your father's house will perish.

Esther fears for her life if she goes to the king. And what Mordechai tells her is nothing short of astounding. In essence, he's saying:

It is not we who are threatened here, it is you. Sure, to any outside observer, it looks like you, Esther, are safe; you can remain hidden in the palace while the rest of us die in a single blood-soaked day of genocide. But looks can be deceiving. In fact, the reverse is the case: this is the moment for you to act. If you don't act, Esther, you will be the one endangered. As for us, deliverance will come from some other place…

Mordechai professes to know one thing for sure: with or without Esther, the Jews will somehow survive Haman's decree. He is absolutely confident that divine assistance will come; God will not, in the end, let them down. *But how does he know that?* If the Rabbis are really right — if the tears he cried in the streets, dressed in sackcloth and ashes, were truly Heaven-ordained repayment, as it were, for Esau's tears — how can Mordechai *know* that the Heavenly Court will, in the end, intervene to save his people from Esau's long-delayed vengeance?

A Story of X and Y

I'd like to suggest that a tentative answer to this vexing question can be found if we go back to the two midrashim I introduced you to in our last essay, on **Parshat Vayeitzei**. Both of those midrashim attempt to explicate how Esau's tears affected the future life of Jacob or the future life of his people by precipitating two other moments of "tears" later in history. What I want to do now is visualize those two teachings, almost as if they were lines on a graph.

Let's start with a point. This is ground zero, the moment in the book of Genesis when Esau, overcome by anguish, first realizes what has happened to him, and he cries.

Esau's Tears

Now let's draw some lines. Our first line will be horizontal, drawn along an x-axis. It will start from our first point, "Esau's tears," and culminate at an important point in Jacob's own life: the moment he first meets the woman he loves, but senses the possibility that she will be taken away from him in the future. This, of course, is the moment when Jacob lifts up his voice and cries upon meeting Rachel:

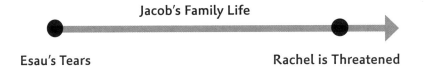

We can think of that x-axis as representing Jacob's own life and the life of his family. That's one axis on which, according to the Sages, Esau's tears will have repercussions. But there's another realm where the repercussions of those tears will be felt, and that is the realm of Jacob's nation. We can think of that as the y-axis in our graph.

This is where the second midrash we were talking about comes into play. We can represent it with a second line, starting, as the other did, at ground zero, but extending vertically, and culminating at a point in the life of Jacob's nation when that nation is endangered, when the great and bitter cry of Esau is echoed by the great and bitter cry of Mordechai:

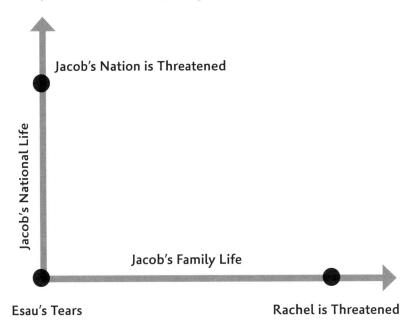

In other words, if we put the teachings of our two midrashim together, we find that the repercussions of Esau's tears are felt along two different continuums: that of Jacob's family, and that of Jacob's nation. Within Jacob's own, personal family, he stands to lose Rachel. Within the realm of Jacob's nation, the entire Jewish people is ultimately put at risk.

Finding the Hypotenuse

Now, take a moment to consider this diagram that we've been constructing. It looks like a triangle, doesn't it? Or the *beginning* of a triangle, at least. We are looking at two lines that form the base of a right triangle. All we are missing is a third line, a hypotenuse — a line that would connect the first two and complete the shape.

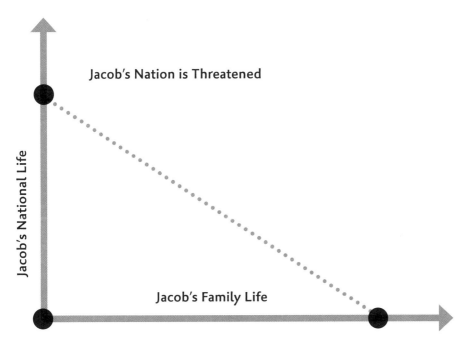

So I want to ask you what might seem a whimsical question: Does such a hypotenuse exist? "What would that even *mean*?" I hear you asking. Well, let me explain.

Up until this point, we've treated these two points (the threat to Rachel, on the one hand, and the threat to Jacob's nation, on the other) as completely independent of one another. Yes, they're both linked to Esau's tears, but they're not linked to each other in any way. But what if they are? The Sages say a relationship exists between every other point of this incipient triangle; what if these two points are related too? In other words, if we could draw a line between them — if we could complete the triangle, so to speak — that might bring the history of Esau's tears to some kind of resolution.

So, does a line like that exist?

Completing the Triangle

Well, let's think about what such a "connecting line" would look like. We'd be looking for a moment in history when Rachel, or some descendant of Rachel, was personally threatened, and at the same time, a more general threat was leveled against the entire Jewish people. Was there ever a moment like that in Jewish history?

Well, you already know that there was, because we were just talking about it. It is the moment when Mordechai speaks to a hesitant Esther, trying to rally her to approach the king. Whose descendant is Esther? She is of the tribe of Benjamin, which means that *she is a child of Rachel*. So add it all up and this is what you get: at this particular moment in history, the Jewish people as a whole stands to be destroyed through Haman's decree. But a child of Rachel (Esther) also finds her own personal life hanging in the balance. She might personally hope to survive by not approaching the king, and by taking refuge in the palace — or she might risk her life in service of her people.

We've found the missing hypotenuse: Mordechai's speech to Esther. And it brings us right back to the question we asked before: in his speech to her, Mordechai expresses supreme confidence that the Jewish people will be saved. But is he right to be so confident, given what the Sages tell us about the antecedent of Mordechai's own tears? If the Heavenly Court, in recognition of Esau's unrequited anguish, had allowed Haman to become a threat, how could Mordechai be so bold and brazen as to think that Haman's onslaught would *surely* be halted?

It seems like Mordechai knows something that we don't. What could that something be?

The Hypotenuse of Hope

What Mordechai knows — consciously or subconsciously — is communicated, ever so subtly, by the words the text of the Megillah ascribes to him. Let's look carefully at these words, and we'll find the mysterious source of Mordechai's seemingly unfounded hope:

Esther 4:14	כִּי אִם־הַחֲרֵשׁ תַּחֲרִישִׁי בָּעֵת הַזֹּאת רֶוַח וְהַצָּלָה יַעֲמוֹד לַיְּהוּדִים מִמָּקוֹם אַחֵר	If you keep silent at this moment, relief and deliverance will come to the Jews from some other place

In most English translations, little here seems remarkable. "Relief and deliverance" will arrive —what could be better than that? But read over Mordechai's statement in the original Hebrew and you'll find something odd about it. In Hebrew, Mordechai says רֶוַח וְהַצָּלָה יַעֲמוֹד (*revach ve-hatzalah ya'amod*). Now, that word רֶוַח (*revach*) doesn't *really* mean "relief." Literally, it means "space," or "distance between one thing and another." So consider this: Why would Mordechai use this particular out-of-place word to describe the salvation he knows will ultimately come to his people? He's using this word, I want to suggest, because he's quoting someone.

The word Mordechai uses for "relief," *revach*, is exceedingly rare. In fact, it appears only one other time in the entire Hebrew Bible. Where? You guessed it: in the story of Jacob and Esau.[1] Yes, Mordechai is quoting from none other than Jacob, who once used the word *revach* in his dealings with Esau. But he doesn't use that word in the part of the Jacob and Esau story we've looked at, the part where Jacob steals the blessing, absconds from the house, and leaves Esau in tears. No, Jacob uses that word much later, in **Parshat Vayishlach**, when, after years of sweat and labor in Lavan's house, he finally confronts his estranged brother for the first time in twenty years:

וַיֹּאמֶר אֶל־עֲבָדָיו עִבְרוּ לְפָנַי וְרֶוַח תָּשִׂימוּ בֵּין עֵדֶר וּבֵין עֵדֶר:	[Jacob] said to his servants, "Go before me, and put **space** [*revach*] between each of the flocks."	Genesis 32:17

What, exactly, is happening in that verse? Well, Jacob may have hoped that Esau would forget the past — that little episode with the blessings — but when he gets word that Esau is coming with four hundred men, he surmises that, for Esau, the past is still very much alive. Jacob fears Esau's army will wipe out his family. So he does what he can to make things better. In particular, he does two things.

A Blessing in Kind

First, Jacob sends gifts to Esau, in the form of flocks of animals. In the verse we've already quoted, he instructs the servants leading each flock to put

---

1   See Ba'al HaTurim to Genesis 32:17.

space (*revach*) between each flock and the next one, so that Esau will be approached slowly, and will see gift after gift coming to him.

This is quite a departure from the past. Twenty years earlier, when he approached his father deceptively with the delicacies he loved, everything had happened so very quickly:

Genesis 27:20

וַיֹּאמֶר יִצְחָק אֶל־בְּנוֹ
מַה־זֶּה מִהַרְתָּ לִמְצֹא בְּנִי

Isaac said to Jacob, "How come you came back from the hunt so quickly?"

But now, rather than presenting slaughtered goats to his father in an act of deception, he presents live ones to his brother, straightforwardly. His mother had asked him to get two *izim* (female goats)° for her to prepare as delicacies for his father; now he would present *a hundred-fold* that number of *izim* to his brother, in an attempt to somehow make things right:

Genesis 27:9

Genesis 32:14–15

וַיִּקַּח מִן־הַבָּא בְיָדוֹ מִנְחָה
לְעֵשָׂו אָחִיו: עִזִּים מָאתַיִם

He selected a present for his brother, Esau: two hundred female goats

Genesis 27:29

Years before, Jacob took a blessing meant for Esau; in that blessing, his father had told him that his brother would bow before him.° Now, as Jacob approaches Esau, it is Jacob who makes a point of bowing before his brother:

Genesis 33:3

וְהוּא עָבַר לִפְנֵיהֶם וַיִּשְׁתַּחוּ
אַרְצָה שֶׁבַע פְּעָמִים עַד־
גִּשְׁתּוֹ עַד־אָחִיו:

[Jacob] went before [his family] and bowed low to the ground seven times, until he reached his brother.

Years before, Jacob took a blessing from his brother. Now he would give one back to him:

Genesis 33:11

קַח־נָא אֶת־בִּרְכָתִי
אֲשֶׁר הֻבָאת לָךְ

[Jacob said to Esau]: Please accept **my blessing** that has been brought before you.

So Jacob's gifts were given with *revach*, space, between each one and the next. And centuries later, Mordechai would use that highly unusual word, *revach*, once more — in the very words he chose to assure Esther that everything would be alright. The *revach* of Jacob's gifts would somehow translate into a different kind of space now: breathing space, precious room between a nation and a force threatening it. Space in which to live.

Prayer

But gift-giving is not Jacob's only preparation for the meeting with Esau — and *revach* is not the only word Mordechai uses to characterize the salvation that is sure to come to his people. Jacob *does* something else too, and Mordechai *mentions* something else too. When Jacob hears that Esau is coming with four hundred men, he also turns to God in prayer:

הַצִּילֵנִי נָא מִיַּד אָחִי מִיַּד עֵשָׂו כִּי־יָרֵא אָנֹכִי אֹתוֹ פֶּן־יָבוֹא וְהִכַּנִי אֵם עַל־בָּנִים:

Deliver me, please, from the hand of Esau, my brother. For I am afraid of him, lest he come and strike me, killing mother and children alike.

Genesis 32:12

Jacob is worried that Esau will destroy everything. His whole family. Mother and child alike. And when he fears that all will be lost, he asks God: הַצִּילֵנִי נָא (*hatzileini na*), *please deliver me from this fate*. With this plea, Jacob conveys his fear, his vulnerability, and above all, his trust that his fate is in God's hands. Centuries later, Mordechai seems, at some level, to remember that prayer. For when Haman threatens young and old, mother and children alike — as Esau once did — Mordechai recalls that key word in Jacob's prayer: *hatzileini*, "deliver me":

רֶוַח וְהַצָּלָה יַעֲמוֹד לַיְּהוּדִים

Revach (relief) and *hatzalah* (deliverance) will come to the Jews.

Esther 4:14

A New Hope

So yes, the Heavenly Court allows Haman's decree to go forward and threaten the Jewish people. It would be allowed to proceed, as the Midrash states, because of the tears Esau shed when his blessing was taken. But that doesn't mean that all would be lost. The tears of Esau were not the *only* part of the Jacob and Esau saga that the Heavenly Court recalled, so to speak. There was a later chapter in the Jacob and Esau story too, and it was *redemptive*. Jacob, who once fled Esau rather than face his wrath, now stays put and meets Esau face-to-face — and in that face-to-face meeting, he does what he can to reconcile with his vengeful brother.[2]

What does he do, in the end? He gives gifts and he prays. But he does something else, too. He cries:

Genesis 33:4

וַיָּרָץ עֵשָׂו לִקְרָאתוֹ
וַיְחַבְּקֵהוּ וַיִּפֹּל עַל־
צַוָּארָו וַיִּשָׁקֵהוּ וַיִּבְכּוּ:

Esau ran to greet him, and he hugged him; he fell on his neck, kissed him — and they cried.

Yes, it had all started with tears, tears of pain that one brother elicited from another. But now, something would take the sting out of those tears; now, both brothers would cry pent-up tears, tears that expressed a mutual recognition of brotherhood. They would cry these tears together.

In the days of Mordechai and Esther, the Heavenly Court would remember these things. They would become a hypotenuse of hope, as it were, in a triangle otherwise defined by suffering. Jacob's gifts, prayers, and tears, his attempt to reconcile with his brother, to face him fully and straightforwardly — all this would become the moral leg on which the nation of Israel would stand when faced by the rage of Eliphaz's descendant. Because of that, as Mordechai declared, even if Esther should choose to

---

2   As a matter of fact, not only did Jacob stay put, he actually sought Esau out. We sometimes make the mistake of thinking that Esau and his four hundred men came upon Jacob, and Jacob had no choice but to face them. But that's not the story that the text tells. Jacob is the one who initiates contact. Recall that Jacob sets out from Lavan's home in Charan, en route to his father's home in the land of Canaan. To complete that journey, he doesn't need to pass through, or even venture near, the land of Seir, Esau's territory. He could easily avoid it. But he specifically sends messengers to Seir and proactively seeks out a meeting with Esau. He seems to be attempting, in one way or another, to meet his brother on better terms than those on which they last parted. Cf. Ibn Ezra and Ramban to Genesis 32:4.

remain silent, salvation would still be assured. *Revach* and *hatzalah* would indeed come to the people from "some other place." It would come from **Parshat Vayishlach**, from Jacob's willingness to face God and his estranged brother squarely and tearfully, in prayer and reconciliation. From all this, a new hope would be born.[3]

---

3   Decades earlier, when Rebecca sent Jacob to Isaac to get his father's blessing, she had tried, but failed, to undo the name Jacob. But isn't it interesting to note that, the night before Jacob reengages with his brother, Jacob struggles with an angel, and as the struggle draws to a close, he discovers that he has a new name for himself: יִשְׂרָאֵל (*Yisra'el*). And the angel explains the name to him: "It is because you have struggled with God and man, and survived" (Genesis 32:29). When you struggle, you confront someone directly, rather than going around them. Indeed, the name itself bespeaks straightforwardness:it can also be read ישר־אל, meaning "straight with God."

In the events of that night and the next day, Yisra'el lives up to his new name: his brother is coming at him with four hundred men. It would be tempting to evade him. To run away. But Jacob is no longer "Mr. Roundabout Man," and he does not choose that path. He chooses instead to meet Esau face-to-face, despite the danger. In doing so, he finally makes his mother's dream real. He finally becomes Israel.

The Greatest Crime That Never Happened?

וַיִּמְשְׁכוּ וַיַּעֲלוּ אֶת־יוֹסֵף
מִן־הַבּוֹר וַיִּמְכְּרוּ אֶת־יוֹסֵף
לַיִּשְׁמְעֵאלִים בְּעֶשְׂרִים כָּסֶף

And they drew and lifted up Joseph out of the pit, and sold Joseph to the Ishmaelites for twenty shekels of silver.

GENESIS 37:28

VAYEISHEV

The Greatest Crime
That Never Happened?

WAS THE SALE OF JOSEPH the greatest crime that . . . *never happened?*
At least one classic commentator, Rashbam,[1] grandson of Rashi, suggests
that this may very well be the case, that *the brothers never sold Joseph as a slave.*

Yes, I know that sounds absolutely outrageous. The Torah comes out
and *says* — in black and white — that Joseph's brothers sold him into slavery;
it's clear as day, right?

Actually, Rashbam argues, it isn't that clear at all. His deceptively simple
reading of the Joseph story upends many of the assumptions we make
about this episode — and the implications of his theory are astounding.

I want to explore Rashbam's theory with you: Why is it so compelling?
What's the thinking behind it? What would it mean for our broader understanding of the Joseph story if we were to accept Rashbam's reasoning?
To that end, I want to engage in a forensic reading of the sale of Joseph
with you. The story is full of knotty, inconvenient details that confuse
the reader in subtle (and not-so-subtle) ways. For Rashbam, these are
clues — building blocks for his theory.[2] Let's take a minute to review the
story and ferret out some of these clues.

What Do the Brothers Have to Hide?

Why don't we begin . . . at the end?

Years have passed since the sale of Joseph. Joseph has risen to the post
of viceroy of Egypt, second in charge to Pharaoh himself. His brothers,

---

1 In his commentary to Genesis 37:28; cf. Chizkuni ad loc. See also Rabbeinu Bachye
   and Malbim ad loc., who advance somewhat similar arguments to Rashbam; cf. R.
   Yosef Bechor Shor.

2 Some of these clues are mentioned outright by Rashbam; others, I would argue,
   are strongly implied by his analysis.

meanwhile, seeking food for their family, have been driven by famine to Egypt, the only power known to have stockpiled grain. Their quest leads them to this high Egyptian official — who, unbeknownst to them, is their long-lost brother Joseph.

While the brothers don't recognize Joseph, Joseph most certainly recognizes *them*. He accuses them of being spies, ignoring their protestations of innocence and their obvious desperation. In the back-and-forth, the brothers mention that they have another brother, Benjamin, back with their father in the land of Canaan. To substantiate their innocence, Joseph demands that they return to Canaan and fetch Benjamin. Until they do, one of the brothers will remain behind, imprisoned in Egypt.

The brothers speak among themselves, lamenting the difficult circumstances they find themselves in. As they do, they consider the possibility that what they once did to Joseph is now coming back to haunt them:

Genesis 42:21	וַיֹּאמְרוּ אִישׁ אֶל־אָחִיו	And they said one to another,
	אֲבָל אֲשֵׁמִים אֲנַחְנוּ עַל־	"But we are guilty concerning
	אָחִינוּ אֲשֶׁר רָאִינוּ צָרַת	our brother, in that we saw his
	נַפְשׁוֹ בְּהִתְחַנְנוֹ אֵלֵינוּ	distress when he pleaded with us
	וְלֹא שָׁמָעְנוּ עַל־כֵּן בָּאָה	but we did not listen; therefore
	אֵלֵינוּ הַצָּרָה הַזֹּאת:	this distress has come upon us."

The brothers seem to see a connection between what they did years ago and what is happening to them now. They stand before the Egyptian official, beseeching him for help. Not only does he turn a deaf ear to their cries, he accuses them of being spies. Why would he do that? Well, years ago, *they* had deemed someone a spy: their brother Joseph, who had brought back

Genesis 37:2

bad reports about them to their father.° And when that someone beseeched *them* for help — when Joseph called to them from that pit — they ignored his anguished cries and his obvious distress. Now the tables have turned: it seems clear to them that the hand of Heaven is repaying them, measure for measure, for their own actions.

But something doesn't quite add up: if the brothers consider themselves guilty for their actions toward Joseph long ago, haven't they committed a more grievous crime against him — one that, inexplicably, they seem to be overlooking? Worse than ignoring Joseph's cries from the pit would be *selling him into slavery*, wouldn't you say? Why don't they hold themselves culpable for *that*? [3]

In other words, if the brothers are of a mind to see the hand of Heaven at work in their predicament, why not take this argument to its logical conclusion — that *they are being punished by Heaven for selling Joseph into slavery*? Why would their present plight be a measure-for-measure punishment for their onetime indifference to Joseph's pleas, rather than for the more egregious crime of selling him into slavery? After all, this high Egyptian official hasn't just turned a deaf ear to their distress; he also intends to imprison one of the brothers, keeping him in Egypt while the rest of the brothers go home to their father. Add it all up: the brothers sold one of their own as a slave to Egypt, preventing him from returning home; now, one of their own will be imprisoned in Egypt, and prevented from returning home. Why would the brothers ignore such an obvious parallel? [4]

That's clue number one.

Where Is Reuben?

Clue number two takes us back to the events leading up to Joseph's sale. It involves a mystery concerning Joseph's oldest brother, Reuben, the first-born child of Leah. To highlight the issue here, I'd like to play a little game with you. We'll call it "Where is Reuben?" In our game, we'll go through the events that lead up to the sale of Joseph, step by step. As we do, we'll

---

3   Remember, the brothers are talking privately amongst themselves, so they have nothing to hide. Joseph, the text tells us, is listening in on their conversation, but as far as the brothers know, no one within earshot can speak their language. They believe, therefore, that their conversation, held in their native tongue, is entirely private.

4   The possibility exists, of course, that they somehow see themselves as justified in having sold Joseph as a slave, but *not* justified in hearing his plaintive cries and turning a deaf ear to them. It's hard to see, though, how they could hold both these beliefs at the same time. After all, if they seriously believe they were justified in selling Joseph, what *should* they have done when Joseph cried out to them for mercy? Going through with the plan to sell him as a slave more or less *required* them to ignore Joseph's pleas. What, after all, were they expecting Joseph to do—meekly acquiesce to the plan? If they were justified in selling him, they were also, of necessity, justified in turning a deaf ear to his pleas — or so it would seem. (Cf. Ramban to Genesis 42:21, who suggests that the brothers may have seen the crime of remaining impervious to Joseph's cries as *greater* than that of selling him.)

pause at each stage to ask ourselves, "Where is Reuben now?" Our final answer will be perplexing indeed.

Let's start from the moment the brothers see Joseph approaching. Their first impulse, you may recall, is to kill him and throw his corpse in a nearby pit. But this plan never comes to fruition, because one of the brothers intercedes:

Genesis 37:21

וַיִּשְׁמַע רְאוּבֵן וַיַּצִּלֵהוּ
מִיָּדָם וַיֹּאמֶר לֹא
נַכֶּנּוּ נָפֶשׁ:

Reuben heard [this plan], and saved [Joseph] from their hands. He said, "Let us not kill anyone."

Reuben proposes an alternative, a Plan B: it would be better, he suggests, to throw Joseph into the pit *alive* and just leave him there, rather than actually spilling his blood with their own hands. Although it sounds like Reuben is merely proposing that the brothers allow Joseph, abandoned, to die *on his own*, the Torah advises the reader that Reuben has a secret motive: he wants Joseph in that pit *alive* because he intends to rescue Joseph later on, to return him safely to their father:

Genesis 37:22

הַשְׁלִיכוּ אֹתוֹ אֶל־הַבּוֹר
הַזֶּה אֲשֶׁר בַּמִּדְבָּר
וְיָד אַל־תִּשְׁלְחוּ־בוֹ
לְמַעַן הַצִּיל אֹתוֹ מִיָּדָם
לַהֲשִׁיבוֹ אֶל־אָבִיו:

"Cast him into this pit in the desert [alive] and don't lay a hand upon him": [he said this] in order to save him from their hands, to return him to his father.

The brothers agree to Reuben's plan and cast Joseph, alive, into the pit. Now, let's stop right there and begin our game: When all this is going on, where is Reuben? The answer is clear, of course: Reuben is talking to his brothers, so he's obviously right there alongside them. Fine, let's continue.

After the brothers cast Joseph into the pit, as Reuben had advised them to, the text tells us:

Genesis 37:25

וַיֵּשְׁבוּ לֶאֱכָל־לֶחֶם

And [the brothers] sat down to eat bread

Stop right there: Where is Reuben? The answer, presumably, is that nothing has changed. The text never said that Reuben left; if he was with the brothers before, he's still with them now, sitting down to lunch.

So we've now placed Reuben at their meal. That's important, because *during* their meal, Judah happens to catch sight of an Ishmaelite caravan on the horizon, headed toward Egypt. Seeing those Ishmaelites, Judah suggests a further revision in plans, Plan C: "Why allow Joseph to die?" he says to his brothers. "He is our brother, after all. Let's sell him, instead, to those passing Ishmaelites!"°

Genesis
37:26–27

Where is Reuben? Well, obviously, he's right there, listening to all this. We already placed him at the meal; all this happens during their picnic.

And the very next thing that happens? The brothers' plan is carried out: Joseph is sold to the Ishmaelites, just as Judah had proposed. And... where is Reuben? Presumably, he's right there, along with all the rest of the brothers. *It never says he left.*

Which makes the next two verses almost impossible to understand:

וַיָּשָׁב רְאוּבֵן אֶל־הַבּוֹר
וְהִנֵּה אֵין־יוֹסֵף בַּבּוֹר
וַיִּקְרַע אֶת־בְּגָדָיו: וַיָּשָׁב
אֶל־אֶחָיו וַיֹּאמַר הַיֶּלֶד
אֵינֶנּוּ וַאֲנִי אָנָה אֲנִי־בָא:

And Reuben returned to the pit, and behold—Joseph was not in the pit! And he tore his clothes. He then returned to his brothers and announced, "The boy is gone! Now what am I to do?"

Genesis
37:29–30

Wait, what's going on? "Reuben returned to the pit"? When did he leave in the first place, that we can now say he "returned"? Wasn't he with his brothers this whole time? Furthermore, why is Reuben so surprised to "discover" that Joseph isn't in the pit? He didn't "discover" anything! *He was right there when the brothers sold him!*

The Torah's language makes it sound as if Reuben must have left at some point and missed all the action: everything that happened with Joseph, his brothers, and those Ishmaelite traders.[5] *But the text never tells us that*

---

5   Indeed, this is the position taken by Rashi (Genesis 37:29): that Reuben did leave his brothers, and was not present for the sale. Rashi suggests that the brothers had a rotation: they would take turns returning to their elderly father, attending to his needs — and this particular day, it was Reuben's turn. Cf. Ramban and *Ohr HaChaim* for other resolutions of this problem.

Reuben leaves. Why omit that crucial detail? [6] The reader is left entirely befuddled as to Reuben's whereabouts. It's as if the Torah is playing a shell game with us, taunting us with this seemingly impossible-to-solve question: *Where is Reuben?* That's clue number two.

Aren't the Midianites Irrelevant?

There's a third clue to be found if we shine a spotlight on some secondary characters: the Midianites.

As we've said, Judah happens to notice a caravan of Ishmaelite traders in the distance, and suggests selling Joseph to them.° The brothers agree to the proposal, and shortly thereafter, Joseph is hoisted from the pit and sold to the very same Ishmaelite traders.° But right before that happens, the Torah throws us for another loop, introducing a *second* group of travelers:

Genesis 37:28	וַיַּעַבְרוּ אֲנָשִׁים מִדְיָנִים סֹחֲרִים And Midianite merchants passed by

These Midianite merchants are, it would seem, entirely irrelevant to the story. To see just how irrelevant they are, take a look at the chart on page 151 and notice how this detail seems to be a complete interruption in the sequence of the story.

So who are these Midianites? Are they innocent bystanders, a group of people that just happened to be passing through? But if that's all they are, we wouldn't need to know about them, would we? We don't know whether it was cloudy or sunny that day, or how many sheep the brothers

---

6   Moreover, if Reuben really *did* leave his brothers, we'd have another problem to deal with: *Why would he do such a thing?* Yes, Rashi suggests that another obligation — fealty to his father — pressed upon him (see note 5). But the Torah makes it clear that Reuben's secret intention is to return Joseph safely to his father. So why would he leave at such a pivotal moment? If the brothers have now chosen to sell Joseph rather than leave him in the pit, wouldn't Reuben want to be on hand to try to sabotage the plan somehow? (He could, for example, "inadvertently" offend the traders and forestall the sale, or follow the traders after the sale and, a few hours later, offer to buy Joseph back at a higher price.) Why would he choose to miss this moment? Indeed, if Reuben was truly motivated by considerations of fealty to his father, wouldn't being on hand, and possibly finding some way to foil the sale, constitute the greatest possible service he could perform for Jacob? (Cf. *Siftei Chachamim* to Rashi to Genesis 37:29, citing Maharshal.)

Genesis 37:26–27

Genesis 37:28

וַיֹּאמֶר יְהוּדָה אֶל־אֶחָיו
מַה־בֶּצַע כִּי נַהֲרֹג אֶת־
אָחִינוּ וְכִסִּינוּ אֶת־דָּמוֹ:
לְכוּ וְנִמְכְּרֶנּוּ לַיִּשְׁמְעֵאלִים
וְיָדֵנוּ אַל־תְּהִי־בוֹ כִּי־
אָחִינוּ בְשָׂרֵנוּ הוּא

And Judah said to his brothers, "What profit is there if we slay our brother and conceal his blood? Come, let us sell him to the Ishmaelites, and let not our hand be upon him; for he is our brother, our own flesh."

Genesis 37:26–27

WHAT SEEMS TO BE HAPPENING

Judah proposes selling Joseph to the Ishmaelite traders he sees in the distance

וַיִּשְׁמְעוּ אֶחָיו: And his brothers listened to him.   Genesis 37:27

WHAT SEEMS TO BE HAPPENING

Judah's proposal is accepted by the brothers

וַיַּעַבְרוּ אֲנָשִׁים מִדְיָנִים סֹחֲרִים   And Midianite merchants passed by.   Genesis 37:28

WHAT SEEMS TO BE HAPPENING

Midianite merchants pass by

וַיִּמְשְׁכוּ וַיַּעֲלוּ אֶת־יוֹסֵף
מִן־הַבּוֹר וַיִּמְכְּרוּ אֶת־יוֹסֵף
לַיִּשְׁמְעֵאלִים

And they drew and lifted up Joseph out of the pit, and sold Joseph to the Ishmaelites.

Genesis 37:28

WHAT SEEMS TO BE HAPPENING

Meanwhile, the brothers lift Joseph out of the pit and do what they said they would: sell him to the Ishmaelite traders were shepherding. We don't know about any of this — because it doesn't matter. So why would the fleeting presence of these Midianites be worth mentioning?

If, on the other hand, they *weren't* simply bystanders, then what role *did* they play in the drama? The only thing we know about them is that they passed by. That doesn't seem very remarkable. If they did something of consequence, why doesn't the Torah tell us what it was?

By way of summary, then, we have three difficulties here: (1) years later, the brothers don't seem to hold themselves accountable for selling Joseph as a slave, even as they castigate themselves for other, lesser sins against him; (2) throughout the story, Reuben's whereabouts are uncertain; (3) Midianites are mentioned, though they seem to be irrelevant.

Where, Exactly, Did the Brothers Eat That Meal?

Here's where Rashbam comes in. He argues that the Midianites aren't irrelevant at all, that Reuben is right where you think he is the whole time, and that the brothers, who never think to hold themselves responsible for selling Joseph into bondage, are being perfectly rational. All these things can be true, asserts Rashbam, if we resolve one final detail in the narrative: the precise location of that meal we were talking about before.

After the brothers cast Joseph into the pit, they sit down to eat. In the words of the text, וַיֵּשְׁבוּ לֶאֱכָל־לֶחֶם (*vayeishvu le'echol lechem*, "they sat down to eat bread.")° It's during their meal that Judah spots the Ishmaelite caravan, bound for Egypt. Rashbam invites us to consider: *Where, exactly, are the brothers sitting when they eat?*

Rashbam's question is one that few of us would think to ask. After all, the brothers cast Joseph into the pit, and the very next thing we're told is that they sit down to eat bread. Sounds like they just spread a picnic blanket right nearby and start eating. But Rashbam asks us to reconsider: Is this really a likely scenario?

We know from the brothers' own words later that Joseph was crying out to them, begging them for mercy — and that they somehow turned their backs on his cries. But imagine for just a moment that you are one of the brothers: you've just taken Joseph, stripped off his cloak, and thrown him, vulnerable and terrified, into a pit in the middle of nowhere. Joseph is screaming, begging you to listen to him. *So ... How's your appetite as you listen to his harrowing screams?* Could you really calmly sit down and eat lunch within earshot of that wailing?

Genesis 37:25

I don't think so. And neither does Rashbam: he makes the deceptively simple observation° that if the brothers were looking for a picnic spot, it seems safe to say they would have found one well out of earshot of Joseph and that infernal pit.

Rashbam to Genesis 37:28

And once we accept that, it changes everything.

Let's read through the verses one more time. As we do, recreate in your mind's eye the scene that unfolds — and try to incorporate this new insight about the location of the brothers' meal.

What the Midianites Did

After a long and painful ordeal, the hard part is finally over: Joseph has been stripped of his coat and abandoned in the pit. Reuben is secretly planning to rescue him later and return him to Father, but as far as his brothers are concerned, Joseph is being left there to die. It wasn't easy to weather Joseph's screams, his cries for mercy — but what's done is done. Judah and the brothers leave the pit now and settle down to eat just over the next hill. Joseph is now out of sight and, as much as possible, out of mind.

The brothers break bread — and just then, Judah sees something off in the distance: the caravan of Ishmaelite traders. He suggests to the brothers that this is an unexpected opportunity, one that makes actually doing away with Joseph an untidy and unnecessary choice:

וַיֹּאמֶר יְהוּדָה אֶל־אֶחָיו מַה־בֶּצַע כִּי נַהֲרֹג אֶת־אָחִינוּ וְכִסִּינוּ אֶת־דָּמוֹ: לְכוּ וְנִמְכְּרֶנּוּ לַיִּשְׁמְעֵאלִים וְיָדֵנוּ אַל־תְּהִי־בוֹ כִּי־אָחִינוּ בְשָׂרֵנוּ הוּא

And Judah said to his brothers, "What profit is there if we slay our brother and conceal his blood? Come, let us sell him to the Ishmaelites, and let not our hand be upon him; for he is our brother, our own flesh."

Genesis 37:26–27

The brothers agree to Judah's plan, and the matter is settled. They won't kill Joseph after all; they'll just sell him to the Ishmaelites and get rid of him that way. Now let's read the very next verse:

וַיַּעַבְרוּ אֲנָשִׁים מִדְיָנִים סֹחֲרִים   And Midianite merchants passed by

Genesis 37:28

So here come these Midianites, the ones we thought were irrelevant . . .
Listen very carefully to what happens next:

Genesis
37:28

וַיִּמְשְׁכוּ וַיַּעֲלוּ אֶת־יוֹסֵף
מִן־הַבּוֹר וַיִּמְכְּרוּ אֶת־יוֹסֵף
לַיִּשְׁמְעֵאלִים בְּעֶשְׂרִים כָּסֶף

And they drew and lifted up Joseph
out of the pit, and sold Joseph to the
Ishmaelites for twenty shekels of silver.

What just happened there? *Who* sold Joseph to the Ishmaelites? The verse
says "they" drew him out of the pit. Ask yourself: *Who's "they"?*

Generally speaking, a pronoun like "they" refers to whichever people
were most recently mentioned. Here, that's . . . the Midianites.

> *And Midianite merchants passed by, and **they***
> *drew and lifted up Joseph out of the pit . . .*

The passing Midianites sold Joseph to the Ishmaelite traders, Rashbam
argues. In other words, yes, the brothers *plotted* to sell Joseph to the
Ishmaelites, but *they never actually did so.* Someone else beat them to it:
those passing Midianites. From the brothers' vantage point over the next
hill, Judah spots Ishmaelites in the distance, heading down to Egypt. But
on the *other* side of the horizon — behind the hill in back of them, let's
say — what Judah *doesn't* see is *another* traveling group of traders, a more
local group of merchants: Midianites.

These Midianites happen to be much closer by, and as they pass within
sight or earshot of the pit and discover a hapless Joseph there, they come
up with the same idea Judah had: *Here's a kid in a pit. Why let him die, when
we can sell him to those Ishmaelites heading to Egypt over there? Let's make
a quick profit!*

The brothers' plan, in the end, is actually executed not by the brothers,
but by *the Midianites.* The Midianites pulled Joseph out of the pit and sold
him, sending him on his way to Egypt.

And what of the brothers? Well, while all this is happening, they're
completely oblivious, totally unaware of what's going on. They're still over
the next hill, eating lunch. All they see is the Ishmaelites off in the distance,
a good ways off. They think they have plenty of time, so they continue
their leisurely meal. No reason to rush anything here.

Only one of the brothers *is* in a rush — and that's Reuben.

Reuben's Rush

"Where is Reuben?" we asked before. The answer is simple: he's right where we'd expect him to be. He's been with the rest of the brothers the whole time, and now he's eating with them. But all of a sudden, he has a reason to hurry.

You see, when Judah outlined Plan C to his brothers, they might have greeted the new plan with a sense of relief. Surely, selling Joseph was a much more pleasant outcome than Plan B, allowing him to die in the pit. But Reuben wouldn't have seen things that way at all. Remember, Reuben has been plotting this whole time to save Joseph and bring him back home to his father. And obviously, his plan depends on keeping Joseph — alive — in that pit. So when Judah convinces everyone to go back to the pit and sell Joseph down to Egypt rather than let him expire in that hole in the ground, all Reuben's carefully laid plans are put in jeopardy.

If you're Reuben, then, what do you do when you hear your brothers agree to return to the pit and sell Joseph? At that point, your only choice is … to get to that pit before they do.

So Reuben leaves the meal early and double-times it back to the pit. That's why the verse says וַיָּשָׁב רְאוּבֵן אֶל־הַבּוֹר, "And Reuben returned to the pit." But when he gets there, as that verse goes on to say, he is astonished at what he finds:

וַיָּשָׁב רְאוּבֵן אֶל־הַבּוֹר וְהִנֵּה אֵין־יוֹסֵף בַּבּוֹר וַיִּקְרַע אֶת־בְּגָדָיו:	And Reuben returned to the pit, and behold—Joseph was not in the pit! And he tore his clothes.	Genesis 37:29

Reuben got back to the pit quickly — but not quickly enough. Unbeknownst to him, the Midianites had gotten there first. *Joseph, mysteriously, is gone!* Reuben is devastated, and he tears his clothes in mourning. Then he returns to tell his brothers the terrible news:

וַיָּשָׁב אֶל־אֶחָיו וַיֹּאמַר הַיֶּלֶד אֵינֶנּוּ וַאֲנִי אָנָה אֲנִי־בָא:	He then returned to his brothers and announced, "The boy is gone! Now what am I to do?"	Genesis 37:30

In the end, Reuben isn't the *last* of the brothers to find out that Joseph has disappeared; he's the *first*. He doesn't know why or how Joseph has disappeared. All he knows is that his brother is gone — and he's devastated by that discovery.

Rashbam and the Three Elephants in the Room

Rashbam's theory elegantly addresses three great elephants in the room: (1) it explains the presence of the Midianites in the story; (2) it explains where Reuben was the whole time, and why he alone makes a return trip to the pit; and finally, (3) it explains why, years later, the brothers don't consider themselves guilty for having sold Joseph. They aren't guilty because *they didn't do it*. Indeed, at the moment of their confession, they are still completely unaware that he had been sold at all. For all they know, Joseph just . . . mysteriously disappeared from that pit.

Does this make the brothers innocent of wrongdoing in the matter of Joseph's sale? Hardly. But it changes the nature of what, precisely, they're guilty *of*. In Rashbam's reading, perhaps the most serious thing they are guilty of is . . . apathy. They are guilty of precisely the thing they later condemn themselves for: *hearing Joseph's anguished cries from the pit and not responding*. They turned away from their brother's anguish — and for this, they come to believe, the hand of Heaven holds them culpable.

Apathy

Indeed, the Torah strikingly draws our attention to the apathy of the brothers in its account of what happens next in the events of Joseph's sale. As we've just seen, Reuben returns to his brothers, who are still eating, and, with anguish, delivers the news to the brothers: *Joseph has inexplicably disappeared from the pit!* How, then, do the brothers respond? Not with shock, dismay, or any similar emotion. Instead, this is their wordless response:

וַיִּקְחוּ אֶת־כְּתֹנֶת יוֹסֵף	They took Joseph's coat,
וַיִּשְׁחֲטוּ שְׂעִיר עִזִּים	slaughtered a goat, and dipped
וַיִּטְבְּלוּ אֶת־הַכֻּתֹּנֶת בַּדָּם:	the coat in its blood. And they
וַיְשַׁלְּחוּ אֶת־כְּתֹנֶת הַפַּסִּים	sent the coat and brought it to
וַיָּבִיאוּ אֶל־אֲבִיהֶם	their father, and they said,

וַיֹּאמְרוּ זֹאת מָצָאנוּ הַכֶּר־נָא
הַכְּתֹנֶת בִּנְךָ הִוא אִם־לֹא:

"We found this. Recognize, please; is it your son's coat, or not?"

Immediately, without batting an eyelash, the brothers set about constructing a cover story. Reuben is grief-stricken and in shock — but the rest of the brothers seem to take Joseph's disappearance in stride. It's the new reality, and they just go about dealing with it.

The way they deal with it, of course, is with deception: they trick their father, falsely suggesting that Joseph has been killed. But for all their deception, there's also a whisper of truth in their words. They show their father Joseph's coat and claim they've "found" it. They're suggesting that they don't know what's become of Joseph — and in broad strokes, that's actually true. In reality, they *don't* know any more than their father does.[7]

In the end, the brothers didn't kill Joseph. They didn't sell him. And there was even a grain of truth in what they told their father about the

---

7   In fact, when you think about it, everyone in the story is at least somewhat in the dark. Jacob doesn't know what happened to Joseph; he is misled into believing his son was attacked by a savage beast. The brothers, for their part, have no idea what actually happened to Joseph; he just mysteriously disappeared. And Joseph? He's in the dark too. For a more detailed elaboration, see the essay on **Parshat Miketz**.

Of course, when Joseph finally reveals himself to his brothers, he does seem to believe that they're the ones who sold him into slavery. He says as much to them, telling them "not to be angry or sad that they sold him to this land" (Genesis 45:4). But as Rashbam would argue, it would only be natural for Joseph to assume that his brothers were behind the sale. All he knows for sure is that his brothers, without explanation, stripped him and left him in the pit, and a few hours later, these Midianites showed up, hauled him out, and sold him to the Ishmaelites. To him, it looks like this was all part of the plan; his brothers must have orchestrated it, casting him into the pit and making some sort of deal with the Midianites to have him sold as a slave.

When all the dust clears, *no single participant in the story really knows what happened to Joseph*. After the sale, Jacob, the brothers, and Joseph are all condemned to move forward in life with an incomplete understanding of what happened in this disastrous episode. They must go forward, working against not only their own fears and guilt concerning the fate of Joseph, but also their own ignorance.

events of the day. But their guilt is indeed still severe. A voice cried out to them from the ground, and they remaiined silent.

The Voice That Cries Out from the Ground

If apathy toward a brother in distress was, in the end, the core wrongdoing of the brothers in the matter of Joseph's sale, then it's worth stopping to consider: *With what degree of gravity does the Torah treat a crime like that?* With quite a bit, the answer seems to be.[8]

One indication of this, I think, are the echoes in the sale of Joseph episode to an earlier story. Where else do we hear of someone who considers killing his brother? Where else are we confronted with the image of ... *a helpless brother calling out from deep inside the earth*? What earlier story in the Torah does that remind you of?

It seems to resonate with what God said to Cain after the death of Abel:

Genesis 4:10   מֶה עָשִׂיתָ קוֹל דְּמֵי אָחִיךָ   "What have you done? Your brother's blood
צֹעֲקִים אֵלַי מִן־הָאֲדָמָה׃   cries out to Me from the ground."

---

8   On Yom Kippur, Ashkenazic Jews recite a series of *piyutim* (poetic additions to prayers) that suggest that the hand of Heaven holds the brothers (and their descendants) culpable for the sale of Joseph. Now, it's unclear how much weight we should attach to this assessment. The *piyutim* in question were composed by medieval poets, and we should be wary of drawing hard-and-fast conclusions from poetry. But at first glance, a reader of those poems might see in them a repudiation of Rashbam's theory: If the brothers didn't actually sell Joseph, how could they be held responsible for that sale by the hand of Heaven?

Is this a valid objection? It might be. But on the other hand, maybe Rashbam would argue that this is the whole point. The brothers may not have sold Joseph, but they *intended* to — and they created the conditions for his sale by casting him in the pit. In legal terms, as the Talmud would put it, they were indirectly responsible for the sale; their act was tantamount to *grama*, indirect causation. Concerning indirect causation, the Talmud (see Bava Kama 60a) rules that an earthly court cannot hold a perpetrator liable — but the Heavenly Court can. Perhaps no greater example of this exists than Jewish tradition's insistence that the brothers — although ignorant of Joseph's ultimate fate — are nevertheless guilty in the eyes of God for the sale of their brother (see Rabbeinu Bachye to Genesis 37:28, and Rabbi Baruch Fränkel-Te'omim's *Margenita de-Rav*, 15b).

And it's not just that one isolated resonance. Consider two more elements of the Joseph story: (1) brothers' (or a brother's) apathy in the face of a calamity that befalls a fellow brother; and (2) an evasive explanation given to Father concerning what became of a brother.

The story of Joseph's sale, when you step back and think about it, really is eerily similar to the story of Cain and Abel. Cain strikes his brother and kills him. Afterward, God comes to him and asks where Abel is. Cain responds with the famous words:

לֹא יָדַעְתִּי הֲשֹׁמֵר אָחִי אָנֹכִי: I don't know. Am I my brother's keeper?   Genesis 4:9

At first blush, it would seem that Cain is lying. *He knows where his brother is; he just killed him!* But maybe it's not a lie. He's living at the very dawn of humanity; no one has ever died before. Cain really *doesn't* know exactly what's become of his brother.[9] To be sure, the outer vestiges of Abel are still present — his lifeless body is there on the ground. But where, exactly, is the Abel who is supposed to inhabit that body? Where is his soul, his personality, his essence? Cain has no idea.

All these elements find their echoes in the Joseph story. Cain's lack of knowledge mirrors almost precisely the lack of knowledge of Joseph's brothers: they don't really know where their brother is either. To be sure, the outer vestiges of Joseph remain; Joseph's cloak, that which used to clothe him, is right there on the ground. But the real live Joseph? The brother who rightfully belongs inside that cloak? They have no idea what's become of him.

Moreover, just as there was a grain of truth in what the brothers told their father, there was also a grain of truth in what Cain told his Father in Heaven. Both claim that the outer vessel of their brother is right there, but they don't know where the essence went. As far as that goes, it's true. It's just that there's a larger story about how things *came to be this way* — and about that larger story, both Cain and the brothers are deceptively evasive.

Evasive *and* apathetic. If you think about Cain's essential sin — what the text *really* seems to hold him culpable for — it's not exactly *murder* in the sense in which we usually think of murder. There's no indication that Cain killed Abel with malice aforethought. Indeed, no one had ever died

---

9   See page 160, footnote 10.

before; Cain wouldn't have known how to kill his brother, even if he'd wanted to.[10] So if Cain isn't guilty of planning a murder, what *is* he guilty of? The answer becomes clear in this exchange between God and Cain:

GOD: *Where is your brother, Abel?*

CAIN: *I don't know. Am I my brother's keeper?*

GOD: *What have you done? Your brother's blood*
         cries out to Me from the ground...

"Am I my brother's keeper?" was the wrong answer. It is here, at this moment, that the Torah seems to want the reader to condemn Cain. His brother is gone, and Cain *just doesn't care*; he seems to believe it's none of his business. Now, maybe you'll protest that there's nothing he could do anyway, once Abel was dead. True enough, but that doesn't seem to matter. Cain should still be casting about for something, anything, he can do to make this desperate situation better. That Cain's response, in this moment, was not shock and dismay, but apathy — that is what condemns him in our eyes.

It appears that the Torah is nudging the reader of the Joseph story to relate in a similar way to the brothers' apathetic response to Joseph's disappearance. Like Cain, Joseph's brothers are not really guilty of murder. Sure, the thought of killing Joseph had crossed their minds, but in the end, they didn't actually do it. For that matter, the thought of selling him as a slave had crossed their minds — but they didn't actually do it. So they're not culpable for murder, per se, nor even for selling Joseph outright. Nevertheless, their actions led their brother to disappear from their lives, possibly forever. What should their response have been?

---

10   It's entirely possible that Cain didn't know what he was doing; he didn't know that the harm he inflicted on his brother would lead to such a terrible, permanent outcome. He was just angry at his brother, he hit him ... and Abel died.

According to one midrash (Devarim Rabbah 2:26), this explains why Cain's punishment was exile. Later passages in the Torah set forth that a murderer who deliberately kills is subject to capital punishment. But one who kills inadvertently, or without full knowledge of what he is doing, is instead exiled from his land (Numbers 35:22–25). Cain's exile, according to this midrash, was the prototype for that law.

Cain's response was disavowal of responsibility ("Am I my brother's keeper?") and so was theirs: they busied themselves creating an alibi by smearing the blood of a goat on Joseph's coat and bringing it to Father. But the moment called for something else entirely. "Your brother's blood cries out to Me from the ground," God had once memorably admonished Cain. When your brother is in anguish, you mustn't be silent. Even if you don't know how to make things right, even if the only thing you can do is let out an anguished cry of your own, in empathetic solidarity with your vanished brother, *that's what you should do.*

This is precisely what the brothers come to understand later. Years later, they are haunted by the memory of a voice that called out to them, in anguish, from the ground — and they hear in that voice a reminder of their enduring guilt:

אֲבָל אֲשֵׁמִים אֲנַחְנוּ
עַל־אָחִינוּ אֲשֶׁר רָאִינוּ
צָרַת נַפְשׁוֹ בְּהִתְחַנְנוֹ
אֵלֵינוּ וְלֹא שָׁמָעְנוּ

But we are guilty concerning our brother in that we saw his distress when he pleaded with us, but we did not listen…

Genesis 42:21

What If?

Let me close with a final thought on the implications of Rashbam's approach. A few years back, I came across a book intriguingly entitled *What If?* It was a collection of essays written by prominent historians, imagining the course of history if a particular twist of fate had gone differently: What if, on a certain rainy Manhattan evening a decade before World War II, the taxicab that merely brushed Winston Churchill had instead veered six inches to the right and killed him? Would Great Britain, and the rest of Europe, have survived the Nazi onslaught? What if Alexander the Great had died at twenty-one instead of thirty-two? Would Greece have been swallowed up by Persia, changing the character of Western civilization forever?

So let's play a little game of "What If?" ourselves. Let's explore a particularly fateful moment in biblical history, one I think Rashbam's theory invites us to wonder about: *What if the Midianites had never happened to pass by?* How would history have proceeded differently? In particular, had the Midianites never showed up, *would Joseph have been sold as a slave to the Ishmaelite caravan?*

Your first impulse might be to say, "Of course he would have still been sold!" The text clearly tells us that the brothers had agreed to sell him — it's just that the Midianites happened to get to Joseph before the brothers could, so *they* ended up being the ones to sell him, right?

But maybe not.

Take the Midianites out of the picture, and what we're left to contend with is a fascinating question: If nothing had stood in the way of the brothers carrying out their plan of selling Joseph to the Ishmaelites, *would they actually have done it?*

And before we instinctively reach for an answer to that question, let's step back and consider the evidence.

Shifting Plans

Consider the following: from the moment the brothers first spied Joseph approaching them to the moment Joseph was actually sold as a slave and loaded onto that Ishmaelite caravan, one thing remained remarkably consistent: *the brothers' plans regarding what to do with Joseph were constantly shifting.*

We've talked about those changes in plans. There was an original plan, a plan born of hatred and disdain, the moment they first saw Joseph approaching: *Murder him and cast his body into a pit.* But soon enough, Reuben dissuaded the brothers from killing Joseph outright, and Plan A gave way to Plan B: *Cast him into the pit alive and abandon him there.* But Plan B didn't last long either; after the brothers threw him into the pit, Judah noticed the Ishmaelite caravan in the distance, and he proposed Plan C: *Let's not kill Joseph at all, even indirectly, by abandoning him in that pit; let's instead sell him to those Ishmaelites.* And the brothers accepted Plan C.

Now, do you see a pattern here?

As time went on, the plans kept getting less brutal, less horrifying. In the last plan they agreed on, Plan C, there was outright sympathy for Joseph:

Genesis 37:27	וְיָדֵנוּ אַל־תְּהִי־בוֹ כִּי־ אָחִינוּ בְשָׂרֵנוּ הוּא	Let not our hand be upon him, for he is our brother, our own flesh.

Now let's extrapolate a step further from our "What If?" scenario.

Plan D?

Had the Midianite traders never showed up, what was likely to happen next? Would the brothers *really* have gone through with Plan C, or would they have thought better of it when the time came for them to act?

Imagine the scene. The brothers have said they want to sell Joseph to the Ishmaelites, so they return from their picnic and approach the pit. Joseph is there. But the task of hauling Joseph out of the pit would have fallen to Joseph's brothers, people who had grown up with him, not impersonal Midianite traders. And what would Joseph have been doing as the brothers grasped his arm and hoisted him back onto level ground? He would have been sobbing, pleading. Would the brothers really have been able to resist Joseph's cries? Would they actually have been able to take the money from the Ishmaelites, tie Joseph up, and hoist him on the caravan, all the while remaining deaf to their brother's anguished entreaties?

We already had Plans A, B, and C. It's hard to believe there wouldn't have been one more plan: Plan D.

What, exactly, would Plan D have looked like? We don't know for sure. Might the brothers have tearfully reconciled with a newly humbled Joseph? Possibly. But even if a true reconciliation wasn't in the cards, perhaps the brothers would have found a way to say "thanks, but no thanks" to the opportunity afforded by that Ishmaelite caravan, and instead reached some sort of working arrangement with Joseph: *Are we really going to sell our own brother? We just . . . can't do that. We've got no choice; somehow, we all have to go home together. Joseph, come home with us — and let's just keep these terrible events between us. Let's all swear that no one will tell Father what happened between us today.*

Tragically, the only thing missing — to keep Joseph with his family, to keep the brothers from bearing this terrible stain of guilt — was *time*.

All the brothers needed was a little more time.

Thinking, Fast and Slow

In his book *Thinking, Fast and Slow*, Daniel Kahneman suggests that we all possess two complementary systems of thought. Kahneman calls these "System 1" and "System 2." System 1 is fast and intuitive, and it can be easily swayed by our emotions. System 2 is slower, deliberate, and more logical. More often than not, System 1 operates automatically, at a primal, subconscious level. System 2, the slower system, operates when we deliberately engage our conscious minds in an attempt to think things through analytically.

System 2 thinking tends to be more reliable than System 1, but its great drawback is that it's *slower*. Each system, therefore, has its place. System 1 thinking helps with daily living: if we had to think slowly and deeply about what simple sentences mean, or how to drive to work, or whether we're going to have Raisin Bran or Cheerios for breakfast, we'd be mentally exhausted by nine o'clock every morning. Instead, we let System 1 take care of the simple things almost automatically. But System 1 also tends to make more mistakes than System 2, so when the stakes get high—when we need to contemplate long-term decisions about money, health, or relationships—we need to engage System 2. We need to pause and let the slower, more analytical part of our brains take over, acting as a kind of check on our impulses and intuitions.

The Kohen's Divorce

Jewish law seems attuned to the need to create these kinds of protections for ourselves. There is a fascinating and somewhat obscure law about Jewish divorce tucked away at the end of the mishnaic tractate Bava Batra, and it suggests a kind of paradigm for how we ought address the inherent flaws in our instinctive, System 1 thinking. The law states that a Kohen (a Jewish priest) who wishes to divorce his wife must use a special kind of *get* (bill of divorce) called a *get mekushar*—a "knotted" *get*. This *get* requires a whole raft of otherwise superfluous signatures, and must be folded and sealed in an inordinately complex manner. Any divorce document used by a Kohen that does *not* conform to the specifications of a *get mekushar* is deemed by rabbinic injunction to be invalid.

What's the rationale behind this law?

The Sages required a *get mekushar* for the Kohen, the Talmud explains, because of the inherently high stakes involved whenever a Kohen makes a choice to divorce. Because biblical law prohibits a Kohen from marrying a divorcée, any divorce issued by a Kohen is unusually ... final. An ordinary couple might reconsider: they might divorce, then decide a few days later that they had acted hastily—in which case they could simply remarry. But not the Kohen. Once he and his wife sever their bond of marriage, any future union between them becomes prohibited.

The *get mekushar*, then, is designed to protect a couple from giving in to heat-of-the-moment, System 1 thinking. What if a Kohen who is experiencing a more or less routine conflict with his wife, a marital problem that's solvable, yields to his impulses in a moment of frustration and serves his wife with a *get*? Such a decision would be tragic; there's no way back from it. And so, the Sages required the Kohen contemplating divorce to commission a complex *get*, one that would take *a long time* to devise. The *get mekushar* requirement, in essence, buys the couple the one commodity that's in scarcest supply: time. Time enough to reconsider. Time enough to work things through. It forces System 2 thinking in a situation where System 1 thinking alone could lead to disaster.

The message of the *get mekushar*: relationships bring out our passions. Avoid at all costs making irrevocable decisions when in the grip of these passions. Slow down. *Buy yourself time.*

The Scarcity of Time

Time, sadly, was a commodity Joseph's brothers didn't have enough of.

Plan A was born in a rush of anger and resentment:

הִנֵּה בַּעַל הַחֲלֹמוֹת הַלָּזֶה בָּא: וְעַתָּה לְכוּ וְנַהַרְגֵהוּ וְנַשְׁלִכֵהוּ בְּאַחַד הַבֹּרוֹת	Here comes the dreamer! Come now, let's kill him—and we'll cast his body into one of those pits.	Genesis 37:19–20

It's not for nothing that they call Joseph "the dreamer." When the brothers see Joseph coming, they respond, in the heat of the moment, to his hated dreams of power and domination, the notion that they will all bow to him, by conjuring up their *own* dream of power and domination. If they had been in their right minds, in System 2 thinking, the brothers would never have contemplated killing Joseph. But they might impulsively imagine doing it. They might *dream* of it: *Here comes Joseph. His accursed dreams have been the bane of our existence. He thinks he's going to dominate us, that we'll all bow to him. Well, what if we dominated him instead? What if we just ... killed him now?*

Horrifyingly, that System 1 thought, that immediate, impassioned response, starts to play out in real life. But as soon as it starts, it gets tempered. Reality has a way of slowly asserting itself. Plan A fades into Plan B. Plan B fades into Plan C.

As time steadily, slowly passes, the brothers pull back more and more on the passions that initially animated their thinking. It's only a matter of *time*, then, before they pull back entirely and reach some sort of sane accommodation with Joseph.

Unfortunately, time is something the brothers don't have in unlimited supply. The Midianites lurk around the bend, just off the main stage of this revenge fantasy. They come on stage and stop the clock, as it were. The Midianites end the unfolding drama just before the brothers can fully snap out of it, before they can settle on *one last* revised plan for their imperiled brother. That one last plan could have brought a measure of sanity, reconciliation, or at least pragmatism, back into a family riven by division, mistrust, and fear. But alas, it was not to be.

God gave us all a System 2 brain, but God doesn't always give us unlimited time in which to use it.

May we learn to err on the side of caution. May we learn to use our time well.

Why Didn't Joseph Write Home?

וַיִּשְׁלַח פַּרְעֹה וַיִּקְרָא אֶת־יוֹסֵף וַיְרִיצֻהוּ מִן־הַבּוֹר וַיְגַלַּח וַיְחַלֵּף שִׂמְלֹתָיו וַיָּבֹא אֶל־פַּרְעֹה: וַיֹּאמֶר פַּרְעֹה אֶל־יוֹסֵף חֲלוֹם חָלַמְתִּי וּפֹתֵר אֵין אֹתוֹ וַאֲנִי שָׁמַעְתִּי עָלֶיךָ לֵאמֹר תִּשְׁמַע חֲלוֹם לִפְתֹּר אֹתוֹ:

And Pharaoh sent for Joseph, and they brought him hastily out of the dungeon. And he shaved himself, and changed his clothes, and came to Pharaoh. And Pharaoh said to Joseph, "I have dreamed a dream, and there is no one who can interpret it; and I have heard it said of you that when you hear a dream, you can interpret it."

GENESIS 41:14–15

MIKETZ

Why Didn't Joseph Write Home?

A version of this essay was originally published in my book *The Exodus You Almost Passed Over*. There you'll find a more in-depth treatment of the Joseph story — and of the many parallels between the Joseph narrative and the Exodus saga.

JOSEPH SPENT MANY YEARS in Egypt as a high Egyptian official, second only to Pharaoh. During all this time, why did he never write home?

This is one of the most perplexing questions of the Joseph saga. If Joseph really loved his father — and it seems that he did — why did he never inform him that he was safe and sound? A postcard, at the very least: *Here I am, Dad, in Egypt. You'll never believe it, but I'm Pharaoh's right-hand man! Weather is fantastic. Wishing you were here.* Something like that. Anything. Why does Joseph maintain radio silence?

It's a question that has been discussed, over the ages, by many commentators.[1] I want to call your attention to a particular interpretation advanced by Rabbi Yoel Bin Nun, a contemporary thinker.[2] He suggests the possibility that Joseph may have been the victim of a terrible misunderstanding.

Let's recall how Joseph ended up in Egypt. One day, his brothers threw him in a pit, and he was sold as a slave. *We* know that Jacob was clueless about what really happened to Joseph; his child just disappeared. But what is less obvious, Rabbi Bin Nun suggests, is that the cluelessness was mutual: Joseph had no idea what really happened with Jacob that day, either.

The Omniscient Reader

To demonstrate that this is so, let me ask you a rather pointed question: What crucial event surrounding the sale of Joseph are *you, the reader,* aware of that Joseph, an actual *participant* in the story, is not?

The event I'm thinking of occurs immediately after Joseph is hauled out of the pit and into a caravan, to be taken down to Egypt and sold as a slave. Right after that, the Torah tells us that the brothers took Joseph's special, striped coat, smeared it with blood, and brought it back to their

---

1 See, for example, Ramban to Genesis 42:9.

2 See *Megadim*, vol. 1, pages 20–31.

father. Their anguished father inferred what the brothers wanted him to: his beloved child had met his end somewhere in the desert.

Genesis 37:33   טָרֹף טֹרַף יוֹסֵף: Joseph has been torn to pieces!

Now, *we*, as readers of this story, know about the bloody coat; *we* know that Jacob has been deceived by his sons. But there's no way that *Joseph* can know this; he's off on a caravan somewhere when all this is taking place. So if you were Joseph, and you *didn't know* that your father had been tricked, how might that affect your interpretation of what happened that day? What terrible, tragic misunderstanding might you arrive at?

Let's replay the events leading up to the sale of Joseph, as Joseph himself might have apprehended them:

> *There I was, seventeen years old, tending sheep with my brothers. There were some tensions in the family, sure. My brothers didn't seem to like me very much. And then I started having these dreams. The first one involved me and my brothers, harvesting wheat out in the fields, when all of a sudden the sheaves of wheat belonging to my brothers started bowing to my sheaf. And then I had a second dream: the sun and moon and eleven stars were all bowing to me. That dream seemed to involve my father, too, so I told him about it. And then, for the first time I can remember, my father became angry at me.*
>
> *He publicly rebuked me: "Shall your mother, your brothers, and I all come bowing to you?"*
>
> *Suddenly, right after that, Father had a mission for me: "Your brothers are tending sheep in Shechem. I think I'll send you to them . . ."*
>
> *Why did Father ask me to do that? It was dangerous. And I was to go to Shechem, of all places!* [3] *He knew my brothers were jealous of me.*

---

3   The mission would have seemed dark and ominous from the start. Shechem, of course, had a blood-soaked history. It was there that the children of Leah had gathered to defend the honor of one of their own, Dinah — and an entire city had fallen by the sword. Now, at a moment when tensions in the family had reached a fever pitch, Joseph, a child of Rachel, would be sent to Shechem, alone and unaccompanied, to meet . . . the children of Leah? Everything indicates that Joseph would have approached his mission with a good deal of trepidation (see also Rashi to 37:14).

*I was scared about going there to meet them, but I complied.[4] I hoped
that things would go well ... but they didn't. I was jumped, thrown into
a pit, and sold off as a slave.*

And there was never any search party.

Add it all up. Joseph doesn't know that his father was deceived into thinking he was dead. Joseph doesn't know, as we do, that his father was horri-
fied, in mourning over the apparent loss of his beloved son. So, given just
what Joseph knows, what false suspicion might he entertain?

Rabbi Yoel Bin Nun suggests that Joseph may have believed that he
had just been thrown out of the family.

*Was it planned in advance? Maybe, or maybe not. Maybe my brothers
had a talk with Father one day and told them it was either me or
them, that someone had to go. Or maybe it happened after the fact:
my brothers came home and told Father that I was safely on my way
to Egypt, that it might be unsavory, but it was the only way the family
could remain intact. It doesn't matter. Either way, I've been thrown out
of the family.*

And it's not as if nothing like this had happened before. Think back just a
few generations in the history of this family. When Sarah felt that Ishmael
was a corrosive influence, soon enough, he was out of the family. In the
next generation, Rebecca had favored Jacob, and before you knew it, Esau
was out of the family. Had the same thing just happened to Joseph?

In Egypt, Joseph would have had a long time to ponder the circumstances of his abrupt disappearance from the family. After a stint as a rel-
atively privileged servant in the house of a nobleman, he found himself
cast into prison for a crime he did not commit, and there he languished
for many years — until, at long last, someone new came into his life. It
was Pharaoh.

---

4   In the text, Joseph says הִנֵּנִי (*hineini*), "here I am," when his father calls upon him
    to meet his brothers in Shechem (Genesis 37:13). In the book of Genesis, *hineini*
    has a chilling echo. It was how Abraham expressed his readiness to go on a jour-
    ney when God, his Heavenly Father, called upon him to sacrifice his son. Here,
    Joseph uses the same phrase to express to his earthly father his readiness to go on
    a journey that might involve sacrifice. The use of *hineini* may be the Torah's way
    of conveying to the reader that Joseph knew something of the dangers of the jour-
    ney before he set out to meet his brothers.

Pharaoh

One day, Joseph found himself suddenly extricated from jail and thrust into the presence of the king of Egypt himself. Pharaoh had been having some dreams that troubled him, and he had heard that Joseph might be able to interpret them. The king asked Joseph to listen to his dreams and tell him their meaning.

The verses that speak of these events hint at just how redemptive Pharaoh's appearance in Joseph's life really might have seemed to Joseph at that moment. The text tells us, for example, that Pharaoh sent for Joseph and had him pulled out of the *bor* (בּוֹר), which literally means "pit."° This is an odd turn of phrase, since, technically, Joseph was not in a *bor*; he was in a prison, described earlier as a *beit hasohar* (בֵּית הַסֹּהַר).° In using the term *bor*, the text seems to blur the lines between the story that is happening now, and a story that happened many years ago. For indeed, there *was* a time when Joseph was in a pit. He was put there by his brothers thirteen years ago:

Genesis 41:14

Genesis 39:20

Genesis
37:23–24

וַיְהִי כַּאֲשֶׁר־בָּא יוֹסֵף אֶל־אֶחָיו וַיַּפְשִׁיטוּ אֶת־יוֹסֵף אֶת־כֻּתׇּנְתּוֹ אֶת־כְּתֹנֶת הַפַּסִּים אֲשֶׁר עָלָיו: וַיִּקָּחֻהוּ וַיַּשְׁלִכוּ אֹתוֹ הַבֹּרָה	And it came to pass, when Joseph came to his brothers, that they stripped Joseph of his coat, the coat of many colors that he was wearing; and they took him, and cast him into the pit

The text seems to imply that when Pharaoh pulls him out of jail all these years later, it feels like déjà vu for Joseph, like he was getting out of that pit at last. After getting a shave and a haircut, Joseph is given a nice new change of clothes by Pharaoh. Here too, the verse seems to evoke memories from thirteen years ago. Right before his brothers threw him in the pit, they stripped him of his special clothes, the beautiful striped coat that his father had given him. Now, once again, he has beautiful new clothes — all courtesy of Pharaoh.

A pattern is taking shape in these verses. A version of the terrible events of thirteen years ago seems to be happening again, but in reverse. Thirteen years ago, Joseph was first stripped of his clothes and thrown in a pit; now, he is taken out of a "pit" and given new clothes.

The pattern of reverses continues. The next thing Pharaoh does is the reverse of something that happened thirteen years ago, before Joseph was thrown in a pit, and before he was stripped of his new clothes:

וַיִּשְׁלַח פַּרְעֹה וַיִּקְרָא אֶת־יוֹסֵף   And Pharaoh sent for Joseph   Genesis
                                                                             41:14

The opposite of being called for is being sent away, and that's exactly what happened to Joseph thirteen years earlier, just before he was stripped of his clothes and cast into a pit: he was sent away by Jacob. His father had sent him to go check on his brothers. That event—his father's decision to send him—was the first in a series of misfortunes that culminated in Joseph's sale into slavery. It was the initial step toward that first "pit."

Thirteen years later, when Joseph was pulled out of a prison cell and brought to Pharaoh, he must have found it wonderful—and not just because it meant the end of his tenure in an Egyptian prison. It was wonderful, too, because in some way, shape, or form, these events felt like the resolution of an earlier trauma, the trauma of the pit. Now, instead of a man sending him away, another man would bring him close. Now, instead of losing his beautiful clothes, he would be given beautiful new clothes. Now, instead of being cast into a pit, he would be pulled out of one.

The man behind all this was Pharaoh.

Through this pattern of reverses, the Torah may well be telling us something about the relationship Pharaoh is beginning to create with Joseph. Pharaoh is acting out a precise inverse of Jacob's role in this story. Whatever disappointment Joseph might have felt toward his own father—How could you have sent me away? Where were you when I was stripped, and begging to be taken out of the pit?—it is all being redeemed by the actions of Pharaoh, who will be a father-in-exile for him. Thirteen years ago, his father sent him away. Now, a new father figure will bring him close.

Three Paternal Gifts

After bringing Joseph into his presence, Pharaoh tells him his dreams and asks Joseph what he makes of them. Here, again, if Joseph were to create a portrait of an ideal father out of thin air, he could do no better. Back in Canaan, Joseph's real father had reacted caustically when Joseph asked him to hear out his dream; but this new father, Pharaoh, asks Joseph to hear his dream, and eagerly awaits Joseph's interpretation.[5]

Genesis 41:15

וַיֹּאמֶר פַּרְעֹה אֶל־יוֹסֵף חֲלוֹם חָלַמְתִּי וּפֹתֵר אֵין אֹתוֹ וַאֲנִי שָׁמַעְתִּי עָלֶיךָ לֵאמֹר תִּשְׁמַע חֲלוֹם לִפְתֹּר אֹתוֹ׃

And Pharaoh said to Joseph, "I have dreamed a dream, and there is no one who can interpret it; and I have heard it said of you that when you hear a dream, you can interpret it."

INITIAL EVENT **REVERSAL**

INITIAL EVENT	REVERSAL
GEN 37:9 Son to father: חָלַמְתִּי חֲלוֹם "I dreamed a dream …"	Rescued from a "pit" **GEN 41:14**
GEN 37:10 Father, hearing son's dream, scoffs at it	Given new clothes **GEN 41:14**
GEN 37:13 Sent away by father	Sent for by new "father" **GEN 41:14**
GEN 37:23 Stripped of his clothes	"Father" to "son": חָלַמְתִּי חֲלוֹם "A dream I dreamed …"[5] **GEN 41:15**
GEN 37:24 Cast into a pit	"Son," hearing **GEN 41:6–36** "father's" dream, takes it seriously

---

5   Thus the pattern of reverses continues, as suggested by the very phrasing of the Hebrew: when Pharaoh tells Joseph of his dream, the Hebrew is חָלַמְתִּי חֲלוֹם,"a dream I dreamed" (Genesis 41:15). When, thirteen years earlier, Joseph tells his dream to his brothers and then to his father, the Hebrew is חֲלוֹם חָלַמְתִּי, "I dreamed a dream" (Genesis 37:9). The order of the statement is reversed.

Joseph successfully interprets Pharaoh's dream. And when he does, not only does the king give Joseph a new job — Joseph will be in charge of administering the grain supplies of the kingdom — he gives him a wife. And he bestows upon him a new name: Tzaphnat-Paneach.°

Genesis 41:45

Now, what kind of person gives you a job in the family business, helps find you a wife, and gives you a name? *That would be your father.*

A New Life

As Joseph rises to power in Egypt, he becomes the son, in a way, of two "fathers." The reader is left to wonder: Is there a competition of sorts between these two men? Throughout his years in Egypt, Joseph seems to retain his devotion to the God of his ancestors (he is quick to mention the name of the Almighty at almost every turn);° but what of his emotional connection to his family? Where do his loyalties lie?

Genesis 41:16, 41:51, etc.

This is the challenge that now faces Joseph. Will the power, love, and acceptance showered upon him by his adoptive father loosen, and ultimately break, the bonds that tie him to his *actual* father and brothers — especially given Joseph's uncertainty over what happened back on that fateful day at the pit? These questions are never more achingly evident than in the name Joseph gives to his first child, born to him in Egypt, from the wife Pharaoh provides for him:

וַיִּקְרָא יוֹסֵף אֶת־שֵׁם הַבְּכוֹר מְנַשֶּׁה כִּי־נַשַּׁנִי אֱלֹקִים אֶת־כָּל־עֲמָלִי וְאֵת כָּל־בֵּית אָבִי:	And Joseph called the name of his firstborn Menasheh, [in gratitude] "that God has caused me to forget my travails, and all my father's house."

Genesis 41:51

If the name of Joseph's firstborn expresses his sense that God has freed him from the tortured memories of his past, the name of his second child expresses his grim determination to make the best of a new future:

וְאֵת שֵׁם הַשֵּׁנִי קָרָא אֶפְרָיִם כִּי־הִפְרַנִי אֱלֹקִים בְּאֶרֶץ עָנְיִי:	And the name of the second he called Ephraim, "because God has caused me to be fruitful in the land of my oppression."

Genesis 41:52

Egypt may be the land of oppression, Joseph seems to be saying. *It wasn't my choice to be here. But with the birth of these two children, I am determined to make the best of it.*

But the names hit the reader like a splash of cold water: in setting up a new life for himself in Egypt, Joseph apparently feels, on some level, that he's closing the door on an old life. Yes, of course, he would still be a God-fearing person — he would continue to hold the values of Abraham dear — but he was an orphan of sorts in a new land; he didn't have a home in Canaan he could go back to.

So why didn't Joseph write home? Maybe it felt like that home was gone. It was home that had turned away from him. All that was left for him was this new home, this "land of his oppression."

It is at this moment — after the birth of these two children, after Joseph seems to have found a measure of peace in starting a new page in his life — that suddenly and without warning, the past comes storming back. For, as the famine Joseph predicted descends upon the civilized world, who should happen to show up at Joseph's door but his very own brothers, seeking grain to bring back to their family in Canaan.

Suddenly, the adoptive son of Pharaoh looks into the faces of his own brothers, the ones who could not stomach him as the favored child of their family. In a flash, the past is not so safely buried anymore. Just as Joseph was starting to get comfortable in his new life and look toward the future, the past rudely intrudes upon his present.

Joseph makes life difficult for his brothers for a while, but he eventually reveals himself to them.° However, even as he does, one question still remains unanswered: If Joseph has until now looked upon Pharaoh as an adoptive father, one whose actions somehow redeem the painful events back home, that's all well and good so long as Joseph's *real* father remains safely ensconced back in Joseph's past. But now, what if Jacob were to join Joseph in Egypt and be reunited with him? If that were to happen, there would be a very real question for this child of two fathers to answer: *Who is your father now? Where do your loyalties lie?*

That is precisely the scenario that unfolds later, in **Parshat Vayechi**. Join me there — we'll pick up these threads and see where they lead.

Genesis 45:3

The Timeless Echo of Judah's Plea

וְעַתָּה כְּבֹאִי אֶל־עַבְדְּךָ
אָבִי וְהַנַּעַר אֵינֶנּוּ
אִתָּנוּ וְנַפְשׁוֹ קְשׁוּרָה
בְנַפְשׁוֹ: וְהָיָה כִּרְאוֹתוֹ
כִּי־אֵין הַנַּעַר וָמֵת
וְהוֹרִידוּ עֲבָדֶיךָ אֶת־
שֵׂיבַת עַבְדְּךָ אָבִינוּ
בְּיָגוֹן שְׁאֹלָה:

And now, when I come to your servant, my father, and the lad is not with us— seeing that his soul is bound up with the lad's soul—when he sees that the lad is not with us, he will die, and your servants will send down the old age of your servant, our father, sorrowfully to the grave.

GENESIS 44:30–31

The Timeless Echo
of Judah's Plea

PARSHAT VAYIGASH features one of the most dramatic moments in the book of Genesis. Joseph's brothers have finished dining with the high Egyptian official who, unbeknownst to them, is in fact their long-lost brother Joseph himself. Joseph has finally given them the lifesaving grain they sought, and it appears that their story is headed for a happy ending. All they need to do now is successfully return home with that grain. But as they're packing up to go home to Canaan, Joseph instructs his palace guards to surreptitiously place a silver goblet in Benjamin's sack. The brothers depart, and shortly thereafter, Joseph dispatches armed officers to track them down. The officers stop the brothers' caravan and accuse the party of theft. A silver goblet is missing from the palace, they say; one of the brothers must have stolen it.

A kind of cold, hard poetic justice is set to play out. Ever wonder why the goblet Joseph used to entrap Benjamin just happened to be a silver one? Is there a reason that the Torah bothers recording that otherwise trivial fact for us? Well, here's a theory: many years ago, Joseph was cast into a pit by his brothers, then hauled down to Egypt into slavery — and payment for the slave was made in silver. The Torah is very specific about that:

וַיִּמְכְּרוּ אֶת־יוֹסֵף לַיִּשְׁמְעֵאלִים בְּעֶשְׂרִים כָּסֶף וַיָּבִיאוּ אֶת־יוֹסֵף מִצְרָיְמָה:	They sold Joseph for twenty shekels of silver to the Ishmaelites, who brought Joseph down to Egypt.	Genesis 37:28

The great crime against Joseph, all those years ago, was perpetrated with silver. That silver, in Joseph's eyes, was an ill-gotten gain; the brothers should never have had it.[1] And back then, his brothers' great crime had remained hidden: no one had discovered that ill-gotten silver, the sum paid for Joseph. All that anyone saw was his bloody cloak. But now, all that would change. Now Joseph would see to it that silver with similar qualities (i.e. silver that by rights belongs to Joseph, but is in his brothers' possession) would indeed be found — and his brothers' crime would be uncovered for all to see. There would be no escaping this time.[2]

The first time around, the exchange of silver had made Joseph, a child of Rachel, into a slave. This time, Benjamin, Rachel's other child, would be threatened with slavery — again by means of silver. Now the circle would be complete.

A Shift in Perspective

Bottom line: perhaps Joseph's decision to entrap his brothers in this particular way suggests that part of Joseph's motivation in framing his brothers with the goblet was, strangely enough, to set things right somehow — to redres a crime they committed against him long ago. We'll come back to these ruminations on the meaning of the goblet from Joseph's perspective in due time, but for now, let's set these thoughts aside and consider things from a different perspective entirely — that of Judah. How do the events surrounding the arrest of the brothers look from where Judah is standing?

Judah's thoughts are not on the past, on crimes committed long ago. He has enough on his hands dealing with a turbulent present. When Joseph's men arrive and accuse the brothers of theft, Judah immediately protests

---

1   Some interesting connections between the two "silvers": the first time around, the silver represented Joseph's "power" (it was exchanged for his service as a slave); Joseph is far more mysterious and powerful now, but once again, the silver represents his "power": it is the cup he is said to use for divination (Genesis 44:15). There's also another parallel: the brothers, as they abscond with Joseph's silver goblet, are on their way from Egypt to Canaan. Where was Joseph taken after he'd been sold for silver? He took the very same trek in reverse, from Canaan to Egypt.

2   There's a deep irony here, though, for Joseph may well be mistaken about the silver. See our earlier essay on **Parshat Vayeishev** (page 145), which articulates Rashbam's theory that the brothers never actually sold Joseph — and therefore never came into possession of that silver. Still, Joseph may well have *thought* that the brothers had sold him and walked off with the silver. After all, they were the ones who threw him in the pit — and for all Joseph knew, they were the ones to profit from his sale.

their innocence. He quite naturally thinks they have nothing to hide, and tells the officers that they are free to search everyone's belongings for the missing goblet. But then he says something he will soon regret:

אֲשֶׁר יִמָּצֵא אִתּוֹ מֵעֲבָדֶיךָ
וָמֵת וְגַם־אֲנַחְנוּ נִהְיֶה
לַאדֹנִי לַעֲבָדִים:

With whomever of your servants [the goblet] is found, let him die, and we will be my lord's slaves.

Genesis 44:9

So sure is Judah that his brothers are innocent, he proposes that the thief, if found, should be put to death. One can imagine his horror, then, when the Egyptians go about their search and find the missing goblet in Benjamin's sack. The despondent brothers are brought back to Egypt, fully expecting the worst. Instead, Joseph — his true identity still a mystery to his brothers — is surprisingly magnanimous. He rejects the idea that the thief should die, and even declines to take all the brothers as slaves:

וַיֹּאמֶר חָלִילָה לִּי מֵעֲשׂוֹת זֹאת
הָאִישׁ אֲשֶׁר נִמְצָא הַגָּבִיעַ
בְּיָדוֹ הוּא יִהְיֶה־לִּי עָבֶד וְאַתֶּם
עֲלוּ לְשָׁלוֹם אֶל־אֲבִיכֶם:

And he said, "Far be it from me to act that way! Only he in whose possession the goblet was found shall be my slave; the rest of you go back in peace to your father."

Genesis 44:17

Deal or No Deal?

Now, let me invite you into a little thought experiment. Imagine that you are Judah at this moment, standing before this Egyptian official. It's up to you to respond to the Egyptian's surprisingly gracious offer. Let's consider the choice before you: *Will you take his deal or not?*

Joseph's proposed deal is a generous one. Remember, it was you, Judah, who had the brilliant idea of suggesting that the guilty party, should he be found, be put to death. Your hastily chosen words have, unimaginably, managed to endanger your youngest brother, Benjamin. But that Egyptian official is now offering you a way out ... or *almost* a way out. An offer is now on the table with far better terms than you, Judah, had proposed. The Egyptian is willing to commute the terrible death sentence looming over Benjamin; he says that the thief should merely be his slave. As for you and the rest of your brothers, you'll return to Canaan unharmed. So, the question is: Deal or no deal? Will you accept this rather magnanimous offer from the high Egyptian official, or will you decline it and take your chances trying to negotiate some other outcome?

It sure seems like a tempting deal to take. To be sure, back in Canaan, you promised your father that, come what may, you would bring the last remaining child of Rachel home to him safe and sound. You even guaranteed that promise, with a dramatic flourish:

Genesis 43:9

אָנֹכִי אֶעֶרְבֶנּוּ מִיָּדִי
תְּבַקְשֶׁנּוּ אִם־לֹא הֲבִיאֹתִיו
אֵלֶיךָ וְהִצַּגְתִּיו לְפָנֶיךָ
וְחָטָאתִי לְךָ כָּל־הַיָּמִים׃

I myself will be collateral for him; you may hold me personally responsible: if I do not bring him back to you and set him before you, I shall stand guilty before you forever.

So yes, there was that promise you made. But that was then, and this is now. When you made that promise to Father, you never thought, in your wildest imaginings, that Benjamin would be so reckless as to steal the silver goblet of the Egyptian grand vizier. And remember, in these first, astonished moments after your arrest, you don't know that Benjamin was framed. All you know is that the missing goblet is there in his sack for all the world to see. Benjamin seems to have no leg to stand on.

Most of us would probably take the deal and, with head hanging low, go back to Father and say something like this:

Look, I know I promised you I'd bring Benjamin back, but no one asked him to go pilfering royal tableware at our last banquet! By rights, he should have been put to death; it is only by the grace of that Egyptian vizier that Benjamin still lives. So yes, Father, of course I'm sorry he's not with us, but what would you have had me do? There was no good option. Let's count ourselves lucky that Benjamin is still alive at all!

No Deal

Genesis
44:18–33

Most of us would probably take the deal. But that's not what Judah does. He rejects the deal, making a risky last-ditch attempt to save Benjamin.° It's an impassioned speech; in it, he summarizes his family's backstory, explaining why it is that Benjamin is so treasured in his father's eyes.

You don't understand, Judah tells the Egyptian. Our father has already lost one child of his beloved wife, Rachel. Benjamin is now all that remains of her. Do you know what will happen if we go back to Canaan without him?

וְנַפְשׁוֹ קְשׁוּרָה בְנַפְשׁוֹ׃	[My father's] soul is bound up with	Genesis 44:30–31
וְהָיָה כִּרְאוֹתוֹ כִּי־אֵין	[Benjamin's] soul, and when he sees that	
הַנַּעַר וָמֵת	[Benjamin] is not with us, he will die	

Yes, there had been a time, years ago, when Judah had allowed a brother, a child of Rachel, to be sold into slavery because Father had loved Rachel more, because Father had loved a child of Rachel more. But that was then and this is now. This time, Judah would confront head-on the terrible truth that started it all:

Father loved Rachel more than he loved my mother, and he loves her child more than he loves me. His very soul seems bound up with Benjamin's. But I accept that; I'm not battling against that anymore. Please, therefore, take me instead. Let Benjamin go back to our father.

It is perhaps Judah's finest moment, and it brings the painful story of the sale of Joseph, at long last, toward a conclusion: when Joseph hears Judah's words, he cannot contain himself. He reveals his identity, assures the brothers that he will care for them, and asks that his father be brought to see him. The family is reunited, and the long charade is over.

But there is more here than meets the eye. Judah's deed, I want to argue, is significant not just for its impact on this particular story, but for its historical resonance over the centuries. If you focus on those deeply poignant and intimate words uttered by Judah: נַפְשׁוֹ קְשׁוּרָה בְנַפְשׁוֹ, "his soul is bound up with his soul." Consider those words and search your mind — and Tanach — for an echo. Where else in the Bible does that striking phrase appear?

Welcome to David and Goliath

As it happens, this very same turn of phrase appears again in the Hebrew Bible, many hundreds of years later, in the story of David and Goliath, as narrated in the book of Samuel. Goliath, you will recall, threatened Saul, the first king of Israel. The fearsome giant had proposed a contest: one-on-one combat between Goliath and a challenger, any challenger that the Israelites put forward. The victor would win the right for his people to enslave the other nation.

Goliath, of course, was not only an imposing giant of a man but a practiced warrior. For days, no one among the Israelites rose to the challenge; combat with Goliath seemed an exercise in futility. But one day, a little shepherd boy by the name of David decided that he would respond to Goliath's challenge. He went out to fight Goliath, and miraculously, he felled the giant with a single stone cast from his sling.

That's the basic story, but let's turn our attention now to the aftermath of the battle.

After David kills Goliath, Avner, the commanding general of Saul's army, takes David — still holding the disembodied head of Goliath — and brings him before Saul, who asks David a very strange question:

| 1 Samuel 17:58 | וַיֹּאמֶר אֵלָיו שָׁאוּל בֶּן־מִי אַתָּה הַנָּעַר וַיֹּאמֶר דָּוִד בֶּן־עַבְדְּךָ יִשַׁי בֵּית הַלַּחְמִי: | Saul said to him, "Whose son are you, my boy?" And David answered, "The son of your servant Yishai, from Bethlehem." |

This question Saul asks David—"Whose son are you?"—seems utterly inexplicable. After all, Saul knows who David is. If you go back a few chapters in the book of Samuel, you'll see that before all this commotion with Goliath and his challenge, David was already familiar to Saul. David had played the harp for the king; they knew one another. But now Saul questions him as if he has no idea who he is.

Moreover, listen carefully to the question. It's not just a simple request for identification. It's not just "Who are you?" It's "Whose *child* are you?" And David's response is very precise: I am the child of Yishai.

What in the world is happening here?

Trading Places

To begin answering that question, look at the very next verse:

וַיְהִ֗י כְּכַלֹּתוֹ֙ לְדַבֵּ֣ר אֶל־
שָׁא֔וּל וְנֶ֙פֶשׁ֙ יְה֣וֹנָתָ֔ן נִקְשְׁרָ֖ה
בְּנֶ֣פֶשׁ דָּוִ֑ד וַיֶּאֱהָבֵ֥הוּ
יְהוֹנָתָ֖ן כְּנַפְשֽׁוֹ׃

And it happened, as [David] finished speaking with Saul, that the soul of Jonathan became bound up with the soul of David. And Jonathan loved David like his own self.

1 Samuel 18:1

Read those words again; you've heard them before. There are echoes here — echoes of the Joseph story. For some reason, the narrator is quoting none other than Judah. Judah had once said that Jacob's soul was bound up with Benjamin's ... and now the book of Samuel uses the very same language to describe how Jonathan, Saul's son, comes to love David.

Aside from these two instances, nowhere else in the Hebrew Bible do we find such a phrase. Why would the book of Samuel do that? Why lift a phrase right out of Joseph's story and plant it here, of all places — in a story about giants and slings and challenges and kings set many hundreds of years later? What does it mean?

JONATHAN AND DAVID	JOSEPH AND THE BROTHERS
נֶפֶשׁ יְהוֹנָתָן נִקְשְׁרָה בְּנֶפֶשׁ דָּוִד	נַפְשׁוֹ קְשׁוּרָה בְנַפְשׁוֹ
Jonathan's **soul became bound up** with the **soul** of David	[Jacob's] **soul is bound up** with [Benjamin's] **soul**
1 SAMUEL 18:1	GENESIS 44:30

Keep reading; the book of Samuel will do its best to tip you off. Here's the next statement we encounter in the story of Saul and David:

וַיִּקָּחֵ֥הוּ שָׁא֖וּל בַּיּ֣וֹם הַה֑וּא
וְלֹ֣א נְתָנ֔וֹ לָשׁ֖וּב בֵּ֥ית אָבִֽיו׃

Saul took him [David] that day, and would not let him return to his father's house.

1 Samuel 18:2

From then on, Saul keeps David in the palace, right at his side. And what was Jonathan's response? Take a look at the very next verse:

| 1 Samuel 18:3 | וַיִּכְרֹת יְהוֹנָתָן וְדָוִד בְּרִית בְּאַהֲבָתוֹ אֹתוֹ כְּנַפְשׁוֹ: | Jonathan and David made a covenant with one another, because [Jonathan] loved him like his own self. |

And the sign of their covenant?

| 1 Samuel 18:4 | וַיִּתְפַּשֵּׁט יְהוֹנָתָן אֶת־הַמְּעִיל אֲשֶׁר עָלָיו וַיִּתְּנֵהוּ לְדָוִד | Jonathan stripped off the cloak he was wearing and gave it to David |

Now, wait a minute. When else have you heard of someone's cloak being stripped off and given to someone else?

Yes, that would be the Joseph story, too, wouldn't it? Right before the brothers cast Joseph into the pit, they stripped him of his cloak. And just in case you're tempted to chalk it up to coincidence, keep in mind that it's not just the *idea* that's similar; it's the Hebrew phraseology too:

JONATHAN AND DAVID	JOSEPH AND THE BROTHERS
וַיִּתְפַּשֵּׁט יְהוֹנָתָן אֶת־הַמְּעִיל אֲשֶׁר עָלָיו	וַיַּפְשִׁיטוּ אֶת־יוֹסֵף אֶת־כֻּתָּנְתּוֹ אֶת־כְּתֹנֶת הַפַּסִּים אֲשֶׁר עָלָיו:
Jonathan **stripped off** the cloak **he was wearing**	**They stripped** Joseph of his coat, the coat of many colors that **he was wearing**
1 SAMUEL 18:4	GENESIS 37:23

Ripples in Time

The evidence seems undeniable. Throughout the aftermath of David's triumph over Goliath we hear a series of echoes of the Joseph story. But why?

Well, these people we hear about in the book of Samuel — David, Saul, and Jonathan — who are their ancestors? Saul and his son, Jonathan, are from the tribe of . . . Benjamin.° Interesting. And David? David is from the tribe of Judah.° In other words, they descend from the two prime actors in the Joseph story: yes, it's Judah and Benjamin, one more time.

1 Chronicles 2:1–15

Return of the King

Now, what was the great source of tension in the story of Joseph? What was the great fear expressed by the brothers, the fear that started it all?

וַיֹּאמְרוּ לוֹ אֶחָיו הֲמָלֹךְ תִּמְלֹךְ עָלֵינוּ אִם־מָשׁוֹל תִּמְשֹׁל בָּנוּ וַיּוֹסִפוּ עוֹד שְׂנֹא אֹתוֹ	His brothers said [to Joseph], "Do you mean to reign over us? Do you mean to rule over us?" And the brothers hated him even more.

Genesis 37:8

The story of Joseph and his brothers is a story about fear of the future: Who will be king here? *Will Joseph really rule over us?* That fear gave rise to hatred, and one brother was very nearly lost to the family because of that hatred: Joseph was thrown in a pit and sold as a slave. And later, another brother was also very nearly lost to the family: Benjamin was nearly taken as a slave.

That's the way it would have been — both children lost to the family of Jacob — were it not for Judah. Judah brings both brothers back from the brink. He risks his life for Benjamin. And in doing so, he comes face-to-face with the recognition that his father loves Benjamin more, would rather have Benjamin home safely with him than Judah — and, hard as it is, he is able to accept that. *Take me instead of Benjamin*, says Judah. *It's okay; you can love him more.*

When did Benjamin ever repay Judah for that?

It takes centuries, but it happens in the book of Samuel. In the days of the prophet Samuel, the ancient fear has been realized: kings now rule over the people of Israel. And Saul, the man who sits on the throne, is none other than a child of Rachel.

Rightfully, who ought to be the next king, after Saul? It should, of course, be Jonathan, the son of Saul, another descendant of Benjamin. With that in mind, put yourself in Jonathan's shoes as he sees David coming home with the head of Goliath. What does David's triumphant return mean to you?

It *could* lead you to fear. It could lead you to panic. You see your father,

Saul, raise his eyes toward David, impressed; he seems to have taken a special liking to this young warrior. You're next in line to the throne, but look at what your father is doing. Look at how Saul is treating David: "Saul took [David] that day, and would not let him return to his father's house." Saul takes David . . . as his son. He adopts him that day. Gives him his love. *Whose son are you? Don't return to your father's house anymore. You're my son.*

All of a sudden, Jonathan is faced with the greatest threat he could imagine. If anything, his father's show of love for this usurper potentially makes this a moment for an outpouring of *hatred*. There is precedent for that, after all. A father loving some other child more? That once *did* lead to hatred. And when it did, brothers declared, "Will you rule over us?" Well, Jonathan could feel that way too: *Will David rule rather than me?*

But Jonathan doesn't allow himself to see it that way:

<table>
<tr><td>1 Samuel 18:1</td><td dir="rtl">וְנֶפֶשׁ יְהוֹנָתָן נִקְשְׁרָה
בְּנֶפֶשׁ דָּוִד וַיֶּאֱהָבֵהוּ
יְהוֹנָתָן כְּנַפְשׁוֹ:</td><td>The soul of Jonathan became bound up with the soul of David. And Jonathan loved David like his own self.</td></tr>
</table>

The heroism of Jonathan, this child of Benjamin, mirrors the earlier heroism of Judah. In an act of grace and devotion, Judah had once said the very same words about Benjamin; now a child of Benjamin, in an act of grace and love, will say them about a child of Judah.

*No, I will **not** allow myself to be threatened that Father would love another child more than me. Let Father take David. Let him be king. I love David like my own soul.*

And then what does he do? Jonathan *strips off his cloak*, and he gives it to David. What is the meaning of this act? There was a time, long ago, when a child of Rachel had his cloak stripped off by the children of Leah. It was an act of violence, a forcible taking of clothes. But this time, it's not forcible. There is no violence. Now Jonathan — descendant of Benjamin, child of Rachel — willingly strips off his cloak and gives it to the descendant of Judah. It is a moment of healing, a moment in history when — for one brief and shining moment in time, at least — the two sides of the family are reconciled.

A cloak for a cloak, measure for measure. There are two ways, perhaps, to bring healing to this family. One is Joseph's approach, the "measure for measure" of cold, hard justice: *You once willingly took silver that wasn't yours without anyone knowing about it ... now you'll have silver that isn't yours without knowing about it.* That's one way, maybe. But there's another kind of "measure for measure" that can bring balance to a family: a payment in kind, modeled by Judah and emulated later by Jonathan, that has nothing to do with the scales of justice. It has to do with love. It all boils down to what you want most: vindication or reconciliation.

In Judah's actions, and later, in Jonathan's, we find a precious pearl of a moment, a moment when a man — facing the greatest possible threat to his own ambitions, to his own place in his father's heart — turns his back on his own welfare, and loves his brother from the other side of the family like his own self.

In the end, Judah's actions carry the day — they were moving enough to bring Joseph to reveal himself, moving enough to echo powerfully in history, to be remembered by the son of a king from the tribe of Benjamin. And moving enough, perhaps, for us to remember them too — so that we, thousands of years later, can, in our own families, let go of vindication and somehow learn to leave behind the temptation of hatred for the hard-won path of love.

Jacob, Joseph &
the Echoes of Eden

וַנֹּאמֶר אֶל־אֲדֹנִי יֶשׁ־לָנוּ
אָב זָקֵן וְיֶלֶד זְקֻנִים קָטָן
וְאָחִיו מֵת וַיִּוָּתֵר הוּא
לְבַדּוֹ לְאִמּוֹ וְאָבִיו אֲהֵבוֹ:
וַתֹּאמֶר אֶל־עֲבָדֶיךָ
הוֹרִדֻהוּ אֵלָי וְאָשִׂימָה
עֵינִי עָלָיו: וַנֹּאמֶר אֶל־
אֲדֹנִי לֹא־יוּכַל הַנַּעַר
לַעֲזֹב אֶת־אָבִיו וְעָזַב
אֶת־אָבִיו וָמֵת:

And we said to my lord: "We have an older father, and a son born to him in his old age. His brother is dead, so he alone remains of his mother, and his father loves him." And you said to your servants: "Bring him down unto me, that I may set my eyes on him." And we said to my lord: 'The lad cannot leave his father; for if he should leave his father, his father would die."

GENESIS 44:20–22

Jacob, Joseph & the Echoes of Eden

PARSHAT VAYIGASH opens with Judah's impassioned speech to the high Egyptian official who is really his long-lost brother Joseph. A fascinating undercurrent to that speech, I think, reminds the reader of events that occurred a long time ago — way back in the Garden of Eden.

The most overt connection between the two narratives is the phrase Judah uses to characterize Benjamin's inability to leave his father:

לֹא־יוּכַל הַנַּעַר לַעֲזֹב   The lad cannot leave his father   Genesis 44:22

The phrase לַעֲזֹב אֶת־אָבִיו (la'azov et aviv), "to leave his father," is constructed in precisely the same way as a phrase we hear back in the Garden — a phrase that describes marriage, of all things:

עַל־כֵּן יַעֲזָב־אִישׁ   This is why a man leaves behind   Genesis 2:24
אֶת־אָבִיו וְאֶת־אִמּוֹ   his father and his mother

Man leaves his father and mother and clings to his wife, the continuation of that verse tells us, because he perceives his wife as completing him. For some reason, that phrase now shows up again, in Judah's speech about Benjamin. Very strange.

A Further Echo

That lone echo of Eden might be dismissed as mere coincidence, but there is another. Listen carefully to the opening words of Judah's speech to Joseph:

Genesis 44:20

יֶשׁ־לָנוּ אָב זָקֵן וְיֶלֶד
זְקֻנִים קָטָן וְאָחִיו מֵת
וַיִּוָּתֵר הוּא לְבַדּוֹ לְאִמּוֹ

We have an older father, and a son born
to him in his old age. His brother is dead,
so he alone remains of his mother

"He alone remains . . ." Judah is speaking of Benjamin here, and the word
לְבַדּוֹ (*levado*), "alone," used by Judah to describe him, conjures up mem-
Genesis 2:18 ories of the Garden too. Back in Eden, Adam was *levado*, alone, and God
had not thought that good, so He created Eve to be Adam's companion.°
Now, for some reason, Judah is using that word to describe Benjamin. A
composite picture seems to be coming together:

ADAM	BENJAMIN
לֹא־טוֹב הֱיוֹת הָאָדָם לְבַדּוֹ	וַיִּוָּתֵר הוּא לְבַדּוֹ לְאִמּוֹ
"It is not good that the man should be **alone**"	"he **alone** remains of his mother"
GENESIS 2:18	GENESIS 44:20
The first man created was alone	**Benjamin is "alone"**
יַעֲזָב־אִישׁ אֶת־אָבִיו וְאֶת־אִמּוֹ	לֹא־יוּכַל הַנַּעַר לַעֲזֹב אֶת־אָבִיו
a man **leaves behind his father** and his mother	"The lad cannot **leave his father**"
GENESIS 2:24	GENESIS 44:22
Man will leave his father behind	**Will Benjamin leave his father behind?**

But what would this mean? Benjamin isn't getting married. There's no
romance in our story. Why would such echoes exist? What is the Torah
trying to tell us?

Jacob

If we widen the scope of our inquiry just a bit, there's a clue: as it happens, Judah's speech about Benjamin has *multiple* resonances. We hear echoes not just of Adam — Benjamin's ultimate ancestor — but of Benjamin's more recent predecessors: in particular, his father, Jacob. Listen again to that phrase in which Judah describes Benjamin as being alone:

וַיִּוָּתֵר הוּא לְבַדּוֹ   And he alone remains   Genesis 44:20

Consider that phrase and ask yourself: Where have you heard it before? Well, you've heard it with reference to Jacob; the father of both Benjamin and Judah was described in these very terms. Just before he encounters his estranged brother, Esau, Jacob meets up with a mysterious man and battles with him in the dead of night. As that battle is about to begin, we are told:

וַיִּוָּתֵר יַעֲקֹב לְבַדּוֹ   And Jacob was left alone   Genesis 32:25

The resonance is unmistakable. Only twice in all of the Hebrew Bible is the unusual word *vayivater* ("and he was left") paired with *levado* ("alone"): in the description of Benjamin, in Judah's speech, and in the description of Jacob, the night before he meets Esau. So here's a thought: Could there be a kind of triangle developing here?

Adam and Eve

Benjamin
(as described by Judah)

Jacob
and the angel

Indeed, strange as it may sound, the Jacob and Esau stories and the Adam and Eve stories seem to be intertwined too. For example, go back to the Adam and Eve story: Right after God declares that it is not good for Adam to be alone, what happens next? He brings Adam a whole parade of animals and asks him to identify them. Among them, Adam is led to believe, he will perhaps find a companion. Well, shift gears now and think about the story of Jacob, just as the text describes him as being "alone." What had Jacob done immediately before that? He had sent his brother a bunch of animals, of course:

Genesis
32:14–16

וַיִּקַּח מִן־הַבָּא בְיָדוֹ מִנְחָה
לְעֵשָׂו אָחִיו: [טו] עִזִּים מָאתַיִם
וּתְיָשִׁים עֶשְׂרִים רְחֵלִים מָאתַיִם
וְאֵילִים עֶשְׂרִים: [טז] גְּמַלִּים
מֵינִיקוֹת וּבְנֵיהֶם שְׁלֹשִׁים פָּרוֹת
אַרְבָּעִים וּפָרִים עֲשָׂרָה אֲתֹנֹת
עֶשְׂרִים וַעְיָרִם עֲשָׂרָה:

And he took of that which he had with him a present for Esau his brother: **15** two hundred female goats and twenty male goats, two hundred ewes and twenty rams, **16** thirty nursing camels and their colts, forty cows and ten bulls, twenty female donkeys and ten foals.

Esau would have had no idea where all the animals were coming from, no means of identifying them with anyone. It would be almost a guessing game:

Genesis
32:18–19

וַיְצַו אֶת־הָרִאשׁוֹן
לֵאמֹר כִּי יִפְגָּשְׁךָ עֵשָׂו
אָחִי וּשְׁאֵלְךָ לֵאמֹר
לְמִי־אַתָּה וְאָנָה תֵלֵךְ
וּלְמִי אֵלֶּה לְפָנֶיךָ:
וְאָמַרְתָּ לְעַבְדְּךָ לְיַעֲקֹב

And he instructed the first [group of servants], "When Esau my brother meets you, and asks you, 'Whose servant are you? And where are you going? And whose animals are these?' then you shall say, 'They are your servant Jacob's.'"

Genesis
2:19–20

Adam, too, was involved in a guessing game with the animals; Adam, too, had to identify all of them.° And yet, Adam found himself uninterested in the animals. They were not the mates he was looking for. Similarly, Esau finds himself uninterested in the animals. Like Adam, he just wants to send them back where they came from:

יֶשׁ־לִי רָב אָחִי   I have enough, my brother;   Genesis 33:9

יְהִי לְךָ אֲשֶׁר־לָךְ:   keep what belongs to you.

After his failure to find a mate among the animals, Adam is alone again. Something significant happens to him in the middle of the night. He is put into a deep sleep, and God fashions a true companion for him:

וַיִּקַּח אַחַת מִצַּלְעֹתָיו   And He took one of his ribs   Genesis 2:21

Does this remind you of anything that happens to Jacob? After Jacob sends all those animals to Esau, he, too, is alone at night. And then something important happens to him in the middle of the night, when he's alone: he struggles with someone. He emerges from the struggle feeling wounded — and isn't it interesting how the Torah characterizes that wound?

וַיִּזְרַח־לוֹ הַשֶּׁמֶשׁ כַּאֲשֶׁר   And the sun rose upon him as he   Genesis 32:32

עָבַר אֶת־פְּנוּאֵל וְהוּא   passed Penuel, and he was limping

צֹלֵעַ עַל־יְרֵכוֹ:   upon his thigh.

The word for "was limping" is צֹלֵעַ (*tzole'a*), a word that sounds curiously like צֵלָע (*tzela*), "rib," the very body part snatched from Adam in the middle of the night by God, out of which He constructed Eve. Adam had a post-surgical wound from the loss of that rib ... and Jacob seems to experience a wound "in kind."

ADAM	JACOB
Adam is given animals to name	**Esau is given animals to identify**
GENESIS 2:19–20	GENESIS 32:18–19

לֹא־ט֛וֹב הֱי֥וֹת הָֽאָדָ֖ם לְבַדּ֑וֹ "It is not good that the man should be **alone**"	וַיִּוָּתֵ֥ר יַֽעֲקֹ֖ב לְבַדּ֑וֹ "And Jacob was left **alone**"
GENESIS 2:18	GENESIS 32:25
Adam, without Eve, is alone	**Jacob is alone**
וַיִּקַּ֗ח אַחַת֙ מִצַּלְעֹתָ֔יו "And He took one of his **ribs [tzela]**"	וְה֥וּא צֹלֵ֖עַ עַל־יְרֵכֽוֹ׃ "And he was **limping [tzole'a]** upon his thigh."
GENESIS 2:21	GENESIS 32:32
Adam had a wound	**Jacob had a wound**

Completion

What's going on here? Why are these stories — Jacob and his confrontations with the angel and Esau; Benjamin in Judah's speech — so deeply connected to the story of Adam and the creation of Eve? There must be a common denominator here. What is it? I think it might be "completion."

To be sure, when we look at the "triangle of resonances" I outlined above, the three events in question don't seem to have much in common: Adam is alone after naming the animals; Jacob struggles with the angel; Judah defends Benjamin. But if you move forward one step in each narrative, if you consider what is *about to happen*, then the common denominator suddenly jumps out at you: Adam is alone ... and is *about to* meet Eve, another person, who will complete him. Jacob is alone ... and is *about to* meet Esau, his estranged brother. And Benjamin too is "alone" (all, seemingly, that remains of his mother) ... and, although he doesn't know it yet, he is *about to* meet his long-lost brother: he and Judah are about to discover that the high Egyptian official before whom they are pleading is, in fact, Joseph.

There is something about each of these protagonists that is very deeply "alone." Each is fragmented in some essential way. Each of these men has "another half," as it were — a person he is deeply connected to, someone who completes him — and each is separated from that person.

For Adam, that person is Eve, a woman created from his own rib. Without her, he is quite literally missing his feminine side. He is only a part of what he needs to be. With her, he is complete:[1]

| עַל־כֵּן יַעֲזָב־אִישׁ אֶת־אָבִיו
וְאֶת־אִמּוֹ וְדָבַק בְּאִשְׁתּוֹ
וְהָיוּ לְבָשָׂר אֶחָד: | This is why a man leaves behind his father and his mother and clings to his wife, and they become one flesh. | Genesis 2:24 |

But it is not only when we are missing a spouse that we feel alone and fragmented. We can also miss a brother. When we become estranged from someone in our family, the sense of loss and fragmentation is palpable.[2] When, against all odds, we find a way to seek one another out again, when brothers somehow find a way to put aside that which separates them and find one another again, the pull that brings them close is magnetic, virtually irresistible:

| וַיָּרָץ עֵשָׂו לִקְרָאתוֹ
וַיְחַבְּקֵהוּ וַיִּפֹּל עַל־
צַוָּארָו וַיִּשָּׁקֵהוּ וַיִּבְכּוּ: | Esau ran to greet him, and he hugged him; he fell on his neck, kissed him—and they cried.[3] | Genesis 33:4 |

---

1 I elaborate on the story of Adam and Eve in the Garden of Eden, and the nature of the "completeness" they experience with one another, in **Parshat Bereishit: Does Man "Acquire" Woman?** (page 9).

2 The Torah seems to suggest that the basis for the connection between brothers is actually quite similar to that between a man and his wife. Think back to the way that Adam characterizes his connection to Eve when he first meets her: "*bone* of my *bones* and *flesh* of my *flesh*" (Genesis 2:23). Later, Lavan will pick up on this language when he meets Jacob for the first time: "You are my *bone* and my *flesh* ... are you not my brother?" (Genesis 29:14–15). Brothers, of course, are the archetypal example of sharing flesh and blood. And if a relationship with an *ordinary* brother brings a sense of completion, the union of flesh and flesh, bone and bone, then this holds all the more true for Jacob's relationship with his brother Esau, for they are *twins*.

3 Cf. Bereishit Rabbah 78:9, Avot de-Rabbi Natan A 34.

And consider what happens right after this embrace between Jacob and Esau. Jacob approaches the city of Shechem, and when he does, he is described as *shalem*, complete:

Genesis 33:18

וַיָּבֹא יַעֲקֹב שָׁלֵם עִיר שְׁכֶם
אֲשֶׁר בְּאֶרֶץ כְּנַעַן בְּבֹאוֹ
מִפַּדַּן אֲרָם

And Jacob arrived complete at the city of Shechem that is in the land of Canaan, having come from Padan Aram

Taken at face value, the Torah's description of Jacob in these terms is superfluous and puzzling. Why tell us that he was "complete?" Indeed, a number of English translations choose, probably for this very reason, to shade the meaning of *shalem* away from "completeness," and toward "safety": Jacob arrived *safe* in Shechem, which is to say, he no longer felt threatened. But the literal meaning of *shalem* is not "safe"; it is "whole"— and perhaps that is precisely the intent of the text:[4] Jacob, having just reconciled with his brother, was finally whole in a way he hadn't been for many long years, ever since he left home.[5]

A similar dynamic would play out for Benjamin. He too once had a soul mate in life, someone whose destiny was deeply entwined with his own: his brother Joseph. Together, they were a pair:

Genesis 44:27

אַתֶּם יְדַעְתֶּם כִּי שְׁנַיִם
יָלְדָה־לִי אִשְׁתִּי:

You know that my wife [Rachel] bore me two children.

---

4   See Shabbat 33b, Bereishit Rabbah 79, *Tzror Hamor* Naso 6.

5   The text seems to suggest as much when, in connection to Jacob's arriving "complete" in Shechem, it emphasizes where Shechem is and where Jacob is coming from: וַיָּבֹא יַעֲקֹב שָׁלֵם עִיר שְׁכֶם אֲשֶׁר בְּאֶרֶץ כְּנַעַן בְּבֹאוֹ מִפַּדַּן אֲרָם, "And Jacob arrived complete at the city of Shechem *that is in the land of Canaan, having come from Padan Aram*" (Genesis 33:18). All those long years in Padan Aram, in Lavan's house, Jacob had not been complete; he had been fragmented, estranged from his twin brother. Now, though, "coming from Padan Aram," and arriving back home in Canaan, Jacob finally achieves a measure of wholeness.

And yet, fate would separate Benjamin from Joseph: Joseph would be sold off as a slave and eventually become "estranged" from the family, building a new life for himself in Egypt. To be sure, even in Egypt, Joseph remains a God-fearing man — but now, as Judah faces off against him in the episode of the silver goblet, reconciliation with his family seems to be the furthest thing from Joseph's mind; he is truly estranged from them.

And yet, through the power of Judah's words, Joseph is transformed. Judah describes the "aloneness" of Benjamin: how Benjamin and his father lost their beloved Joseph, and how Jacob is so deeply connected to Benjamin, he feels he absolutely cannot lose him.[6] Joseph's heart seems to melt at the portrayal, and, in tears, he unmasks himself, revealing himself to be Benjamin's long-lost "other half." Like Adam and Eve or Jacob and Esau, Joseph and Benjamin find themselves drawn to each other, embracing with tears of joy as they revel in their newfound sense of "completion" in finding one another:

וַיִּפֹּל עַל־צַוְּארֵי בִנְיָמִן־אָחִיו וַיֵּבְךְּ וּבִנְיָמִן בָּכָה עַל־צַוָּארָיו:	He embraced his brother Benjamin around the neck and wept, and Benjamin wept on his neck.	Genesis 45:14

Full Circle

Joseph's embrace of Benjamin is dramatic and emotional, but it also serves as a hopeful entry point into something larger. For look what happens right after Benjamin and Joseph embrace:

וַיְנַשֵּׁק לְכָל־אֶחָיו וַיֵּבְךְּ עֲלֵיהֶם וְאַחֲרֵי כֵן דִּבְּרוּ אֶחָיו אִתּוֹ:	And then he kissed all his [other] brothers, too, and cried upon them—and afterward, his brothers spoke with him.	Genesis 45:15

There was a larger circle of brothers from whom Joseph was estranged,

---

6 See **Vayigash I: The Timeless Echo of Judah's Plea** (page 179) for a deeper exploration of Judah's speech before Joseph.

and Joseph now reaches out to embrace them, too. It is as if Benjamin is a stepping stone for Joseph, a way back into connection with the larger family. Having been enticed to unmask himself by Judah's poignant words about Benjamin, Rachel's other child, Joseph goes further, and seeks to reconnect not just with Benjamin, but with his other brothers too — the children of Leah. He kisses them and cries upon their shoulders.

But now look at the conclusion of that verse, and you'll find words that seem almost like a letdown from these soaring heights of emotion:

Genesis 45:15　　וְאַחֲרֵי כֵן דִּבְּרוּ אֶחָיו אִתּוֹ:　　And afterward, his brothers spoke with him.

It seems strange that the Torah would feel a need to add those final words: "and afterward, his brothers spoke with him." It seems like the ultimate anticlimax. Here are Joseph and his brothers: they haven't seen each other for years; they used to be antagonists; the brothers had thrown him in a pit; he, in turn, had very nearly taken them all as his slaves — and now they reunite in tears and hugs. Why add "and afterward, his brothers spoke with him"? What did they speak about? We don't know, and the Torah doesn't bother telling us. So why is it so important to relate this seemingly trivial detail?

Unless it's not trivial at all. Go back to the very beginning of the Joseph story, and you'll see that the Torah is, with a grand arc, closing a circle. How, after all, did the estrangement, the hatred, between Joseph and his brothers initially express itself? *Through the brothers' inability to speak to him:*

Genesis 37:4　　וַיִּרְאוּ אֶחָיו כִּי־אֹתוֹ　　And the brothers saw that it was he who
　　　　　　　　אָהַב אֲבִיהֶם מִכָּל־אֶחָיו　　their father loved from among all his
　　　　　　　　וַיִּשְׂנְאוּ אֹתוֹ וְלֹא יָכְלוּ　　brothers—and they hated him, and could
　　　　　　　　דַּבְּרוֹ לְשָׁלֹם:　　not speak to him in peace.

At the very beginning, the brothers' hatred of Joseph was so intense that they "could not speak to him in peace." But now that silence in the relationship is finally gone. The brothers, at long last, *can* speak with him:

וְאַחֲרֵי כֵן דִּבְּרוּ אֶחָיו אִתּוֹ׃   And afterward, his brothers spoke with him.   **Genesis 45:15**

In harking back to the origins of the rift between brothers, their one-time inability to speak with one another, the text seems to be suggesting that the deafening silence of hatred is finally over. But whether the wounds of the past will truly and finally heal, or whether the reconciliation of **Parshat Vayigash** will prove to be merely a passing truce in a longer war — this we do not know yet. Joseph and his brothers will spend a long time together in Egypt, and what transpires later will decide this issue. For now, though, a little slice of wholeness has been brought back into a family torn by pain. Thus: What, in the end, did Joseph and the brothers speak about? *It doesn't even matter.* Brothers are once again on speaking terms — and for now, that is a victory of unimaginable proportions.

The Fence of Thorns

וַיִּקְרְבוּ יְמֵי־יִשְׂרָאֵל
לָמוּת וַיִּקְרָא לִבְנוֹ
לְיוֹסֵף וַיֹּאמֶר לוֹ אִם־
נָא מָצָאתִי חֵן בְּעֵינֶיךָ
שִׂים־נָא יָדְךָ תַּחַת יְרֵכִי
וְעָשִׂיתָ עִמָּדִי חֶסֶד
וֶאֱמֶת אַל־נָא תִקְבְּרֵנִי
בְּמִצְרָיִם: וְשָׁכַבְתִּי עִם־
אֲבֹתַי וּנְשָׂאתַנִי מִמִּצְרַיִם
וּקְבַרְתַּנִי בִּקְבֻרָתָם
וַיֹּאמַר אָנֹכִי אֶעֱשֶׂה
כִדְבָרֶךָ: וַיֹּאמֶר הִשָּׁבְעָה
לִי וַיִּשָּׁבַע לוֹ וַיִּשְׁתַּחוּ
יִשְׂרָאֵל עַל־רֹאשׁ הַמִּטָּה:

And the time drew near that Israel
must die; and he called his son
Joseph, and said to him, "If now I
have found favor in your sight, put,
I pray, your hand under my thigh,
and deal kindly and truly with me;
bury me not, I pray you, in Egypt.
But when I sleep with my fathers,
you shall carry me out of Egypt,
and bury me in their burying-place."
And he said, "I will do as you have
asked." And he said, "Swear to me."
And he swore to him. And Israel
bowed toward the head of the bed.

GENESIS 47:29–31

The Fence of Thorns

This essay continues themes developed in **Miketz: Why Didn't Joseph Write Home?** (page 169). A version of this essay was originally published in my book *The Exodus You Almost Passed Over*. There you'll find a more in-depth treatment of the Joseph story — and of the many parallels between the Joseph narrative and the Exodus saga.

ON ITS FACE, the story of Jacob's death and burial seems unremarkable. An ailing Jacob summons Joseph and asks that Joseph bury him in the family tomb at Machpelah, back in the land of Canaan. When Jacob eventually passes, Joseph does this, in compliance with his father's wishes. The whole thing seems pretty straightforward.

Given the outward placidity of these events, it's no wonder that the verses detailing Jacob's burial typically get little attention from the casual reader. But this often-overlooked story actually contains great tension and drama: there's a reason it's one of the culminating episodes in the book of Genesis. If we fail to see the drama in the episode, it just means we haven't read it closely enough.

Let's take a closer look.

Ties That Bind

The Torah begins its account of the deathbed conversation between father and son by providing the reader some chronological context for the scene: we are told that it takes place seventeen years after Jacob first came to live in the land of Egypt.° Jacob, who is by now approaching death, calls for his beloved son, Joseph, and makes his desired burial place known to him. He tells his son that he wishes to be buried in Canaan, in the place where his fathers are buried. And the Torah then gives us Joseph's response to his father's request:

Genesis 47:29

Genesis 47:30

וַיֹּאמַר אָנֹכִי אֶעֱשֶׂה כִדְבָרֶךָ:   He said, "I shall do as you have asked."

Now, if you were reading the Torah's account of these events and, just as you got up to this verse, you were asked to shut the book and guess what happens next in the story, what would you say? Or even better, pretend you are Jacob. If you had made this request of your loyal son (*Please bury me with my ancestors, in Canaan*) and he had answered in the affirmative (*Yes, Father, I will surely do what you've asked; you can count on me to bury you in the family tomb*) — if you heard those words from Joseph, how would *you* respond?

I don't know about you, but if I were in Jacob's shoes at that moment, I might've said something like: *Thank you very much, Son. That's really very kind of you. I knew I could count on you.* Something in that ballpark, at least. But that is not at all how Jacob responds. Instead, he tells his son:

Genesis 47:31

הִשָּׁבְעָה לִי   Swear to me [that you'll do it]

That's not very nice, is it? Here's your loyal son, assuring you that everything will be fine and that he'll do exactly what you've asked of him, and you ask him to *swear* that he'll really do it? What a terribly awkward thing to ask of him! Is Jacob intimating that he doesn't trust his son? [1]

Whatever Joseph might think of his father's demand, he takes the oath. And when he does, Jacob does another strange thing:

Genesis 47:31

וַיִּשְׁתַּחוּ יִשְׂרָאֵל עַל־רֹאשׁ הַמִּטָּה: And Israel bowed toward the head of the bed. [2]

---

1   Cf. Ramban to Genesis 47:31.

2   The straightforward translation of מִטָּה (*mitah*) is "bed," meaning that Jacob prostrated himself toward the head of the bed. But the Sages understand it euphemistically to mean "legacy" or "children" (the products of one's "bed").

THE FENCE OF THORNS 209

The sages of the Midrash wondered about this. Why, they asked, does Jacob bow toward the head of the bed? What is the significance of this oblique act? Here is their interpretation:

Rashi to
Genesis 47:31

עַל שֶׁהָיְתָה מִטָּתוֹ
שְׁלֵמָה שֶׁאֵין בָּהּ
רָשָׁע, שֶׁהֲרֵי יוֹסֵף
מֶלֶךְ הוּא, וְעוֹד
שֶׁנִּשְׁבָּה לְבֵין
הַגּוֹיִם, וַהֲרֵי הוּא
עוֹמֵד בְּצִדְקוֹ.

[He prostrated himself to God] because his legacy was whole, insofar as not one of [his children] was wicked—for Joseph was [Egyptian] royalty, and furthermore, he had been captured [and lived] among heathens, and yet he remained steadfast in his righteousness.

[Sifrei Va'etchanan 31, Sifrei Ha'azinu 334]

According to the Sages, Jacob inferred something from Joseph's willingness to commit himself to his father's deathbed request: Jacob saw in it evidence of his son's abiding righteousness. Despite Joseph's many years in Egypt, isolated and away from his family, he had not assimilated into the heathen culture. Jacob now felt his legacy was "complete," and he bowed in gratitude.

Time to Take a Bow

Now, let's take a moment to ponder what the Sages are telling us here. They suggest that Jacob has what amounts to a revelatory moment at the conclusion of this discussion with Joseph about burial arrangements: seventeen years into his life in Egypt, he *finally* realizes that his son has not assimilated into heathen culture. But should it really have taken Jacob that long to realize this?

Put yourself once again in Jacob's shoes at this moment, as he nears death and contemplates his funeral arrangements. Looking back over the course of your life, if you could identify any one moment — and *only* one moment — when you came to realize that yes, your beloved son, Joseph, was still a loyal, God-fearing member of this budding family of Israel, when exactly would that moment have been?

It probably wouldn't be this moment; it would've been seventeen years earlier, when you first set eyes on your long-lost son after two decades of being apart. Back then, Joseph ran to greet you, embraced you and cried, set your family up in Goshen, and took care of your every need. *Look at Joseph,* you might have said to yourself at that moment, when you first laid eyes upon him. *He's still a God-fearing man, devoted to his family. Power hasn't made him forget his roots.* Surely that's when Jacob should have realized what a good son Joseph was. Why then do the Sages say that it is only now, on his deathbed — seventeen years later — that Jacob recognizes this?

The sages of the Midrash seem to be telling us that our first-blush assumptions about this are wrong. It is actually *this* moment — this discussion about burial, at the end of Jacob's life — that is the *real* moment of truth for Joseph, in Jacob's eyes. *This* is when he truly finds out what kind of person Joseph is. Apparently, despite everything Jacob already knows about Joseph — that Joseph had taken care of the entire family, had provided them with the food they desperately needed in order to weather the famine — despite all that, there is some *other* area of concern that Jacob still has about Joseph, one that, in his mind, somehow dwarfs all other considerations. He needs to know that Joseph will bury him in Canaan. He needs Joseph to *swear* to him that he will do this.

But what is so important about this burial request? Why, exactly, would this one request tell Jacob what he felt he needed to know about Joseph?

The answer may lie in the events that immediately precede Jacob's deathbed request, the events recorded at the end of **Parshat Vayigash**.

More than the King Needs to Know

Back in **Parshat Vayigash**, we hear how Jacob, after years of believing Joseph to be dead, is told that his long-lost son is actually alive, and has risen to power in Egypt. After the disbelief subsides, an elated Jacob sets out to see Joseph. He arrives in Egypt, and is given an audience with Pharaoh himself. Jacob blesses the king, and Pharaoh engages Jacob in what one might almost call polite small talk: he asks Jacob how old he is. But strangely, Jacob doesn't reply the way we might have expected him to:

Genesis 47:9	וַיֹּאמֶר יַעֲקֹב אֶל־פַּרְעֹה יְמֵי שְׁנֵי מְגוּרַי שְׁלֹשִׁים	And Jacob said to Pharaoh, "The days of the years of my sojourning are 130 years.

> וּמְאַת שָׁנָה מְעַט וְרָעִים Small and disappointing have been the
> הָיוּ יְמֵי שְׁנֵי חַיַּי וְלֹא years of my life. They have not even
> הִשִּׂיגוּ אֶת־יְמֵי שְׁנֵי חַיֵּי equaled the years of the lives of my fathers,
> אֲבֹתַי בִּימֵי מְגוּרֵיהֶם: in the days of their own sojournings."

Why is Jacob in such a bad mood? Why say all that to Pharaoh, who is seemingly only trying to be nice, complimenting Jacob on having lived to an advanced age? [3]

The answer would seem to lie with Jacob's understanding of his destiny — a destiny as yet achingly unfulfilled. Decades earlier, Jacob had received a promise from the Almighty: he would have many descendants, and these descendants would be given the land of Canaan as their ancestral homeland.° Jacob's destiny was to settle in the land of Canaan, have children, and begin to build the nascent family of Israel in its homeland. And, as a matter of fact, this seems to have been precisely what Jacob was aiming to do, when he returned with his family to the land of Canaan after a long sojourn in the house of his father-in-law, Lavan. He was coming home, hopefully for good:

Genesis 28:13–14

> וַיֵּשֶׁב יַעֲקֹב בְּאֶרֶץ And Jacob **settled** in the land where
> מְגוּרֵי אָבִיו בְּאֶרֶץ his fathers had **sojourned**, in the
> כְּנָעַן: land of Canaan.

Genesis 37:1

This would be Jacob's great triumph: his ancestors had all lived in Canaan, but they had lived there as sojourners; they weren't permanent residents.[4] Jacob would be the first to really *settle* there, he hoped. The verbs in the verse make that clear: Jacob *settled* in Canaan, in the land where his forefathers had only *sojourned*. Returning from Lavan's household, Jacob thought his life's mission was nearly in reach; all he had to do was settle down with

---

3   See Ramban to Genesis 47:9.

4   See e.g. Genesis 23:4, where Abraham characterizes himself as a "stranger and a sojourner" to Ephron and his men.

his children and let them build a nation in their own land.[5] But that was before the sale of Joseph. Now, as he stands before Pharaoh, preparing to take up residence in the land of Egypt, Jacob is, on the one hand, grateful for his good fortune: through Joseph's rise to power in Egypt, he and his family will be assured of food to survive the famine. But Joseph's position in Egpyt and the family's dependence on him also means something else. It means the dream is starting to fade. Slowly, inexorably, with the best of intentions, Joseph had brought everyone back there along with him. Now everyone was living there, strangers in a strange land…

This is on Jacob's mind, apparently, as he stands before Pharaoh. He seems to have a sense that he has not lived out his dream. He is in the sunset of his life, and still only a sojourner like his forefathers.[6] Wasn't he meant to settle in Canaan and begin the work of nation-building? But he wasn't able to do it. Yes, he and his family would survive here in Egypt; they wouldn't starve. *But is this really where he was supposed to be?*

When Making It Better Makes It Worse

Jacob and his sons finish their conversation with Pharaoh, and then the text tells us something curious. Jacob's sons had told Pharaoh, in that conversation, that they had come to "sojourn" in the land,° but Joseph gives his father and brothers something that no sojourner or stranger could ever have:

Genesis 47:4

Genesis 47:11

וַיּוֹשֵׁב יוֹסֵף אֶת־אָבִיו	Joseph settled his father and brothers,
וְאֶת־אֶחָיו וַיִּתֵּן לָהֶם	and gave them ancestral holdings in the
אֲחֻזָּה בְּאֶרֶץ מִצְרָיִם	land of Egypt

---

5   This, indeed, is what the sages of the Midrash (Bereishit Rabbah 84:3) seem to have in mind when, commenting on the words "And Jacob settled," they add: "Jacob sought to settle down in tranquility … but [was foiled], for the the troubles of Joseph [and his sale] descended upon him." See also *Kli Yakar* to Genesis 37:1; cf. Ramban ad loc.

6   See Rashi to Genesis 47:9; cf. Sforno ad loc.

Ancestral holdings are the deepest type of land ownership described in the Bible. Later, this particular word, אֲחֻזָּה (*achuzah*), will be used to characterize Israel's possession of the land of Canaan.° But Joseph is pro- Numbers 32:22
viding an *achuzah*, this deep and profound type of land ownership to his family — in Egypt.

Joseph seems keen to ensure that his family *won't* be mere sojourners in Egypt. They will feel like they *belong* there.[7] It does not seem coincidental that Joseph makes this small adjustment in his family's immigration status immediately after he overhears his father complaining to Pharaoh about living the life of a sojourner at the end of his years. Seemingly, Joseph wants to make it better. He doesn't want his father and his family to feel like displaced persons. He wants them to feel at home, so he gives them an *achuzah* in Egypt.

And so it happens. The family of Joseph takes possession of land in Egypt, and, over time, they prosper and become numerous there. On the face of it, the family is now secure. They are living near Joseph. Things couldn't be any better.

In Joseph's eyes, making his family into landed gentry in Egypt must have seemed like a great privilege. But there is at least one man who understands that there is a dark side to all this: Jacob. The family's destiny lies in Canaan, not Egypt. *But how will they ever get there?* They came down to Egypt with seventy souls. But as Jacob nears death, years later, there are hundreds of family members. The family is wealthy and privileged. They are landowners. Jacob's grandchildren have grown up there; Egypt is all they know. What will ever make them leave?

This is the background for Jacob's fateful talk with Joseph about his burial. Look at the progression of ideas in the biblical text: tellingly, it is right after we are told° that the family "took hold" of the land "and were Genesis 47:27
very fruitful" in Egypt that we hear of Jacob's decision to summon Joseph to discuss his burial arrangements.° As the Bible presents it, the former Genesis 47:29
leads directly to the latter.

So Jacob has that deathbed conversation with Joseph. In it, the man who tried, but was unable, to settle his family permanently in Canaan makes a final plea to the son who has helped them all survive, albeit on

---

7   See Ramban to Genesis 47:11.

foreign soil. If Jacob cannot "take hold" of the land of Canaan in life, he will at least be enveloped by it in death. He summons Joseph and asks him to bury him in the land of Canaan, in the cave where his forebears are buried. Joseph says he will, but that's not enough; Jacob asks him to *swear* to it. Earlier, we wondered why a solemn oath would be necessary, but now we can understand why.

Who Is Your Father Now?

I mentioned in a note in the beginning of this essay that we'd be picking up on themes introduced in **Parshat Miketz**. In the essay on **Miketz**, we established something about Joseph and his relationship with Pharaoh.

The king of Egypt becomes, in many ways, like a surrogate father to Joseph. He gives him a job. A chariot. A wife. A new name. He's there for Joseph in his most desperate hour, saving him from languishing for a lifetime in the palace dungeons. But now Joseph's relationship with Pharaoh complicates things. In theory, it was all well and good for Joseph to bear a strong allegiance to this "father," Pharaoh, and be a good son to his real, biological father, Jacob — as long as the interests of his two "fathers" were not in conflict. *But what would happen if they ever were?*

Well, now is that moment. This is when Pharaoh's and Jacob's interests diverge; there's just no way to make both men happy anymore.

Consider this: Who, exactly, is Jacob in Egypt's eyes? He's the father of Egypt's savior, Joseph — which means that Jacob is Egyptian royalty. When he dies, all Egypt mourns him for seventy days. How would Pharaoh feel about a state funeral in a little backwater of the Middle East called Canaan? Imagine Queen Elizabeth dying and being buried in Madagascar. Things like that don't happen. To make such a request of Egypt's king would be outrageous. It would be dicey, to say the least.[8]

---

8   Cf. Ramban to Genesis 47:31. The absurdity of the scene is evident in the biblical text, when the actual burial takes place a short while later. When, ultimately, Jacob's funeral procession travels toward Canaan, there are so many Egyptians in the crowd that neighboring nations looking on don't even see an Israelite funeral; they see an Egyptian one. They exclaim in wonderment: *What a huge mourning entourage this is for Egypt!* (Genesis 50:11)

Joseph's Choice

Nevertheless, Jacob asks to be buried in Canaan, and Joseph answers in the affirmative. He tells his father he'll do it. He *swears* he'll do it. And then Jacob bows toward the head of the bed.

Now we can appreciate what the sages of the Midrash meant when they said that Jacob was bowing in gratitude:

יוֹסֵף מֶלֶךְ הוּא,
וְעוֹד שֶׁנִּשְׁבָּה לְבֵין
הַגּוֹיִם, וַהֲרֵי הוּא
עוֹמֵד בְּצִדְקוֹ.

Joseph was [Egyptian] royalty, and further-more, he had been captured [and lived] among heathens, and yet he remained steadfast in his righteousness.

[Sifrei Va'etchanan 31, Sifrei Ha'azinu 334]

Rashi to
Genesis 47:31

We asked earlier why it took Jacob seventeen years of living in Egypt to re-alize that Joseph was "righteous," that he had not assimilated into Egyptian culture. Why did Jacob not realize this the moment he first set eyes upon him, the moment Joseph first embraced him, cried, and promised to take care of the family's every need? *That* seems like the moment Jacob should have realized what a good son Joseph was. Why is it only *now* — seventeen years later — that Jacob recognizes this?

But it makes perfect sense. This really *is* the moment that Jacob knows, fully and without reservation, that Joseph is a loyal son. Providing for the family was one thing. That choice did not really require him to put his re-lationship with Pharaoh under any strain. After all, Pharaoh was fine with Joseph providing for his family. But a state funeral in Canaan? Trying to honor *that* request could come at a real price for Joseph. When Joseph says he'll do it, *swears* he'll do it, Jacob understands what that means. In a contest between competing fathers and their respective interests, Joseph has chosen Jacob.

Where Is Home?

In truth, Jacob's request to be buried in Canaan isn't just about the disposi-tion of his body; it's about the destiny of his family. The Israelites weren't meant to become God-fearing Egyptian aristocrats; they were meant to serve God as a sovereign nation in their own land. Jacob's real question for Joseph, his child who rules over Egypt, is this:

Are you on board with that vision? Are you willing to publicly back our family's allegiance to another homeland, to a larger national mission that doesn't include Egypt as a place of residence?

Joseph's answer to his father's burial request is in the affirmative. He understands the family's destiny, and despite the personal sacrifice it might entail, he will do his part to uphold it.

The Fence of Thorns

Jacob dies, and Joseph fulfills his promise to him. He leads a burial procession — an Egyptian state funeral — on a long journey back to Canaan, back to the cave at Machpelah. According to the Sages, however, something intriguing happens along the way.

The biblical text tells us that before Jacob is buried, he is eulogized in a place, on the east bank of the Jordan, with an odd name: it is called *Goren Ha'atad*, which means "a threshing floor surrounded by thorn bushes." Why is it called that? Rashi, quoting the Talmud, explains that the place gets its name because of something remarkable that happens at Jacob's funeral.

As the sages of the Talmud tell it, during Jacob's burial procession, all the kings of Canaan and the princes of Ishmael assemble to ambush and attack the Israelites, who had gathered at this spot to eulogize Jacob. But then, the would-be attackers see something that makes them halt in their tracks:

Rashi to Genesis 50:10

כֵּיוָן שֶׁרָאוּ כִּתְרוֹ שֶׁל יוֹסֵף תָּלוּי בַּאֲרוֹנוֹ שֶׁל יַעֲקֹב, עָמְדוּ כּוּלָן וְתָלוּ בּוֹ כִּתְרֵיהֶם, וְהִקִּיפוּהוּ כְּתָרִים כְּגוֹרֶן הַמּוּקָף סְיָג שֶׁל קוֹצִים.

Joseph's crown was hanging on Jacob's casket, and when they saw this, all [these kings and princes] stood up, [put down their weapons,] hung their own crowns on it, and surrounded his casket with crowns, like a threshing floor surrounded by a fence of thorns.

[Sotah 13a]

What do the Sages mean to say with their cryptic story? Why are these kings attacking? And why does the sight of Joseph's crown make all these kings halt their attack — and join their crowns to his?

Consider this: Who, exactly, do the Sages say are attacking the children of Jacob? They aren't just any random attackers. They are the kings and princes of Canaan and Ishmael.

Think back to the founding fathers of these nations, Canaan and Ishmael: What was the common denominator between them? They were both dispossessed children.

Thrown Out of the Family

Canaan was the son Noah cursed and threw out of the family.° Ishmael was the son of Abraham, also thrown out of his family.° Both of these dispossessed children now come to attack other children, children their own fathers had loved and legitimized.

Genesis 9:25

Genesis 21:9–21

Shem was accepted by Noah. Isaac, a descendant of Shem, was accepted by his father, Abraham. And now, generations later, as the descendants of all the accepted children gather for Jacob's funeral, the kings of Ishmael and Canaan, the dispossessed children, come to attack them. But then something halts them in their tracks: the crown of Joseph, hanging over the coffin of Jacob.

Joseph was a child who thought himself dispossessed too. But when he had his chance, Joseph didn't do away with the "accepted children." He clawed his way, somehow, back into the family. It took years, but he made it. And when the fateful moment came for him to choose:

With all your wealth, power, and prestige, are you a son of Pharaoh or a son of Jacob? Whose family do you call your own? —

Joseph chose his own family, the family of Israel, with all the difficulty this choice entailed.

Joseph buries Jacob in Canaan. In so doing, he puts his crown, as it were, on his father's casket. Joseph puts his crown — his prestige and his favor with Pharaoh — at risk for his father. As the Midrash puts it, when the kings of Canaan and Ishmael saw that crown, they stopped the attack, and with humility, joined their crowns to Joseph's.

Only Joseph holds the moral force to take the venom out of an attack of dispossessed children. And remember: not only does he fend off these kings, he wins them over; they join their crowns to his. One wonders if the Talmud is painting a picture not only of the past, but of a possible future, a future where there is hope for reconciliation between Israel and the descendants of dispossessed children who make up Israel's extended — but estranged — family. If, after all the pain, anger, and misunderstanding in his past, Joseph can solemnly give Jacob honor — if, after everything, he can wed his destiny to that of his family — then perhaps other fragments of dispossessed families can find in Joseph an example to emulate. If Joseph can make it back, perhaps there is hope for them too.

Want more?

Explore Rabbi Fohrman's thoughts on the weekly parsha with his beautiful animated video courses.

Check out **www.alephbeta.org**

Maggid Books
The best of contemporary Jewish thought from
Koren Publishers Jerusalem Ltd.